THE
PRESENCE
OF
ABSENCE

THE
PRESENCE
OF
ABSENCE

Kitchen table talks about parenting,
leaving fundamentalism, and the
very messy business of living with loss

DESIREE RICHTER

UNIVERSITY OF NEW ORLEANS PRESS

Published by University of New Orleans Press

Cover design by Kevin Stone

ISBN: 9781608013005

University of New Orleans Press
2000 Lakeshore Drive
New Orleans, LA 70148

504-280-7457

Dedicated to the kids and to all those in grief,
which is basically all of us.

CONTENTS

Welcome to This Book!

Welcome to this book. This opener used to read "Welcome to this (sort-of) book" because for a long time, this manuscript felt like a sort-of book. That's probably because I didn't start out to write a book. These kitchen table conversations began as a series of private journal entries that I wrote as I navigated that messy business I like to call "Whatever the fuck living with long-term loss actually is."

The idea of conversations came later in the process because I want you to feel like there is not much distance between the me who wrote this book and the me who is living the losses and gains recounted in its pages.

I am from the South. I am a third-generation Southern woman who grapples with the complicated nature of that identity.

I grew up traversing field and farm every Christmas only to arrive at the twelfth notch of the Bible belt at the stroke of midnight—I'm talking deep South Alabama, y'all. My kin and I would roll up to the back carport. The screen door would open, and my mom's mom, who is as Southern as they come, would greet us. Her hug was a bit standoffish. I think I know why now, but I think she put her love into a big pot of gumbo. As a child of five or six, I didn't completely understand that fact. I only knew that these words would greet me:

"Honey, eat this gumbo. I made it for you."

I didn't want the gumbo. I didn't want anything but to put my road-weary little brain down to bed and sleep off several states' worth of sitting in the way back of my parents' station wagon.

Didn't matter. I was gonna eat that gumbo.

Little known fact: In the South we created a breed of women for whom the phrase "butter wouldn't melt in her mouth" readily applies. But it is also a little-known fact that we invented non-consensual eating. Non-consensual eating means that you are going to take at least one helping of that gumbo, them butter beans, that bacon, and you're gonna like it. You're gonna compliment the cook, and you are gonna eat seconds.

If this form of hospitality is a bit passive-aggressive, at least someone is trying, from the confines of their culture, to give you something good.

And with that eating comes the conversation. At that kitchen table, the family stories were retold ... or withheld. The conversations around mealtimes both revealed and shrouded the family truths. Secrets sat down alongside the second helpings of pie. Stories of loss and remaking settled into my bones, though as a child, I didn't always understand their import. This book is my own re-telling of the individual story of my own great loss. And, while I hope to inhabit a gentle form of my native hospitality, I really heartily welcome you to this book.

So, grab yourself some sweet tea, or whatever suits your fancy, sit down on the front porch of your heart, and consider yourself warmly invited to the kitchen table of my heart.

What I have attempted to do with these essays is not dissimilar to the way that members of various church councils united the scriptures on which I cut my teeth. I wonder what it must have been like to sit at the table of, say, the Council of Rome in 382 AD and cast a vote for or against canonization. I imagine a few fights broke out. To take a disparate set of texts written by different authors over the long haul and tie them together in some way is no small feat. In a sense, I came to my own council, calling to the table the various versions of myself. I cast my vote to canonize certain parts of my original texts, whilst other ideas have been relegated to the apocryphal. I've had to ask myself, similar to the council that decided we didn't need the story of little Jesus turning mudpies into sparrows, whether or not another story of how grief knocked me on my ass for nearly two decades really adds to the point of this book.

And what is that point?

Wish I could tell you.

This book covers a lot of terrain including leaving my fundamentalist belief system in middle age, maintaining a relationship with my son, Elijah, who passed away when he was two, and learning how to parent my four remaining children in ways that are not fueled by the fever dream of fundamentalism. But this book was born of a hell of a mess; as such, parts of it which remain a bit untidy—sort of like that unpainted section of concrete in my basement apartment that stays dusty no matter how many times I clean it. (Hint: not that many times.) The untidiness that remains expresses itself as me thematically "stepping on my tale," as it were. I've tried not to repeat myself verbatim, but if I am going to give you an actual glimpse into bereavement over the long haul, part of that peek is the repetitiveness of certain grief motifs. So I have revisited certain ideas over and over, examining them from slightly different angles. Continuing the comparison to Scripture, consider that the resurrection story exists in all four Gospel accounts. Each rendering deepens the meaning.

My hope is that any tale-stepping yields a complexity of perspective about the topics this book attempts to wrangle. Grief, loss, and healing from loss and fundamentalism all dovetailed with parenting, artmaking, and sexual awakening. If at times this book reads more like you are inside the mind of someone who is still struggling to make some damn sense out of it all, that's because I am. Feel free to nod and eyeroll to your heart's content if everything you read is just oh so obvious. And don't forget to bring your favorite li'l long-term, wicked mess of a struggle that you just can't figure out how to tidy up.

If you are looking for a how-to book on recovering from

grief, this ain't it. This book does not land in a final resting place where the healing is complete. No memorial will ever be erected in honor of my grief, no granite slab bearing an epitaph: "Here lies Desi's grief." This book chronicles the movement of grief from the unbearable to something that is integrated into my psyche. If there is help in this book, it may come from seeing how it relates to your own process of living with your great loss.

Let's get the hardest part out of the way first. I am a bereaved mother. I lost my firstborn son in an accident in the fall of 2000. He went to bed one night and didn't wake up. He was two years old at the time. Think of that information this way: when you read a book like *Into Thin Air*, you know that people are going to end up dying on Mt. Everest. You don't read the book to find out that people died. You read it because you know you are going to learn something about the nature of people and maybe even life.

Similarly, this book is not about the plot points of Elijah's passing. I just summed them up in a single sentence, but hidden beneath that sentence is the unraveling of a mother, a marriage, and a faith. The reality of that single sentence was a catapult into a future that was so foreign to me I spent well over a decade in an epistemological and emotional no man's land. I'm no longer a full-time resident there, but perhaps part of the reason I am choosing to tell my story is to speak back to the grief-phobic notion that if you aren't doing significantly better by a certain point in time, your grief is pathologically complicated. I wholeheartedly disagree. Grief is complicated. Period. And healing is possible. Period. But linear notions of healing are not helpful, and with this book, I hope to normalize the idea that a person can be simultaneously whole and broken, healed and still hurting over a loss—in a word, *human*.

I used to say that Elijah's death acted as a great schism—a bifurcation between the life I thought I was going to live and the one I am now straining toward. I don't see his loss that way now. For one thing, I don't think that making Elijah's early death the

4

main point of his life honors my son. Rather than fixating on Elijah's untimely death, I am more interested in honoring the fullness of his short life. Elijah's death will always live in me. But his death is not *about* me. This idea has been hard-won, but at the end of the day, none of our kids' lives are about us, are they? We are simply stewards of their spirits. And that is true regardless of how long they are physically on this earth.

Two decades of living without Elijah has given me a front-row seat to living in the liminal space between grief's first blow and healing. In movies, grief is portrayed as widows falling apart at funerals, or mates stoically lowering their fallen one into the ground—then onto the next scene. Rarely do we see a person working out their grief in real time, moving through life's mundanity while subsisting as a crater of loss. Yet, isn't this what we all do? Don't we all walk around the world with the specters of our loved ones shackled to our souls? We grocery shop, fuck, fill out applications, all the while grappling to get out of a gaping hole of grief. For my part, I finally quit trying to claw my way out of the hole. I decided to order takeout and re-decorate.

I used to see Elijah's loss as an event that cleaved my being—like lightning splitting my life in two. Sometimes I still do. There was BED and AED, before and after Elijah's death. I felt so utterly unidentified with my old self that I wrote her a eulogy—because I am normal like that. The result of integrating Elijah's death into the whole of my life is a psychic metamorphosis that, most days, feels less like a bifurcation and more like soul-composting. It's tempting to draw a straight line from who I was when Elijah died—devout right-wing, fundamentalist wife, mother, and missionary—to who I am now—a left-leaning, sex-positive single mom who dreams of a gentle back half to her life.

It would be easy to say, "She lost her son, and she couldn't deal, so she lost her faith." That might be strictly true, but there is a lot more to the story than that. This book shares my perspective from both sides of the fence. In writing it, I have revisited my former worldview. At least intellectually. In this sense, these essays share something else similar to Scripture. Just as the Bible is an amalgam of sundry perspectives, these pieces are written from the perspectives of three Desis. There is Fundamentalist Desi, who believed in her God. There is Unmoored Desi, who struggled for about ten years to hold onto that faith in the wake. Finally, there is Present Desi—the one peering into these pages, revisiting the other two Desis with much kindness.

Even though each Desi believed radically different things, I don't think they are actually three different versions of me. I have come to the belief that the essence of my psyche—sweet, sensitive, seeker—has remained constant. For me, healing means that I can see an arc to my story that didn't exist when I was in the throes of a grief-induced psychic rending. My present pro-clivities about sex, religion, parenting, and pretty much every-thing else make me look like a different woman on paper. But my essence has remained the same. So, perhaps this book represents an attempt to dovetail the seemingly disparate selves, to unite them into something as complex as humans actually are.

Dovetailing, like the little bird embedded in the word, seems to be an inherently peaceful process. Unlike shoe-horn-ing, which seems very violent, dovetailing shaves of bits of this and that between two pieces of wood. Under the care of a master carpenter, those pieces somehow fit, snugly and tightly, together. In my case the years have winnowed off some of the sharper edges of these psyches to coexist so that I can now say, "I am a mostly peaceful mess of a woman."

Let's begin the journey to that peaceful dovetailing not with where I once was, but where I am now: New Orleans.

Heartbreak City

"They got all the cancer and just had to take the left breast. No chemo, no radiation. She's gonna be fine."

You would think that this tender statement was shared with me in a hospital waiting room, after weeks of surviving on gut-rotting vending machine coffee and Oreos. The doctor would emerge from the operating room looking all battle worn and victorious. He would look steadfastly into our eyes, weary grin in place, and announce, "It was a long haul, but we got it all." In this scenario the doctor is also hot because apparently hot doctors make tragic situations better.

However, this relief-soaked news was not rendered up to me by a ride-or-die buddy or close kin. Or a hot doctor.

It was uttered by my Uber driver. Ray, the rather talkative Uber driver.

No shade to Ray, but he's not my Uber driver type. I much prefer the slightly stoned, lo-fi spinning driver, the type who seems to understand that if I need an Uber, it's because I don't want to need an Uber. Today, I especially don't want to need an Uber because it means I am dealing with Gigi.

Gigi is not one of my many offspring—five in total. "Five?" you say. Yes, five, all birthed from my womb. Why five? Because I was a very good fundamentalist, that's why. And I was damn fertile. Downright fecund, really. Moreover, my babies were all those easy sleep-through-night models who rapidly became the loves of my life. Sorry, current love interest. You are sixth in line.

But this opening isn't so much about my many offspring or my lack of long-term partner. It's about Gigi. Gigi is my rarely working 2002 Jeep Wrangler. I bought Gigi around Christmas in 2021, and I have driven her for exactly three months. No, really: the pine needles from that Christmas tree still adorn her floor like she and I just took our first ride home together, full of the promise of many camping tips, joy rides, and regular ole A-to-B drives to come. Let's just say Gigi's story hasn't exactly panned out the way I expected.

Some people would call Gigi a lemon, but I prefer to think of Gigi just doing a lot of hot (engine) girl shit. What do I mean? Let's just say that if Gigi were human, she would have a propensity to post memes of herself on Friday evenings at one of her spa-garages. If anyone has seen "Can't drive now, doin' hot girl shit" pop up on your feed, let me know what Gigi is doing on her little getaways. I suspect she is getting her pistons manicured, or her struts massaged, or her O-rings orgasmed. I've quit asking because Gigi is pretty tight-lipped about these types of things.

Gigi's escapades, which have included a new head gasket, rebuilt engine, new radiator, another new head gasket, and a myriad of new, more minor parts, remind me of something my dear friend Jenna once dropped into a conversation we were having about dating: "They tell you things at the beginning." Jenna didn't really dive into the types of things people have told her, but I think she means little things like, "I am not looking for anything serious," or "Monogamy isn't really my thing." I am starting to think that people might actually mean these things that they say on their third glass of pinot.

If Jenna is right (and she usually is), then Gigi might have been trying to tell me something at the beginning. I just noticed during one of my rare drives with Gigi that she has a little light in the upper right corner of her display, one I'm beginning to suspect has been there all along. It's rather hard to read, but if you look real close it says "Part time." Part time? Really? Is that even a trouble light? Apparently it is, and apparently Gigi meant it, and if I had just *literally* read the sign, I could have saved myself and Gigi a world of trouble.

If only I had known that Gigi and the last few of my lovers really *meant it* when they were flashing "Part-time," I would have heeded that information. Because nothing about my life is part-time—not parenting, not working, not loving, not existential dread. I am a very full-time kind of girl. Gigi, apparently, is not. I don't want a part-time man or a part-time car that seems to be on a one-Jeep attempt to solve the ship of Theseus paradox. If a Jeep that is, like, 112 in car years has all of her parts replaced, is she still the same vessel?

Gigi's most recent Heraclitus-inspired, hot-girl shit required an extended vacation with a mechanic on the Westbank for reasons that are apparently "undiagnosable." In fact, they are so "undiagnosable" that the shop owner refused to even try. In other words, Gigi's mechanic broke up with her.

Hence, I am in the car with Ray, the rather talkative Uber driver, retrieving my car from the Westbank. For the New Orleans uninitiated, the Westbank refers to a side of the Mississippi River. Sounds logical, but, surprise! The Westbank is not west of New Orleans. In fact, it's mostly east of the city proper. Whenever I am driving toward the Westbank in whatever rental that is decidedly not Gigi, the digital compass informs me of this fact. I think this little parcel of land is thus named because it actually *is* West of something or other farther back up the Mississippi. But even slow-moving muddy waters make big bends, and I think the Mississippi's story took a plot twist somewhere around New Orleans. So, what was once west is now east, or sometimes south.

And that is the perfect metaphor for how we tend to think that the points of our life's compass are ever fixed, but the river of life slowly bends—though the current of change may run slowly, one day we wake up and find our compass points have disarranged. We may exist in this state of Compass Rose soup for quite some time. When new compass points finally land, they point us in totally different directions. The people who get the joy of living with us while we try to reorient just love it, likely saying things like, "I don't know who you are anymore." Yeah, sister, me neither.

This long arc of the river's bend is exactly what happened to me. And when that river spit me out, I found in New Orleans a new true north. I would not live in New Orleans if I hadn't lost Elijah. My river would not have bent toward this city. I would not be sitting in this Uber listening to Ray, the rather talkative Uber driver, talk.

Initially, I was mildly annoyed by Ray. In the span of about six minutes, I had learned that a.) Ray delivers mail for his day job, b.) he has a new dog, c.) he had to put the old dog down because of brain cancer, and d.) he was going to smoke a bowl when he got off and take his dog to the dog park. *Brother, I don't care.* I started caring when Ray began talking about his wife.

"She's Sicilan, so she's goin' stir crazy and finding all sorts of work to be done. There isn't any."

I care now because Ray is doing this thing that I have repeatedly observed in members of my adopted city: Ray is reckoning with loss in *not*-private. His acknowledgement comes with no bravado. Ray is pushing sixty-seven, and he wears the look of a New Orleanian who has seen some shit. He's weathered the storms and stayed. This acknowledgement of hardship is no attempt at a sympathy grab. It's a simple truth transmitted through Ray's glance in the rearview mirror.

Ray has no idea that I am a bereaved mother. It's just not the kind of thing I lead with, ya know? But I am pretty sure that if I told him, it wouldn't phase him. Yeah, I am liking Ray more and more, just like I like Brad the security guard at Canseco's, who in one breath asked me out and in the other told me he had buried his father two weeks prior. Both of these things he did without missing a beat while loading my cat litter into my car.

I have never lived in a city where complete strangers talk

about their dearly departed with such ease, often in tandem with a stubborn playfulness. And I fucking love that about the people in this city. Ray and others epitomize the optimistic embrace of *Laissez les bons temps rouler*. In a town that makes its living on tourism, "Let the good times roll" is a well-commodified, Mardi Gras-themed catchphrase. But for New Orleans residents, the sentiment transcends its t-shirt selling status in the Quarter. When I tried to whine to Ray about Gigi, he listened for a second and then replied with a hint of a grin, "I'll complain when I'm dead."

Ray's words didn't feel like toxic positivity. Rather, they felt like a little bit of *Laissez les bons temps rouler* threaded into Ray's (and so my) day. Ray was rolling, literally, with the times. In fact, he drives Uber so that he can keep that cash flow rolling for his wife in the manner to which she has become accustomed. How much do we love Ray?

As a new arrival, I thought it was good times bringing to me New Orleans: a new job, a new Christian community with whom I could try to embody the Franciscan ideal of "Preach the gospel at all times. If necessary, use words." I thought I was coming to New Orleans to reanimate my flagging faith, to start anew with my family. But now, I am not so sure it was good times that brought me here after all. I would not live in New Orleans if I had not lost Elijah. And, having lost my son, I was desperate to not lose my religion too.

So, ten years after Elijah's death, I fled to the land of *Laissez les bons temps rouler*. It was in the literal full-blown fanfare of this expression that I—a very White, very deep South, Alabama-born transplant—first landed in New Orleans. And here, just a bit of advice: If you are a faltering fundamentalist trying to hang onto your faith, don't move to New Orleans in the middle of Mardi Gras. Consider me your cautionary tale. Of course I didn't know then that the death gurgle of my fundy faith was at hand. I was soldiering on—a bereaved mother who still wasn't even sure she deserved to be on the planet let alone be in, to paraphrase Tennessee Williams, one of America's three cities during its most famous celebration. I was green to the city, and I was hurting. Questions I had long repressed refused to rest. I was bone weary in my soul, marathon-grief fatigued, feeling the weight of too many unanswered prayers—but mostly just missing my boy.

I suppose some DSM-IV wielding soul would say, given the time that had passed since Elijah's loss, that I had complicated grief—to which I would reply, "There is nothing complicated about waking up to find your two year old died in the night while you slept peacefully down the hall." There is only the unrelenting presence of his absence. There is also nothing complicated about the idea that living with such a nuclear bomb of loss would lead to a very complicated healing journey that some days feels like I am right back in the thick of the trauma.

Grief expert and bereaved father David Kessler has a wonderful response to people who ask, "How long is this going to hurt?"

"How long is your loved one going to be dead?"

And that is a response that I find both absolutely true and strangely comforting. Perhaps if we treated the bereaved with more dignity and actually provided them with the unmitigated freedom to feel as sad as they need for as long as they need, they might find a way to flourish even in their heartbreak. Instead, we loan them three days of bereavement leave, a few warm casseroles, and the link to a Facebook support group. Then, should these measures fail, we label grievers' inability to recover within some bullshit timeframe as "complicated grief."

So, in my very uncomplicated state of long-term sorrow, I was ill-equipped to assess the nuanced complexity of the city when I arrived. Hell, I was generally just happy to sit at home, nurse my baby, and wonder about small problems like, "Why *does* the neighbor's dog holler daily like a donkey being ritually sacrificed?" Yeah, that's where I was when my family landed in New Orleans in 2010, the Friday before Fat Tuesday, on a night when six parades rolled. Six!

The movers took one look at the traffic, dropped the bed-frames on the floor, and fled. I was just well-off and stick-up-my ass enough to be annoyed. But my then husband knew better. He got us out of the house and we drove our minivan down to Napoleon and St. Charles—the family friendly portion of the parades. He walked into the fray with the three older kids, having Sharpied our cell phone numbers on their hands, just in case. (In case of what, exactly? I wondered.) I parked said minivan several blocks away and strolled my sleeping six month old into the scene. Keep in mind we had just moved from Ft. Hawkins, Georgia, the literal birthplace of the Trail of Tears, then driven all day with the kids, ages ten, eight and six and nursing. It was in this bone-weary state that I encountered my first ever Mardi Gras parade.

It was resplendent in every way you have ever seen depicted. And then some.

I noticed the float first, a well-lit double decker from which the krewe threw plastic bejeweled strings of beads. My heart followed their arc, intuiting that these little trinkets were imbued with some mid-air magic. I *wanted* them. And in those days, I rarely wanted anything.

The street was lined with ladders, babies perched atop them in boxes, high-stepping high school bands, beer-holding bros. All arms outraised ready to receive. The scene rivaled a massive Pentecostal gathering. Only instead of speaking in tongues, people were petitioning riders with "Throw me something, mista!" The roaming altar call was not to penitence but to revelry.

Into this raucous sea I steered my infant's stroller. I found my family. People could tell we were new and thrust my kids to the front of the crowd. As I watched pole dancers in flesh-colored suits, I learned that the definition of family friendly in New Orleans is a little bit . . . different.

The locals assured us: "Don't worry. No one will be flashing for beads on Napoleon."

I mouthed an "Oh."

As the fanfare began to seep in, my road weariness was replaced with wonder. I felt gloriously anonymous, invited to the altar of revelry even though, or maybe because, no one really knew me. I didn't know much about this place, but I knew one thing.

I was home.

Thirteen years later, I still can't claim a deep knowledge of this city like many of my New Orleanian friends can. Take Sarah. Sarah has been roaming this city by bike since she was seven years old. Slow down and take that in. Sometime in the eighties, a little *seven*-year-old Sarah and her gaggle of cousins pedaled their way through the French Quarter, getting into all manner of scrapes, settling scores, seeing it all. Sarah knows all the curves of the Crescent City, the sinews of each street. The history of this place is not something she recites so much as embodies. There's no separating that girl from her city, and damn the man or storm that would try. When I need a lesson in joie de vivre, I see if Sarah is free.

These days, my two youngest kids and I live below my friend James in a little place on the bayou. James is a New Orleanian of a slightly different breed. Most mornings I wake up to hear him composing something that moved way beyond trad jazz about twenty years ago. James, in his mid-sixties, is a minor jazz deity. About forty years ago, he dropped out of college, came to play, and never left. Though he wasn't born here, he has that essence shared by Ray, Sarah, and the security guard at Canseco's who has a crush on me. James has the everyday *Laissez les bons temps rouler* runnin' up and down the neck of his upright bass. That man has more optimism in his well callused left thumb than I could ever hope to hold. Get James talking, and you will talk about his two favorite subjects: complexity, and how in the eighties musicians used to make their rent every night. James remembers when jazz was transgressive and defiant. For him, it still is.

James also holds two distinguished positions in my heart:

1. Best quote about coitus whilst popping a blue-berry into his mouth: "It's summer in New Orleans. Somebody oughta be fuckin'."

2. He also holds the very distinguished position of being the only man I've ever dated whose love remains just as constant after we stopped sleeping together. After a very platonic porch hang, he always says "I love you, baby." The words ring just as true as they did when we were lovers. Score one for com-plexity. Score another for lettin' the good times roll in a variety of directions.

Laissez les bons temps rouler may be in full regalia for Mardi Gras, but a quieter embodiment of this sentiment resides in the hearts of her people year-round. This artful revelry is nothing like the string quintet in Titanic serenading as the ship sank. It is not the solemn Cellist of Sarajevo soothing citizens from the center of a bomb crater after a terrorist attack. It does usu-ally involve a smidge of debauchery, over-the-topness, and the sanctioning of behaviors that my twenty-three year old self would have been unable to accept, let alone praise.

Now, I think that *Laissez les bon temps rouler* represents a very conscious choice that New Orlanieans have made to revel—not because it's all just going swimmingly, but because they repeat-edly choose life in the wake of loss. And when I say "life" I don't mean "do the dishes, get to work on time, the show must go on." I mean collective, cultural practices that actually make us feel that we are alive. *Laissez les bons temps rouler* is a direct admon-ishment not to ignore the hard times but to dance with them: "Baby, you better let those good times roll 'cause the hard times are 'bout to roll in right in their heels."

Hell, this is what that back half of Mardi Gras prepares us for. The whole shebang, with its pomp and circumstance just done up right, with glitz and balls and floats that will make you question whether Macy's even knows what a parade is supposed to be, is all preparation, a great cathartic exhale gearing up for a lenten season that culminates in, drumroll please . . . the actual grief of God Himself. I ask you: Does it get any more epic than that? The coin flips at exactly midnight on Fat Tuesday, so be prepared to trade in the beaded bedlam for repentance and ash.

This perfectly orchestrated theater is the expression of the existential tensions we humans embody, and I love that it gets played out writ large in bawdiness, beads, and balls. We've got floats for miles, to the tune of around eighty parades every Mardi Gras. We've got a military precision trash sweep operation that rolls right behind every one of these parades. Anonymity, allowing for unfettered expression, is part of the ruse, and anyone riding on a float unmasked will be fined. I'm pretty sure that if there's one law we will enforce, it's: wear your (Mardi Gras) mask.

It's all incredibly healthy, if you ask me. And it's why, when people wonder, "Why would you live in a city so vulnerable to hurricanes?", as they did again in the wake of 2021's Hurricane Ida, I shrug and really don't offer much of a response. If you have not experienced the great catharsis of anonymously letting your heart hang out, if you haven't authentically *Laissez les bon temps rouler*d with strangers wearing costumes that reveal their truths while concealing their identities, then it won't make sense to you. If you only see the cracked infrastructure, dirty politics and a good place to get wasted for your bachelorette, then New Orleans will not make sense as a place to actually inhabit. Sure, I would love to not have to budget a yearly "nail-in-tire" tax on top of all Gigi's other expenses, but it's a small price to pay for living in a place that heals me.

While our city is famed for her playfulness, I've found it is the perfect place to live if your heart is broken. New Orleans is not just a place you come to party; she is a balm for the broken-hearted, a place of respite for those who are inundated with loss.

New Orleans heals as she loosens the mental reigns of the tighty-whitey, stick-up-our collective ass, efficiency-take-all milieu that encapsulates much of post-industrial America.

Without actually ever taking to task the vestiges of that assembly-line approach to living, New Orleans simply observes them— much in the way that my grandma would stand barefoot in her pink muumuu, under her pecan tree, watching the antics of her many grandkids. My gran would shake her head in bemusement, reach into her clothespin bag, and let the sun kiss the laundry in a way that Tide has tried to imitate for over fifty years. Like her, New Orleans watches the world's antics. She is not in denial about how the world is; she simply chooses to keep attending to the beauty, the heartbreak, the joie de vivre that humans have stupidly attempted to automate out of life.

She's a beauty, but she ain't for everyone. Moving fast is not really in the fabric of the city. Those potholes and live oaks growing through the sidewalk? They can be seen as evidence of infrastructural decay (they are) or as a lifting of the scrim called collective societal denial about grief. This denial pushes the bereaved to hurry through the hardship, denying their own humanity as they try to cope. We try to pave over grief, but it pushes its way up through the concrete like the roots of the live oaks that line the streets of my adopted city. Some of us even pave superhighways over our loss, trying as quickly as possible to whatever we were before loss dismantled us. And by some of us, I mean me. Something about those roots poking up through the pavement reminds me that grief doesn't need a highway; it needs a slow, cracked sidewalk where you can tread as slowly as you need.

So, more advice: Don't come to New Orleans to party for partying's sake. That's what Vegas is for. Come if you are heartbroken and you need the kiss of sweet olive on your brow as you walk in the not-quite cool of the eve. Come to New Orleans if you are ready to let the blues split your ache open. Come if you are willing to sip a Sazarac on a hot summer night while the tears pool on your collarbone. Go to mass even if you don't believe a word of the liturgy. Dress up to the nines one day and wander a swamp the next in your oldest pair of cut-offs.

Don't come to New Orleans to ferret out your grief, because New Orleans knows that grief is illogical. New Orleans will allow you to embody your grief and not tell a soul about it—but when someone you don't know says, "Hey baby," or "What's up boo?", you and that person will share a kinship that is bestowed when two souls meet in passing and warmly affirm each other's dignity.

New Orleans fosters this kinship because she is no stranger to loss and so no taker-for-granted of communion. Because New Orleans is a city of heartbreak. This city has had her heart broken so many times the air is tinged with the fragrance of loss. Sorrow is misted into the air like the scent of magnolias in spring. Between some combination of geography, human folly, and chance, New Orleans has been uniquely plagued by, well, *plagues*—disasters both ecological and human made.

In 1755, when the Acadians were kicked out of Nova Scotia in Le Grand Derangement and settled around New Orleans, they did so with great upheaval. We think of the heritage they maintained, but I think it is telling that in order to settle for good, they underwent a name change. Acadians became Cajuns? The Acadians were pushed into the area, while the Chitimacha, once the most powerful tribe in the region, were forcibly removed. Long before coastal erosion was a whisper of a worry, Bienville made war on the tribe, eroding their lands with a twelve-year-long war.

Only a year after the slaughter ended, the first enslaved Africans landed in America by way of New Orleans, which became the largest center of slave trade in the United States. Over 135,000 humans were trafficked prior to the Civil War—all on the banks where sunscreened-slathered tourists now schlep to the festival of the week. I count myself among that number.

Sanitizing these cultural plate tectonics sells gumbo but belies the fact that Heartbreak City is as apt a moniker as The Big Easy—maybe even more so.

Sometimes natural and human choices have dovetailed into

a tour de force of disaster. Just three months into the War of 1812, French consul Louis Tousard chronicled a hurricane rivaling Katrina in magnitude if not destruction. Of the Hurricane of 1812, he penned: "During the night a hurricane more horrible than any event, that even the oldest among us could remember, destroyed all the construction in the harbor; knocked down buildings; and took roofs from nearly all the houses in the city."[1] Heartbreak whirled in within the midst of a war that would claim the lives of approximately fifteen thousand.

I joke with my kids that we live in a city of plagues. Each spring we get real spry as we step around stinging caterpillars. We batten down the hatches against swarms of formosan termites eager to chomp down on our historical homes. But, banter aside, New Orleans is a city that has literally succumbed to plagues. Covid-19 is far from our first. Over the span of eighty-eight years (1817–1905), yellow fever ravaged the city, claiming over forty-one thousand lives.[2] These numbers, so easy to zip into a few sentences, represent individual heartbreaks stacked end to end.

Heartbreak City hasn't outlived her lineage. In 2023, we were the murder capital of the United States, and our state was long known as the incarceration capital of not just this country but the world; meanwhile, we rank third in the US for HIV infections and are still suffering the economic and medical impacts of Covid-19. The loss of our children pains me most. We exist in a time where grieving mothers are laying their babies to rest because of stray bullets and other babies are carjacking SUVs in Uptown. Clearly, loss is not just a personal thing but a collective one. Heartbreak City is alive and well.

I do not wish to sweep aside these ailments and, from a place of extreme privilege, romanticize a city that, in many ways, is pretty damn fucked up. But I would not be honest if I did not acknowledge that in my experience, Heartbreak City is a healer nevertheless—a wounded healer, most certainly, and perhaps I love her all the more for that.

That's it!

Heartbreak City is a wounded healer. In her sensuality, I found my way back to the land of the living. In her mysticism, I found peace with the fact that I will always have one foot in the land of the living and one on the other side. She embodies the reality that has felt true for me ever since Elijah left: No matter how whole I may become, I am simply not all here. The loss of my little boy dismantled me, or what I thought was me. Ever since we placed Elijah's ashes in a little graveyard in Florida, I have felt that much of me lies in repose with his remains. Do you ever feel like that? The veil between the living and dead was lifted for me the day we laid my boy to rest under a crepe myrtle tree.

Elijah's grave is tidily hidden from the bustle of my former city. Not so of the graveyards in New Orleans. Here, the living walk among the dead, treading our way around their exclusively above-ground sepulchers and sacred spaces. I really can't imagine another place that physically intertwines the living and the dead like New Orleans does. In this city, it is not uncommon to have a trip across town interrupted by a corpse-carrying carriage followed by umbrella-toting, rug-cutting second-liners.

It feels so appropriate to have my day upended in this way. As I wait for the second-line to clear, I could either observe the passing, honor the life, or join in the parade. For a few moments, I can bring the burden of carrying on in the wake of Elijah's death to the collective by humming a few bars of "Just a Closer Walk with Thee" along with the band. Hell, catharsis is built into the fabric of everyday life. Why isn't *that* in our city's brochures? Shouldn't "New Orleans: come cry in our courtyards and twerk it out at Tipitinas" be at least one of our mottos?

I don't know. I only know that the sorrow in the air here has been a balm to me. The flip side of the laissez-faire attitude for which we have been named "The Big Easy" is that New Orleans will simply let you *be* in whatever state you are in. We let the arc of sorrow run as long as it needs to, and well, if that sorrow does you in, we will let your ashes flow down the delta and be carried out to sea. It's not that New Orleans doesn't care; it's just that New Orleans will not try to fix you. In fact, perhaps the great wisdom of this city is that it knows that much of what we call "broken" should really be called "being a human." This sentiment is the sediment from which our inclusivity springs, not from any ideological motivation. It's really just, "Honey child, you are one of God's creatures. Now come on down here to the levee and eat this mess o' crawfish." I really can't imagine another way. I don't even want to.

At first, New Orleans allowed me to find a way to do something that approximated living. Her full-on embrace of merriment was the jolt my system required to awaken from my grief-induced stupor. My melancholy needed the daily reminder that a life with deep grief can still be a life worth living. This is a truth that I am still learning to accept.

Though I don't think my grief itself has been complicated, my relationship to my grief has been. Elijah's death was a ground zero of loss. Many other losses have come to reside in that crater. In some ways, I am not so different from my Jeep. If Gigi is testing out her ship of Theseus paradox here in the only city I know of where you can go off-roading while remaining on the road, I feel like a one woman test-case for that paradox. If your worldview flips so fundamentally that you have replaced almost all of your old beliefs about the nature of reality, are you still the same person?

And when you split your time between Costco and the crypt, are you ever wholly of this earth again?

In the first year after Elijah died, people expected the rawness. Though I no longer speak to many people from my fundamentalist days, my then community was there for me in ways that can only be described as angelic. The meals, the flowers, the odes to Elijah, and the embraces carried me through the early days. I was allowed and even encouraged to wail. But, as is the norm, those early casserole-infused attempts to comfort me waned. I had to start carrying the weight of my grief more or less alone. As I picked up that weight and tried to function, the only way I knew to do so was to mute it, or, worse, make it grist for some "to God be the glory" mill.

This caused my grief to involute. Something worse than depression set in. Repression is a bitch, y'all. My senses dulled. Even though I was parenting my other four children, I did so with too much awareness of how easily it could all end. Balancing the truth of a loved one's demise with pushing toddlers around Sam's Club is no easy task. I failed at it repeatedly. And when my last large-scale heave at making something good come of Elijah's death failed, when my strength was failing, New Orleans came along. Or rather, a job for my ex-husband came along. When I landed in the city, carrying my nursing baby in tow, I felt it. The embrace. The tango of hope and heartbreak that causes some people to step off of a plane for a weekend fling and make it their mission to live here.

My healing started in the shade of a December day one month before the Mardi Gras move. I was a wraith when I came to New Orleans on that trip, ostensibly to narrow down our new home choices to a few near Audubon Park. I was worn down, weary with the work of grief and trying to carry on. The canopy of oaks lining St. Charles Avenue softened the early winter sun. And that mild sun nestled into the nooks and crannies of the city, beckoning me, awakening my curiosity. The humid air soothed the cracks in my dried out soul.

My happiest memory from that first foray into the city is a simple one, a delightful hour passed on a sprawling porch, sipping a latte while my baby rested. They napped, I did nothing at all. Into the sheer exhaustion of soldiering on, a bit of wounded healing seeped.

The city was still fresh off her latest and perhaps greatest heartbreak: Katrina. She was still disheveled in some places, seemingly distraught in others, but her pulse beat beneath pavement. God, what a testament to how healing actually works—

one plot of land at a time cleared of debris, one tree replanted, and even then you can't rush the roots to reclaim their hold beneath the sod. Each gutted house was restored not to its former glory but to a different one. I could not at the time give testament to the many hours of work that it took to take her from watery graveyard to where she was on that December day. But something in her state called to me. It was her life, existing out of the composted sorrows of so many who have had their hearts broken here.

I know that my sorrow is not their sorrow. I know enough to not conflate my own particular missing of this small boy with any other grief. Still, the universal and the particular do intersect, don't they? Though my grief and New Orleans' is not the same, New Orleans' acknowledgement and honoring of sorrow—in her music, her history, hell, even her streets—has allowed me to walk hand in hand with my own. My sorrow has moved from being all I feel to being a part of who I am. Just as the graveyards exist across the way from the dancing halls, my sorrow is only a stone's throw away from my sensuality, my silliness, and even my ambition. I can wake full of sorrow in the morning and be ready to slip into something sexy at night. Tears may take me down to the floor on a Tuesday afternoon, but the bayou will beckon to me in the morning. New Orleans never asked me to solve my grief, but she did show me how to be a lady with it, and for that I am forever indebted.

By mid-pandemic, I think some wondered whether New Orleans could make it this time. Had our culture bearers, hospitality bringers, hell, most of us just been through too much? Would the next storm or surge be our undoing? Had twenty months of masks and ICUs and babies on ventilators cracked our foundation? In other words, would New Orleans continue to find her way? My answer, both then and now, is yes. When Katrina came and we truly became the city that care forgot, we took up the reins of our own care. I think that the same care existed through the pandemic, exists still. Yes, we are frayed, we are a city that carries our trauma on our sleeve. Isolation was not good for our hearts, and I still feel the grief. The hard times came rolling in like a hellhound on greased roller skates. And they decided to come and sit a spell.

In the midst of this travail, I guess no one gave the ocean the memo that we all were goin' through some shit already, and I'm not sure she would have cared. Enter Hurricane Ida. I don't know why the algorithm came up with this particular name, which is of German etymology. You know what Ida means? Industrious. Yup. Fucking Industrious decided to dovetail with whatever the hell we'd all been doing since March 2020. Of course Ida was going to be a category four. What else would you expect from a storm named Industrious?

Perhaps another day I'll write about the great exodus of 2021, wherein we re-learnt to avoid the rookie mistake of stopping to pee in Atlanta *ever*. I only bring up Industrious because that storm took another swipe at Heartbreak City. And she lost.

I don't want to come across as cavalier, especially as I write poised on the edge of another hurricane season. But I believe in the resilience of this city. New Orleans was forged in heartbreak, and I think her resilience resides in something ancient. Something in this soil is mystical, and I sense it stirring. I feel it in the drum circle on Cabrini bridge, in the way the customers at Cansecos are singing again in the aisles. The weather is turning, and with it, we are regathering our strength. Ida was a bad bitch, but at least she was a kind of blow that we know how to treat. We know how to care for people after the storm. Problem is, Covid is a long haul and takes a special kind of caring—but the question just becomes, where else can we be creative? What better city to show that even with trauma embedded in our sinews, we can open to the waves?

No. New Orleans is not done. And I intend to be here to see what shape her beauty takes next, knowing that her ancient strength is never as far off as some would like to think.

Perhaps this witnessing and sharing in her struggle is part of how I continue to honor and heal from my own loss. So: Let the good times roll.

Slaking the She-Beast

Before New Orleans began to heal me, before I knew I would need healing, before I was a bereaved mother, I was simply a mom. A twenty-five-year-old girl who labored in a hospital bed in Columbus, Ohio. It was winter. And in that excruciatingly cold January, an exhausted and exultant Desi held her newborn to her breast.

"Killer blue eyes," remarked the OB. Elijah, so alert and open, had entered the picture.

This birth was expected, hard-won. Elijah, so wanted, so eagerly awaited, was immediately nursed, held, loved. But Elijah's birth brought with it an unexpected other. This four-footed being arrived quietly alongside my firstborn, then padded off into the shadows of my psyche without a sound. There she lay in wait, purring out the words, *Protect, protect.* . . . While I was busy lullabying and patty-caking the days away with my baby, I had no idea that this She-Beast resided in the inner recesses of my amygdala, sharpening her claws and waiting to emerge if ever Elijah were threatened.

Emerge she did, on the playground one fall day. Elijah was a toddler who was trying to make his way up the ladder of one of those older metal slides. You know, the ones that have mostly been torn out of playgrounds because they are like ten feet tall and their sides could barely keep a teddy bear, let alone a toddler, from hurtling over the edge? Elijah did his best, but his chubby legs were ill-suited to the task. At fifteen months, he was one of the wobblier kids attempting the ascent. I watched from the ground, far enough away to allow his climb, yet close enough to catch him if he fell.

Isn't this what parents do? We may pick different distances from which to hover, but most of us hang back a little, ready to assist, hoping to mitigate damage if our kids take a tumble.

Incoming!

Out of nowhere, a slightly older but much burlier kid arrived on the scene. The kid moved fast and shoved Elijah to one side, scuttling my son's shaky climb in pursuit of his own. As Elijah went down, I saw red. My first urge was to throttle the brat. No, my first urge was to tend to Elijah, who shook off my attempts to kiss his boo-boo. So, I dusted him off, and, of course, Elijah turned his perfectly fine little cheeks toward the sky and began another upward lumber.

I returned to my post. Outwardly, I encouraged him, "Go on, buddy," but beneath my gentle veneer, the She-Beast still bristled, hackles raised, maw baring fangs.

Down, girl.

She finally slinked back to her lair, peering at the scene through half-closed eyes. She fixed one of them on Elijah and the other on the kid who remained oblivious of his near miss. As she watched, I mused: *So, that's a new emotion.*

Over the years, I have come to accept that this part of my psyche is hard-wired as a biological preemptive. She's not very nuanced, but she is focused. Living by her first word, "protect," she scans for all manner of dangers. In her milder moments, she held Elijah's other hand as we crossed streets, taught him that stove tops are hot and outlets are "owie," and stood watch over him at the mall while he threw pennies into the fountain and made wishes. We both took delight in being with Elijah, enjoying his burgeoning personality and vocabulary.

But even in these tamer times, the She-Beast is the yang to the nurturing yin. Her appearance became a constant over the years—not just for Elijah, but my other four children as well.

Ada saw the She-Beast in action when she was around nine years old. A neighborhood boy had crossed the ditch that separated her school playground from his home. He grabbed his crotch and slung a few lewd comments at my daughter. Ada didn't know what they meant. But I did. The beast brought out her tongue-o'-nine-tails and delivered one hell of a lashing.

"You will *never* speak to or even *look at* my daughter again. I can see your house from here. If you so much as enter this playground ever again, you will find cops at the door. Understood?" My voice was low. A snarl lurked beneath my words. "Go home."

"Yes, ma'am."

Had he owned a tail, I am certain it would have been tucked between his legs. He couldn't get home fast enough.

The She-Beast emerged again when another man catcalled both me and Navis at the same time in my corner grocery store. And the She-Beast unfurled her claws the day my second son was diagnosed in utero with a mysterious ailment that made it impossible for him to swallow amniotic fluid. That one kind of confused her though, because there was no flesh to tear apart. So instead she paced around while I labored. When Isaiah emerged, blue and silent, into the world, she thrashed, flailing at the unnamed ailment that had threatened him. She watched as the doctors plunged needles into his chest and pulled five hundred ccs of fluid out of his pleural cavity. As he slept, a neonate intubated in the intensive care unit, she kept watch over his bed, bemused by the tubes and monitors, but on guard, nonetheless.

And She-Beast was definitely there on the night that I helped build the bed that claimed Elijah's life. She whispered that something wasn't quite right about the bed. And there was me ignoring that intuition, singing Elijah a lullaby, and sleeping peacefully through the night. She nudged me to check on him. I did, around midnight. When we awoke, he was gone, and with him the whole world.

Except for the beast.

When Elijah passed, I expected the sorrow. I didn't expect her rage.

While She-Beasts may be helpful as metaphors for understanding what is happening when our brains move into fight or flight on behalf of our offspring, a She-Beast is still a beast. She has but one purpose: to ravage the enemy with a vengeance. Teeth and claws and take over.

So what is a She-Beast to do when the very person who brings the child into the world, the mother whose marrow exists to protect him, becomes the accidental agent of his demise?

When Elijah died, her anger extended to the universe at large, to God, to gravity and vectors and whatever had allowed Elijah to succumb. But the beast didn't stop there. Beasts know things in their breasts, and this one knew that I was in part responsible for my son's death. With that knowledge, those teeth and claws turned inward. They tore into my psyche. They ripped at the fabric of my mind. When Elijah died, the She-Beast began to devour from within.

There is always a sense of guilt when a parent outlives a child. But when the mother is involved accidentally in the death of her baby, she is left not only with waves of hysteria, grasping endlessly for her child, but also with a malignant self-hatred that oozes into her bones. At least, this mother was. I remember talking with my friend Celeste not long after Elijah died and asking her, "What kind of mother lets this happen to her child?" I don't even remember Celeste's response, but I do remember there was no soothing me.

I've since learned to stop asking these questions. Grouping mothers into good and bad and measuring their worth by what their offspring do or become is not only cruel, it uncomplicates the contexts in which both parents and children are operating. When I asked the question "What kind of mother lets this happen to her child?", I was not asking a new question. I was only extending this question into a new context.

The circumstances surrounding Elijah's death were far more complicated than can ever be answered by a single question. And I have since learned that even having the answers doesn't ease the absence of the people we grieve.

It is normal to try to make sense of a catastrophic loss. But, when ruminated upon, those questions can become defense mechanisms that keep us from the real work of grief. In reality, the only scenario that would have sufficed was "Surprise! This whole situation has been a modern-day adaptation of the Book of Job. We felt that a protagonist gender reversal was in order, and in order to make your performance believable, we couldn't actually tell you that everything is fine. But you did swell, and now you can go back to your regularly scheduled life."

What I needed, even more than such a divine intervention, was Elijah. I needed his rosebud kisses and chubby hands and chipmunk grin. I needed to watch him explore a hole in a tree and decide that it was where Winnie-the-Pooh lived. As my then husband aptly put it, I needed my chief smile-maker back.

I cannot speak to the tears of widows and orphans, but I can speak to these tears. They are hot. They are accompanied by deep primordial sounds that I didn't know my small frame could house. They are a swirling river of loss that you are some-how supposed to navigate while making fish sticks for your remaining kids. They are aching arms reaching around to hold your baby and finding only a crater of emptiness inside your heart. They are a hundred birthday candles you will never see blown out, the college essay you will not help your son write. They are the next dumb Disney movie that you won't watch with your child and get sick of them reenacting. They are the inconsolable tears of a mother bereft.

The day we found Elijah dead, my father—the fundamen-talist preacher of hellfire—came to me. Heartbroken, he held me outside on the grass where neighbors and church folk had gath-ered in solidarity with us. He sat with me in our living room where only hours earlier I had cradled Elijah's body while we waited for the police to arrive. In those moments, my father had no sermon to share, no platitudes to utter. My dad reached beyond the rhetoric of the pulpit and found the one Bible verse that put words to my groans. As he rocked me, he whispered, "Rachel weeping for her children because they are no more."

He was right.

I wept for my son, but my tears did not heal me. I used to think that because I cried so much, I began grieving Elijah early on. But I now think that much of what I then called grieving was actually the She-Beast shredding my soul with self-loathing. Those tears were not clean grief. They were tears tinged with self-flagellation. There was no mercy in them, no relief, for I thought that anyone who hurt Elijah deserved none. My boy. My little chubby-legged, musically gifted, playful, cherubic, blue-eyed son was gone. And I was culpable.

The police ruled the death an accident, and no charges were filed. For the sake of my remaining children, I'm so grateful for this. And they were, of course, right—this was the last thing myself or ex-husband intended to happen. My mind understood this fact. But I wanted justice for Elijah. I was torn between this desire for justice and a need to heal. These two opposing vectors tore at the continents of my psyche, a sort of reverse plate tectonics of the mind.

We planned a funeral that honored Elijah, played all of his favorite songs, eulogized him eloquently, buried him under a crepe myrtle tree reminiscent of the ones I used to climb as a child. In this early grief, I never drank much. I didn't turn to drugs. I sought solace in my religion, and I didn't stop parenting. I got up and nursed baby Ada, held her close. We took down the bed and turned Elijah's old room into an office. But I wasn't whole. I wasn't right. I wasn't a human anymore. I was a gutted corpse who had buried my sanity under a crepe myrtle tree in Florida and topped it off with a Winnie-the-Pooh headstone bearing the words "Little Man."

But Elijah was no man. He was little more than a baby who

never would be a man, a lamb who was led to suffocate in an ill-conceived bed. Elijah was a victim. She-Beast knew it and growled a new word at me: "Murderer."

Of course, I wasn't a murderer.

I was an unwitting cause of an accident. There is even an acronym for people like me, who live with the harm we have caused: CADI, or causers of accidental death or injury. While no one brings this little tidbit about themselves up at cocktail parties, the truth is, there are many of us. There exists on this globe a substantial subset of people who have inadvertently hurt others, who have unwittingly been party to their deaths. CADIs are created in a single moment when a perfect storm of circumstance brings them into contact with another human. The accidents happen in an instant. One moment, two humans are living their lives. The next, someone left is dead, and the survivor is left traumatized with the knowledge that a life has been snuffed out, and they are to blame.

Some of us were involved in car accidents. Others lost people to pools or guns in our homes. The common thread between us is that none of us had any intent to cause harm. Both we and those we harmed are victims.

Once I was able, I dragged my shell of a self to a CADI support group. I spoke my stories, whispered my shame. I grappled with my guilt. That support group is the one place I have felt seen in my whole grief as a CADI. I didn't stay too long, but that group helped me believe on my best days that I am a good person who was part of a horrible accident. It's easy to fall prey to simplistic clichés when we are bereaved. And no wonder that, as a CADI, I was searching for footholds of meaning, and ideas like "living for two," whatever the fuck that means, can be appealing. Attending the CADI support group did not provide me with an intellectual foothold. It simply made me feel less alone in my trauma. On my worst days, I believed that two tombs should have been dug because for a very long time whatever I did after causing an accidental death, certainly didn't feel like living.

Traumatic deaths often give birth to traumatic grief. As a mother who was involved in an accidental death, I am double bereaved. I lost not only my son; I also lost my sense that I am capable of adequately taking care of my own children. For a mother who wants nothing more than to nurture her babes, to protect them from all harm, this secondary loss has in some ways been as devastating as the first. I lost the ability to trust my gut. I was left with a searing sense of helplessness where it mattered the most: the actual, literal preservation of my children's lives. I believed myself to be the worst of mothers, a pariah of our species. I believed I deserved to be reviled, to be locked up in some sort of special prison for mothers like me, where we would be sentenced to hear (on infinite repeat) the screams of the children we had hurt.

No such prison existed, so the She-Beast and I created it. We sentenced me to lifelong sorrow. If Elijah couldn't live, then neither could I. After birthing and caring for Elijah's every need, my heart had become so knit to him. His every cry. His every need. His whims. My life force felt bound to his. Without him, I became my own judge, jury, and executioner. Had it not been for my daughter who remained and the three children who came after Elijah, I may have carried out that sentence in the flesh. As it was, I lived in a sort of existential limbo. I created a sort of schizophrenic existence where I tried to care for my remaining children while at the same time trying to kill what remained of my own life.

Needless to say, it didn't work.

But it did make me very, very unwell. And the truth of Elijah's loss, the need to mourn it fully, as fully as one can, eventually thrust through my self-imposed prison.

The experience of feeling like both a victim and a perpetrator is incredibly disorienting. I know that life often calls us to hold two contradictory truths in tandem. But I think, for a CADI, the fact that a human being can be ordering a latte one minute and skidding to a stop too late the next is some-thing the Fates could not have done a better job designing if they had woken up on a random Tuesday, held a staff meet-ing, and decided that inspiring war and famine had grown a wee bit tedious: "Wouldn't it be more fun to watch a sin-gle human mind involute on itself by having to grapple with two equally painful, equally 'true,' seemingly diametrically opposed truths? Watch this."

And that, fellow humans, is how cognitive dissonance was born.

If we, even for a moment, allow ourselves to hold onto the hot-poker reality that we all have the power to accidently end life—and if we fully focus on the fact of our fallibility, again, for even a moment—traumatic responses are not only to be expected, they might just be warranted. Go stare down that truth with a good bourbon if you are feeling particularly "deep" on a given day. And then close that line of thought down immediately if you want to do anything other than sit in a paralyzed stupor for the next fifty-three years.

I am not being hyperbolic about the idea that our intent does not equal outcome. This truth is inherent in the word acci-dent. I live as one who didn't see the danger. Worse, I engi-neered the danger with wood and screws and love—yes, with *love*. The very fact that I could intend love, act out of love, and that the upshot of my love could cause irreparable harm is a very inconvenient truth indeed. We can mean well, and we can fuck it all to hell.

Humans who mean well are doing harm all the damn day. When I was a fundamentalist, I meant well. One could argue that I meant the highest "well" of all. What more "well" could I have intended other than to help sinners move from the hands of the angry God and onto the road that leads to the pearly gates? This truth is why I don't get on board with peo-ple saying that fundamentalists are disingenuous, even those in politics. When I voted pro-life, pro-Bush (twice), I wasn't doing so because I was trying to cause harm. When I was teaching my kids that being gay was wrong, I wasn't trying to do harm.

But I *did* cause harm. In my attempts to "rescue" people, I harmed them. My fundamentalism refused to accept fundamental parts of their identities. I was kind of like a flat earther, but the earth was other people's experiences, other people's truths. In "flattening" my worldview to a literal interpretation of an ancient text, I consistently asked anyone who wasn't straight, cis, or Christian in *exactly* the way I was to, you know, just not be that anymore. And if such people were having too hard a time lopping off part of their souls, then the solution was simple: maybe they had a demon. Literally.

Now, demons in the olden days had much much better names: Legion. Beelzebub. Molek. When my own demons were getting cast out as a teen, they went by much more boring words: "anger" and, get this, "masturbation." (Fortunately, the out-casting didn't work.) In the world I grew up in and once taught to my own children, sexual "deviancies" weren't just sins to be eradicated, but acts imbued with demonic gusto. I came from the "pray the gay away" generation of Southern Baptists. We weren't exactly sure what gay was, other than not right. What I have learned is that you are not loving someone when you are constantly trying to change them. Yet many still construe this type of rejection and pressure as "loving" the so-called sinner, as "meaning well."

Realizing just how fallible I am has humbled me. An outgrowth of knowing my own power to harm has made me try on this revolutionary new skill: *listening*, one method of un-flattening. This includes the ways that the She-Beast and I teamed up to flatten myself.

I know that some harms cannot be repaired. So, if we are given the opportunity to repair on the micro or macro level, then we are being given a gift. We get to learn, to make things better. Isn't this part of what it means to be human? When we begin to understand that unrepaired rifts create a schism between our soul and God (yes, God), then listening can move us into learning, and learning can move us into action and, hopefully, healing. Healing ultimately comes from letting ourselves feel deeply and then letting those feelings move us from sackcloth and ashes to kinder ways of moving through the world.

This includes kindness to ourselves.

My self-forgiveness, the slaking of the She-Beast, wasn't easy, but it was necessary. Though Elijah's death had eviscerated me, though my most poignant belief was that I deserved to die—that death was both my judgment as an accidental perpetrator and my right as a bereaved mother—my children deserved something else. Whatever that mother looks like is the mother that I am resolved to become. This bitch is messy. She is no beatific vision of placidity. She listens to her kids when she makes a mistake that hurts their hearts, listens to the ways her past actions created circumstances that led to their trauma. Because there's one thing she is fiercely committing to being: *here, fully present for her children.*

Each of my remaining children is as precious as Elijah. They are all beacons of innocence and now, as they grow older, experience. And these children deserve a mother who is as healthy as she can possibly be.

In order to become the mother who is here now for my children, I had to be willing to embrace the story of my son's passing. All of it. It's a story I've been digesting bit by bit for over two decades. Doing so unmade me, but in a more transforming way than the She-Beast's grief-stricken evisceration. When the woman who bore a child becomes the woman who buries him, she becomes an entirely different creature altogether. At first, she is simply haunted. She is gaunt. She is lean of soul. But that woman finally figured out that in order to be a mother to the four children who remain, she had to remove her claws from her own heart.

And so, in order to embrace the work of loving my chil-

dren fully, I chose to pardon myself for the "sin" of not seeing.
I am coming to see that it wasn't a sin at all. This pardoning
did not happen all at once. In fact, it is a daily decision. But
that pardoning created space for She-Beast and I to coexist
again. We are still figuring out her new job description. Gone
are the days when my children needed her in her original
manifestation. I sometimes wonder if there is not a different
sort of beast that is needed now.

In Madeline L'Engle's *A Wrinkle in Time*, three kids—Meg,
Charles Wallace, and their friend Calvin—are called upon to
save the earth from impending darkness. . . as you do when
you're the protagonists in a young adult novel. At one point
late in the tale, Meg finds herself on a strange planet, feeling as
if she has failed her brother, herself— basically all of humanity.
The mission is balancing on a knife's edge. Meg's baby brother
is worshiping at the altar of a giant mind control brain. Meg
herself has just endured an iciness of soul to which she almost
succumbed. She has figured out that the grownup on the scene,
her father, cannot save her. In the middle of this coming-of-age
moment, Meg encounters a beast.

Meg is initially frightened of this tentacle-wielding, furry
creature. But in order to be saved from the effects of the brain, it
is this beast, not a man, that saves Meg. Meg's iciness didn't need
reason. This beast does not wield claws but soup, song, and long
enfolding arms. The logic of our language makes no sense to the
beast. The ways in which humans perceive light and word only
seem to muddy the truth. The point is that this beast soothes
Meg, not by solving anything, but by the power of sweet minis-
tration. Aunt Beast is her name, and the moniker is perfect.

One might think that a mother would be called for in this
situation. But even though Meg's mother is painted as a bastion of unfailing love, perhaps Madeline L'Engle knew a few
things about mothers. A mother might hover a bit *too* much.
An auntie will love you and let you be.

In my own case, I hope that She-Beast has been replaced by

something more like Aunt Beast—something fiercely nurturing, rather than fierce for blood. I would like to think that the days of baring teeth and claws are done. While that instinct to protect at all costs is still there, I have learned to temper it. The beast and I coexist. Self-compassion is the scar tissue that covers the wound she caused.

Twenty-three years after Elijah went to bed and did not wake up, she and I inhabit this precarious place of letting my children climb much higher ladders, of letting them leave home, as two of them recently have. All of my kids are now old enough to make some intractable grown up mistakes of their own. I am acutely aware that it is not only I who might make the slight wrong turn of the wheel, but them. I stand back from the ladder knowing that my arms are not strong enough to break their falls. The natural laws of gravity, velocity, and gene mutation bend for no mother, no matter how much she loves her children. In becoming the woman I am now, I come to accept this truth: Learning to live is learning to lose again and again and to keep opening up our hearts despite this harrowing reality.

A few years back, I was talking about Elijah with my friend Matthew. Of course, one doesn't talk about these things freely or often because they are just too heavy. They lift that flimsy curtain that veils us from the existential void and threatens to send our lizard brains into a permanent state of fetal recoil. The tendrils of this loss regrow in very peculiar ways. The painful thoughts reinvent themselves in ways that I can't even imagine until they are upon me. Sometimes they coil around me until I recognize them for what they are: vestiges of my old self-loathing—the She-Beast remembering again the taste of my blood.

It took two bottles of wine and a whole lot of small talk for Matthew and I to finally get around to the topic. Even then, I backdoored my way into the subject. When I shared my fear that losing Elijah meant I was unworthy of being loved, Matthew took absolutely no time to look me right in the eyes and reply, "Desi, this is the very reason you deserve it all the more."

I don't know if Matthew is right, but his words landed. They brought me sorely needed comfort. I utter his words when my thoughts turn dark. They help me be tender with myself. If there is one truth I've come to embrace in the via dolorosa of this loss, it is that tenderness is a balm for the bereaved. Apply it liberally for a long time and as often as necessary. Maybe Matthew wasn't exactly correct. Maybe I don't deserve love more than any other human. But what happened to my baby boy, what happened to me, doesn't make me deserve it less.

This thought is progress. It is another decision. It is claws retracting. It is enough.

Damn, I Guess it was a Tragedy?

In the decidedly not cool of the eve, my lover and I sit in two tall chairs that adorn his porch. It is most definitely late summer in New Orleans—the time when we are all truly tired of peak Louisiana heat and planning for hurricanes. Tonight, we cut the heat with a nicely chilled white he brought home from work for the occasion. Two or three candles flicker in dusk, reminding me that I am indeed on a romantic rendezvous.

To this little tryst, I wore a slip of sunset colored dress and leather sandals—hand-me-downs from one of my grad school colleagues. But my lover doesn't know that. He definitely doesn't know that most of my clothes are thrifted or that I spent a good half hour rummaging through my closet to find this little number that matches the sky. There are lot of things my lover doesn't know about me—little things like, for instance, my full name, my aspirations as a writer, or the fact that I am carrying the weight of one too many dead dreams in my chest.

It's not that I am trying to be guarded about my past; we are just early in this process, and I have found that sharing certain tidbits about myself too soon, like that I was raised in a high control group or that I used to wonder if being a martyr was *the* way to go out, doesn't usually lead to the desired relational results.

I need this tryst more than my lover knows. At the time of this meeting, I was still recovering from my breakup breakdown, which is exactly what it sounds like. After my divorce, I fell hard into the arms of a gentle man who was willing to do, well, pretty damn near everything for me. Even though I tried to tell him things at the beginning, like, "I think I might be too sad to be in a relationship," he assured me that all was well. And it was—until a wee bit of woundedness crept into the crevices of our relationship. By a wee bit of woundedness, I mean that I brought to that first relationship every unmet expectation of my fundamentalist marriage, a sense of existential loneliness that took root in the crater Elijah had left when he passed, and a whole slew of post-divorce issues. Let's just say that I might have been a tad much during this phase of my post-fundamentalist journey.

I am not shaming myself for being in great pain, but I will also say that being in constant agony is perhaps not the best foundation upon which to build a partnership. "Hey baby hold my drink while I let this guttural wail rip through me for a few. Now, where were we? Oh yes, the seal documentary." I think my boyfriend needed me to get better faster than I could. Turns out that it takes more than two years to rebuild an entire belief system. Who knew? He was kind, but, like many of us, he was ill-equipped to deal with a partner navigating a dark night (after night, after night) of the soul. After three years and change, we split, and I found myself floundering a bit.

That's a lie. I was a complete dumpster fire of a human. At times I wasn't sure if I was grieving my breakup, my worldview, my son, my former self, or just my whole effing life. In retrospect, that last one feels about right. My therapist said that it is normal for new grief to open up old wounds. Awesome—as if knowing that I was going to re-grieve everything from the time that one kid in fifth grade said I walked funny to the day my boyfriend no longer wanted to touch me was somehow helpful, but according to my therapist, "You will always be grieving something."

Now, I love it when a therapist drops truth into the muddy

depths of a grieving psyche, but sometimes I wonder if "You will always be grieving something" might not have been the best thing to say to a woman whose hobby list could read "Taking long walks on the beach and spending Friday afternoons in a fetal position." Maybe it would be better to just lie and say, "Give it a few months, honey. You'll be fine."

My favorite fetal position hang spot is apparently the kitchen floor *right* in front of the fridge. I don't know if I am hoping to reach for a nice little post gut-heaving snack or if it just feels right that if I am going to crumple, it should be onto the crypt-like surface of kitchen tile. All I know is that whenever grief decides to take me low, it's to the kitchen floor I go. Tell me, therapist, is that also normal?

To be clear, my therapist wasn't wrong about the grieving thing. I think I just needed comfort more than I needed words. And this idea should be of comfort to anyone who is trying to help someone in the throes of deep grief: If you think you don't know what to say, run with that thought. If you think you do know what to say, you're probably wrong. Best to say nothing and just be there. That's it.

If it helps, you can think of your grief-stricken loved one like a special Squishmellow who comes with a tag that says, "Hi, I'm Griefy! I don't really do much. All my hobbies have taken a back seat to my current passion for writhing in agony and soaking your sheets with tears. To care for me, make me a bit of tea and shut the fuck up while I look wretched. Then make me some more tea."

My therapist did balance out the idea that I would always be grieving something with the idea that grief would become more manageable one day. Which day, exactly, I wonder? Is it Tuesdays, because Tuesdays are usually pretty sucky since they are giving rise to Wednesdays, and Wednesdays are when you don't have any leftover weekend high to run on and Friday still feels pretty far away. If grief could be better on Tuesdays, that would be awesome.

Obviously, this is not what my therapist meant. She meant that the waves of grief would grow smaller in time and you can do a gradually better job of acting like a normal human. In fact, if you play your grief cards right, most people (like your new lover, for instance) won't know that you are grieving at *all*.

To exemplify this idea, my therapist used the sweetest little metaphor of a grief box: "Once you have grieved something, you put it in the box. You can choose to open the box and revisit the painful times in your life, but they aren't so painful anymore." I nodded, picturing a little bejeweled, art-deco box with the words "Grief Box" etched on the lid.

So, let me get this straight: *I* am not supposed to crawl into a big box and ask someone to shovel dirt over me. Rather, I'm supposed to let my grief-waves roll through me over and over—early in the morning while picking out oatmeal, at 11:43 p.m. while watching that scene in *Supernatural* where Castiel finally confesses his love for Dean and goes directly to superhell—maybe even on a porch while sipping pinot gris and hoping to get laid. Ostensibly, doing so will shrink the grief down to a size that will fit into one of these little grief boxes. Sorry, grief, I have other plans tonight. Get back in the box, please.

Please believe me when I say that I would pay through the nose for even one of those little gilded gems. Actually, I would love to own ten of these little darlings, which I would line up on my mantle and use as stocking holders near my Christmas tree.

My kids would walk by and say, "Dearest Mama, are those little bejeweled boxes holding some wondrous Christmas treat?"

"No, my sweet angels, those are my grief boxes, where I keep my life's sorrows on lockdown and revisit them at a time that is wholly convenient to me. I just thought that they would help usher in this season of cheer. Plus, the cats peed on the old ones, and they are wholly unusable."

At any rate, no one informed my grief that these little boxes existed, or that my grief was supposed to shrink down to fit into them. So instead, grief wrapped itself around my DNA and informed every aspect of my life for about twenty years.

In this early breakup-breakdown phase, grief reminded me again what a diva she is. She doesn't care how busy you are. Exciting job opportunity? Grief doesn't care. Need to pull a sixty-hour workweek? Too bad. Parenting four kids? So what. Your Grief Diva especially doesn't care about your newfound freedom or that beckoning "opportunity for growth." Grief takes center stage and upends your best laid plans. Grief waltzes in with a contract you didn't know you signed and says, "Pay up."

Here's what I mean. If you give yourself to love, you are signing a blood pact of which Faust himself would approve. In showing up for the magic of intimate connection, you are in effect saying, "I allow my heart to be sewn to another. Each day, I will stitch another seam that knits my heart to my beloved. I will do this moment by moment, day after day, for as many years as I am allowed. Every inside joke we make, each time we set up the hexagonal pieces for a rousing game of Settlers of Catan, every romp in the sack or trip to the library is another stitch in the seam that knits our hearts together. I do this knowing that one day, the great seam ripper of loss will come along, and in a single moment leave me with less than half of my heart.

"In exchange for the mystery of deep connection, I agree to have the fabric of my heart violently torn in two. I agree to not only miss my beloved but also undergo a psychic rendering of cataclysmic proportions. It won't matter if the person I love is a child, a best friend, or a lifemate. It also won't matter if the person was fucked up, or the relationship was doomed from the beginning. Either way, I will bleed."

Is it any wonder that the joke, "What do you call people on their second marriage?" rings so true? By the way, the answer is ... *optimists.*

In those early months of my post-breakup breakdown, I managed to look pretty okay most days. I got up and did the normal humaning things like brushing my teeth and drinking my coffee. I was still trying to figure out an entire new worldview because the old one was, well, completely wrong. I was also trying to do a little thing called finish my freaking dissertation. My grief didn't care. I also began dating again, and that's when I learned that grief is a lot like Gigi the last time she broke down after her four-month-long recovery from an accident. I thought we had patched her up, but as soon as she spent an hour on the open road, she left me stranded with a red hot engine exactly halfway between New Orleans and Baton Rouge.

Yeah, that's a lot of what grief is like. You think you have your heart patched up enough to open it up. You take it for a spin on the open road only to find yourself stranded on a hot stretch of interstate halfway between the man who used to be your boyfriend and the one you are hoping will be your next. If you are lucky, you wake up next to your fridge in a fetal position and you find yourself scrolling through your exes' exes for some sort of Instagram intel about why it didn't work out. Hint: probably because I was a cocktail of post-fundamentalist complicated-PTSD and codependency.

I was about six months into stitching the fabric of my heart back around itself when I first saw him. It was in a coffee shop where I had fled to avoid my ex-boyfriend. Yes, fled. I didn't flee him because he was an asshole (he wasn't). It's just that when he moved out, he stayed in our mutual neighborhood. On a given day, I might run into him at our little grocery store, or see him walking his new puppy on the bayou, or, my personal favorite, strolling hand in hand with a date under the live oaks on Esplanade. This just wouldn't do as I was desperately trying to get my heart to understand that this boy was long gone. So, I fled to this little coffee shop on the outskirts of the neighborhood and began the diligent process of acting like I was not a shell of a human. This was best done gripping a cappuccino and plunging into writing the world's most tedious of tomes: an academic literature review.

One day while I sat, pounding through yet another sexy study showing that teachers hate standardized testing, he appeared.

Tall. Lanky. Salt-and-pepper hair. I felt an instant attraction. Before I met my lover, I thought I knew what attraction meant. But when I say I was attracted to this man, I mean that I felt like an invisible magnet the size of Montana was in my abdomen, drawing me toward him. And I couldn't make it stop. I tried, because it was incredibly annoying to be pounding away at my absolutely riveting literature review and somehow know without looking up that my crush had entered the premises.

Thoughts like *Baby, I'd like to teach to your test* would creep into my psyche only to be replaced with more mundane musing like, "I wonder what this stranger does for a living?" or "What would happen if I ended up in line behind him and my finger 'accidentally' found its way to those salt-and-pepper locks?"

My lover lived in my diary as Mr. Salt-and-Pepper for a while. "Mr. Salt-and-Pepper just walked in, and I think maybe he just looked at me. Or not. Maybe he is looking at the internet password, but he doesn't have a laptop." I wrote a few entries like these when I was forty-seven . . . or maybe I was sixteen, because that's about how school girl-silly I felt over this burgeoning crush. For his part, Mr. Salt-and-Pepper seemed completely nonplussed.

One of our first unbearably flirty conversations went something like this:

Me: Soooo, you ordered both orange juice and black coffee. That tells me a lot about you.

Him: Oh.

Me: Yeah.

Now you can see why I am surprised that suitors are not clamoring to put a ring on the fount of banter like this.

So, how did Mr. Salt-and-Pepper and I move from this orange juiced-coded, palpable sexual tension to an actual porch date several months later?

It is at this point that I will utter the words that came to my mind one fateful spring morning during the ascendance of my crush: *Damn you, Brené Brown.* For the uninitiated, Brené

Brown is a social science megastar who encourages people to (of all things) actually embrace vulnerability. Ick. According to Brown's research, vulnerability is a gateway to human connection and human connection is more important than my three morning cappuccinos.

On said morning, I had just seen Mr. Salt-and-Pepper offer someone in need some kindness, which of course made me once again think that my fingers belonged in his hair, when I came across these words by Brené Brown:

"Vulnerability is not winning or losing; it's having the courage to show up and be seen when we have no control over the outcome. Vulnerability is not weakness; it's our greatest measure of courage."[3]

I repeat: *Damn you, Brené Brown.* The last thing I wanted to do was be vulnerable in my love life. At this juncture in time, I didn't feel like I was exposing my underbelly. I felt like my *whole body* was underbelly. Being vulnerable about my feelings felt like the worst possible thing to do. And it also felt unavoidable if I was going to heal. So I did it. I opened up my bag, pulled out the stationery that I always kept on hand (men find this irresistible), and penned these words:

"Today, I noticed that you performed a simple act of kindness, and I wanted to tell you how moved I was by it.

And also, I think you are incredibly handsome, and I have a huge crush on you.

My name is Desi

[insert phone number]"

I handed the note to and quickly exited the premises. And then, I waited.

Mr. Salt-and-Pepper also waited—a full eighteen hours and thirty-seven minutes—to respond (trust me, I know):

"It is often in the small kind acts of strangers that I have taken solace in dark times.

I too have noticed that you are easy on the eyes.

My name is . . ."

We will just keep calling him Mr. Salt-and-Pepper because someone once told me that I am supposed to have boundaries.

Several months and incredibly awkward conversations later, Mr. Salt-and-Pepper texted and asked me to share some wine at his abode. Hence, we return to the opening scene on the aforementioned porch.

On this sultry night, my lover wears a white linen shirt, unbuttoned just enough to tease. He is a silver fox with an MFA (of course he is)—that bohemian intellectual type that I find pretty much irresistible. This setup with the wine and linen intermingling with the last vestiges of summer sultry all make me want to be wearing less of this five-dollar dress.

I still never know when this lover will call. He comes, he goes, but when he comes we share the kind of connection that makes me want him to stay. I am pretty sure he won't, but there is a good bottle of wine to be drunk, and conversation to be had, connection to be explored. No matter the events surrounding our meetings, I have consistently felt the most incredible desire to disrobe; this evening is no different.

Our talk tonight is of tragedy, specifically of the Greek variety. Mr. Salt-and-Pepper, normally more of the listening type, dives into the subject with an unusual gusto. (Dear Diary, is it a red flag if a man becomes particularly animated when discussing tragic heroes?)

"The tragic hero is a basically good human who becomes a pawn of the gods," he says. "The thing about tragedies that make them *tragic* is not the fact that really bad things happen. No. Tragedy ensues when circumstances are perfectly engineered by the gods to bring the hero low—so low that he really can't recover from the blow."

My lover is not mansplaining; he wields genuine authority

over his topic and doesn't miss a beat of refilling our glasses and making quite the intimate theater of this little gathering. I get the sense that he is enjoying curating this scene, and as he is doing a fantastic job ushering me into the erotic, I decide to let him.

Perhaps I lean into the great attraction I feel for this man because it reminds me that I am much more than a grief-stricken, middle-aged mother of four (five? four? I never can get that part right). I am not kidding here when I talk about sexual healing. I am a believer. I need a way to come to my senses, and I mean that in the old-fashioned taste, touch, see, hear, and smell sense of the word. With this man, sex is full-on present, embodied play.

However, the erotic isn't the only thing present in this sultry little scene. Tonight, my grief is riding shotgun with my lust. Ah, hello there, Grief Diva, my old friend. Grief Diva waltzes in and reminds me that she doesn't really care whether I am in the boardroom or the bedroom or the grocery store. Grief resides in the deep waters of our hearts, and even the slightest wind can dredge up a little swell.

Grief Diva and I used to have a standing date for a lovely tango at Walmart because I had taken Elijah to the bathroom there once and he had fallen in the potty. Elijah liked his privacy, which was of course fine, but in Walmart, they didn't have any of those snap-on seats that little tooshies need to stay situated, so I had planned to stay in the stall with him. Elijah wasn't having any of it.

"Door shut!" he commanded. "Oh, please," he added.

Elijah was always tacking on that "Oh please" to the back half of his requests. Elijah, a social animal in transition. Let me explain: Babies are pure want wrapped up in your Auntie Beth's homemade blankie. We grownups have learned to superbly hide our wants in order to fit in with society and keep therapists in business. Babies, not so much. Like all older toddlers, Elijah was somewhere in the middle. He still led with the want: "Door shut!" And then he remembered that those magic words meant to make the adults in his life bend to his will: "Oh, please."

I love that about Elijah. The in-betweenness of that stage of his life. My other kids all grew into the more proper, "May I please . . ." version of the statement and, as young adults, are well on their way to engaging in America's Olympic sport of suppressing their true desires in favor of capitalistic notions of what constitutes success. But don't worry, I got them all therapists and grief boxes too, so we are good.

Anyway, I left Elijah to his solitary pottying only to hear him whining but a moment later. I went in and there he was, legs dangling over the edge, rump submerged. As I pulled him out, he collected himself and wisely intoned, "Don't fall in the potty."

Yeah, kid, and be careful what you wish for.

For years, the memory of that moment flooded me whenever I went to Walmart, so I was really happy when I found out that Sam Walton is Satan's lackey and started to avoid shopping there.

Let's return to the porch, where my wine pouring lover pontificates about Greek tragedy. Also, let's upgrade him from here on out from Mr. Salt-and-Pepper to Mister Linen, because his white linen shirt is perfectly framing the muscles in his forearm as he balances the bottle over my glass.

To summarize, what makes Greek tragedy so damn tragic is that the hero is basically a pretty good human—not perfect by any means, but someone you wouldn't mind being your Uber driver on your way to pick up your prodigal Jeep on a random Sunday. According to Mister Linen, for reasons that remain pretty much a mystery, the gods choose to fuck with the hero—a mostly decent human. To make matters worse, this puny human is warned of the fuckery by an oracle, or a seer, so they *know* that a particularly horrible thing is going to happen to them. On hearing the news, they spend pretty much the whole play trying to escape their fate. Spoiler alert: They never do.

According to Mister Linen, the tragic hero's ultimate demise is as much a given as the fact that the sun will rise. No matter what decisions the protagonist makes, he is doomed from the start to meet the decreed end. In fact, the tragic hero will often orchestrate the events that lead to their demise. In trying to avoid their downfall, they will set in motion the plot points that lead to it. Oedipus will kill his father and marry his mother while trying to avoid doing just that. Antigone will die for her resolve to properly honor the dead. If tragic heroes have hubris, we can hardly fault them. Despite their flaws, they are still trying their damndest to do right by their kin, their country, their loves. And, despite their best efforts, they will fail.

If this is the essence of tragedy, then we are all just a little bit tragic, aren't we?

While my Mister Linen explains all of this, I vacillate between the desire to unbutton his shirt a bit more and this thought: "Dude, you have *no idea* how close this hits to home."

Mister Linen's speech does stir up my grief, but more than that, his speech and the wine muddle together to bring new clarity. His words gave me a new heuristic through which to view Elijah's loss.

Here's what I mean:

I have often described the events that gave rise to Elijah's accident as a perfect storm.

- If we had gone to church that Saturday instead of staying home . . .

- If I had pressed my opinion harder that we should not build our son a bed . . .

- If I had just bought the bed I had seen on sale a few week's prior and put him in it . . .

- If I had listened to the whisper in my gut telling me that something was off . . .

- If I hadn't been conditioned to ignore that whisper because I believe I was evil . . .

- If we hadn't slept in the guest bedroom . . .

- If I had not turned on the air filter . . .
- If we had built the bed in the daytime . . .

If a single one of these ifs had transpired, we might have seen the flaw in the design. And Elijah would still be here.

If, if, if . . . the ifs spiral around themselves, creating a double helix of doom that embeds itself in the soul and leaves the bearer of these thoughts with the impossible task of trying to untangle the events—as if doing so would somehow make the loss more bearable. Those who are acquainted with great sorrow know this game all too well. The "if only" game never ends, or at least never ends well, because the ifs only serve to keep the bereaved stuck in a cycle of rumination. The suffering plays on an infinite loop.

With Elijah's death, like the Greeks described, I felt like an unwitting pawn in a game that my grief-addled brain could not understand. In my belief system at the time, God was not necessarily trying to destroy me—although, I mean, he *could have been*. While Judeo-Christian God is usually cast as more distant than those of pagan pantheons, according to scripture, God did seem to hold some individual fates in his hands. In the Exodus story, God personally paved the way for the miraculous release of the Israelite slaves. The whole Moses parting the Red Sea moment was preceded by God hardening Pharaoh's heart not once but six times. I am not saying that Pharaoh's story was tragic, because he seemed to be quite the twatwaffle, but my point is that God does seem to doom some people for the larger plan.

So, like the Hellenic gods and goddesses, Jehovah had no trouble dipping his fingers into the affairs of the little people. But unlike His historical predecessors' capricious meddlings, God's fingers were for weaving some apparently disparate threads together for the good of His people. And, to my way of thinking at the time, I was one of those people. Understand that as an Evangelical Christian, my God was no far-off deity. He was "a loving Heavenly Father who has a wonderful plan for my life." The relationship I had been fostering with this Heavenly Father (who we called Abba—Daddy) felt exceptionally personal. I talked to him as much as I did my own dad.

As an Evangelical, I believed I had a direct line to God. The old gospel song "Jesus on the Mainline" epitomizes this idea:

Jesus on the mainline, tell him what you want
Jesus on the mainline, tell him what you want
Jesus on the mainline, tell him what you want
Tell him what you want today.

Well, Jesus, what I wanted was to have a beautiful fundamentalist family and a firstborn son who would have become quite an ambassador for Christ. I wanted years with my son to love the shit out of him. I wanted to be a good wife and mother to all my kids and help bring "revival" to our country. Trust me when I say I was not tracking toward being a midlife sometimes-atheist who vacillates between schlepping around her guilt-laden grief and sliding into the sack with unfettered joy.

Want to create some universe-sized daddy issues? Paint God as your cosmic Daddy, talk to Him about damn near everything for thirty plus years, believe He can read your thoughts, is leading you toward some greater good, believe your firstborn is a special gift from your Daddy—and then be the unwitting instrument of that child's demise. Sounds like the stuff Sophocles could have had a heyday with back in the day. Grappling with the fact that Elijah had not just died but that I had put the screws into the bed that killed him felt like too much to handle. I couldn't make the pieces square.

Though I had been conditioned to believe that God had some higher purpose in allowing this perfect storm, that purpose seemed elusive, as elusive as the language of naming the event. Was it an accident or a test of faith? Neither explanation did that night justice. Tragedy, though—now that felt more like it, especially given the years of fallout that ensued as I grappled with Elijah's loss.

And it is this realization, this language, that began to dawn on me in the sultry dusk. In the corners of my mind, the question formed: "Was it a tragedy?"

I am not sure that a human can really answer this question—at least not while in the middle of their own life's story. But the language of tragedy provided me with a lens through which to understand the perfect storm that led to Elijah's death. It underpinned a part of my meaning-making around Elijah's death. For years I had felt very alone in these musings, but considering Elijah's loss through the lens of Greek tragedy pushed against this: If a whole artform exists to describe this feeling of engineered loss, then perhaps I was less of a pariah and more like an everyday person.

And yet . . .

The truth is that even this many years out, it feels like some cruel trick of the gods to allow me to have had this gorgeous child, to give him a name so laden with proof—Elijah means "The Lord, he is God"—and then to steer the ship right into the rocks. The pain of the loss alone is harrowing enough to send any mother spiraling into grief-stricken insanity, to say nothing of the existential quandary. It is no wonder that when people hear about Elijah's death, they often say, "I can't imagine." I contend that they actually can.

But bereaved mothers don't need to muzzle ourselves and suffer these losses alone. Author Lidia Yugnavitch puts a fine point on this particular psychic rending. Not long after she miscarried her baby daughter, sat down in a grocery store aisle and peed herself. Yugnavitch described this part of her life as her "lost her marbles" phase: "I spent some time wandering around, living under an overpass in a kind of psychosis."[4] She was not right in her head nor heart until her mind could find a way to integrate the reality of her loss into her life. As hard as Yuknavitch's loss of marbles must have been, I rather envy that she was able to do so. I didn't lose my marbles. I superglued them together into a clump with scriptures that only intensified my pain.

Like Yugnavich found a way out of her labyrinth of suffering, so did I. I don't know the details of her journey. I do know that part of mine has been gaining some clarity around this word—tragedy. In the colloquial sense of "extremely, deeply sad," I had long accepted it on face value. But what my sometimes-lover playwright gave me was the language to access exactly what that term means.

The preamble to Elijah's death does indeed feel tragic, in the classical sense, almost flawlessly engineered by a deity that seemed bent on breaking me. Was it?

Many days, I like my life now (score one for Elijah's death not actually being a tragedy), but I remember fearing when Elijah was alive that if I loved him too much, if he became an idol to me, that God might need to take him from me (score one for team tragedy, if that were true). Some would say that my subsequent loss of faith is the true tragedy, but I see it differently. The initial loss itself was a nuclear bomb that cratered my heart, but the sanity threatener was my insidious belief in the role of a deity—my deity—allowing the accident that killed Elijah.

For years, my mind struggled to comprehend how my Abba could allow me to help build a bed that would kill my baby. I fought the good fight for over eleven years after Elijah died. Like a good soldier, I clung to my faith even as it failed to support me. I clung to it until doing so threatened my own sanity, and then one day, in the midst of the quickening, I quietly cast it aside like a shawl that had worn thin from too much wear.

Doing so was another death, but it was also a threshold into healing. Letting go of a God who could be so cruel planted the first seeds of forgiveness for myself. If God wasn't to blame, then who was left responsible? At first, the answer was clear: me. I and I alone bore the responsibility. I was no pawn of the gods. Nor, I eventually realized, was I a monster. I was just a mom who was raised to not listen to her intuition. That mom couldn't see the future; there was no oracle to clue me in.

Many parents have had near misses with their children—have turned their backs for just a moment, received calls of accidents that took their children within a hair's breadth of death. I am not some special case of divinely meted out suffering. Score another one for Elijah's death not being an actual tragedy.

Of course, now I don't literally believe that Jehovah engineered Elijah's death anymore than I think Zeus had a hand in the matter. Losing Elijah was just so bad, so hard, and so big, that my gut still can't let go of the idea that there was something tragic at play. Perhaps that *something* is best described not by the language of tragic drama, but by another T-word: trauma. Everything about Elijah's loss was extremely traumatic. By the time I met Mister Linen, that trauma had been lodged in my body for a good twenty years.

Though trauma lives in our bodies, it can be accompanied by some humdinger thoughts, like "I am damaged goods" or "I have no sense of myself anymore." A complete obliteration of one's sense of self is, apparently, not all that uncommon in survivors of deeply traumatic events. When Lidia Yugnavitch lost her marbles, I suspect it was this traumatic loss of self she was experiencing. Trauma can also cause us to feel hopeless, like, why bother trying anymore? The deck is stacked. Given the enormity of impact of trauma on a body, trauma leading to loss of faith isn't really that much of a plot twist.

Sophocles saw this one coming too and chronicled the twin sense of doom and defiance some trauma survivors grapple with. Just prior to being entombed in a cavern (okay, my day is suddenly looking better), Antigone, fiery to the end, throws down these words of a wounded soul:

> "Why, hapless one, should I look to the gods anymore—what ally should I invoke—when by piety I have earned the name of impious? Nay, then, if these things are pleasing to the gods, when I have suffered my doom, I shall come to know my sin; but if the sin is

with my judges, I could wish them no fuller measure of evil than they, on their part, mete wrongfully to me."[5]

With a banger of a closer like that, is it any wonder that the word "trauma" is a descendent of the Greek word—wait for it—trauma (τραύμα)? Sophocles got it. Antigone's monologue has such an "I give up on trying to figure this shit out" ring to them. I can relate. Can't we all?

The Greeks got something else right, too: the idea of catharsis. Before taking me to bed, my lover rounded out his exegesis of the ancient form with an explanation of what catharsis really is: strictly speaking, a purification that happens through the medium of art, a sort of setting the scales aright. The art acts as a container for what feels too painful to hold on one's own. We, the audience, experience by proxy the emotions of our Antigones and Oedipuses.

Over the years, the term has morphed to mean any strong release of emotion after which we feel better. Art might be involved, but as often as not, we could just be having a big sad all by our lonesome, say, on our kitchen floor. This modern view of catharsis waters down both the initial meaning and the power of the experience. I may have indulged in plenty a cry during my breakup breakdown, but I wouldn't call those cries cathartic. They were the necessary movements of grief, but I was experiencing them as me, the main character of my life's story, having a trauma response. I was completely immersed in the pain of those cries. They involved no self-compassion, no mindfulness, no sense of self-soothing.

Cathartic tears are different. When the emotion is entwined with art, the tears become good medicine: There is a communal sense that we are both bearing and bearing witness to life's greatest wounds. In seeing the other, we are ourselves seen. This is the healing power of old-time catharsis. And without that tiny bit of distance that a stage and a script give us, our pains can be our undoing.

As the wine and Mister Linen's soliloquy neared their mutual ends, life and art began to curl into each other. Two players on the stage of that little porch danced with ancient ideas. One of them was likely just talking about one of his favorite intellectual topics. The other was beginning to feel that perhaps this evening had been perfectly engineered for her own catharsis. The conversation itself became the artful container I needed. I'm sure it didn't hurt that two decades had passed since a twenty-seven-year-old me had put her son to bed. Those years allowed me to see that girl with some kindness, to feel her loss as the woman that her loss had winnowed me into. I saw her from afar and offered her some love. *Oh, sweetheart.*

That night, catharsis didn't involve a large discharge of emotion. Rather, as I sat on that little stage, imbibing the language of tragedy and a good bit of wine, something new began to feel true in my chest. I didn't cry. But the constriction born of compartmentalizing my grief began to unknot. Catharsis also came as I allowed my sorrow and my desire to coexist. On that night, perhaps my grief and sexuality met up and became friends. Grief Diva had shown up and threatened to steal the show.

But once I welcomed her onto the scene, she didn't start bellowing "I Dreamed a Dream" from center stage. Instead, she took off her crown, quietly tiptoed out of the spotlight, and became a part of the chorus of my own quiet catharsis.

Catharsis involves seeing, and though Mister Linen knew nothing of Elijah on that night, I felt seen by him. And talking about tragedy in the abstract made me feel more comfortable allowing my grief into this part of my life. Maybe grief isn't so much a diva as a regular part of our psyches that simply wants to have a seat at the table along with all the others. Whatever else Mister Linen saw of me that evening, I know that he saw the complicated curves of a woman who has grown into herself. And I don't think there is anything sexier than that.

The Return of Ft. Richter: Dispatch from 2020 Lockdown

In 2020, we were all massively, as my kids say, "Goin' through it." This dispatch from the heart of early lockdown is not meant to merely document our experience. (Who needs that? We all lived it?) Rather, this entry serves to show how this intense return to full-time parenting three kids intersected with my parenting identity and with my grief. Here goes . . .

PART 1: GATE ZERO

In December of 2012, just a few days prior to Christmas, the kids and I landed in Charlotte, North Carolina, only to find ourselves marooned. We had been enroute to visit family in Columbus, Ohio, when a snowstorm struck up north. All travel to Columbus was banned while they cleared the roads, landing strips, the edges of plane wings—whatever people with plows and deicers need to clear in these situations. I don't really know because I'm from the South, where we cancel school if the temperature dips below thirty but sit on our porches during gale-force winds sipping libations and listening to Jimmy Buffet.

So, while the Northern folk took hours clearing the way for us, my little brood found ourselves sitting on the ground at Gate Zero. I was sick, having contracted my yearly "maybe it's the flu and Maybelline won't help" illness. Compound a sick mama with a red-eye that was about to stretch into perpetuity along with kids ages twelve, ten, eight, and four, and you've got yourself a recipe for one lovely stay.

Parents are not provided with a tactical guide for how to handle these types of situations. Even if we were, our kids would not read them. Whatever parenting book you have that you want to use as a field manual, good on you, but I guarantee that no matter how well-intentioned, researched, or reasoned that book is, the universe will give you a kid who will show you that the adage "The exception proves the rule" still holds.

At this point in my parenting, I had already stopped seeing the Good Book as a literal tactical manual for all of life's snafus. Since I was no longer trying to raise up little soldiers in the Lord's army, I did not "Lift up mine eyes to the hills" for help. However, as the head of this little troop, I knew two things: 1.) a nap was imperative, and 2.) we needed to hunker down while I slept.

I am pretty much the least sergeant-like of humans on the planet. But I still think that every parent needs the ability to pull a good "ten-hut" outta their hat in situations that involve safety. It doesn't need to be loud, but it needs to ring with a bit of "I got this, and here's what we are doing. We can all journal about our feelings tonight, but right now we gotta get shit done."

Now, was an extended layover in Charlotte really one of those "ten-hut" situations? Probably not. But me and Nyquil had had a meeting of the minds the previous night, and I was doin' my best to stay conscious. And that right there is one of parenting's dirty little secrets, folks: You will not infrequently be thrust into situations that you cannot simply Mary Poppins your way out of. Storms and Nyquil hangovers and weird-ass old traumas are going to come in, even if you are determined to give your kids an idyllic Christmas with their cousins. Them's the breaks, the cards, so to speak, so you play them to the best of your ability and do a Dory ("Just keep swimmin'").

In order to accomplish the mission at hand, I mustered up my best Nyquil hangover-infused order:

"Kids. Circle up. No. A *circle*. Not a rhomboid. Yes, it is impossible to make a pentagon with four people. Who can tell me what 'penta' means. That's right, *five*. Isaiah, that's not a circle.

"Grab your sister. Okay. How many of you are there again? What's your name, little one?

"Okay, now that I have your attention, grab your blankies and suitcases. Bring them all over here."

"Here" was a stretch of territory flanked by mostly empty seats on one side and a wall on the other. This carpeted terrain likely harbored many viruses as gnarly as the one that was taking me down, but I didn't care. I wanted a wall at my back and a way to stretch out. "Here" provided that. Second, what lay beyond on the other side of bland sheetrock was the most important supply we would need for our hunker. Every fort needs to be well provisioned. This one was no different. On the other side of that wall lay not a Jelly Belly. Not a Taco Bell or airport bar. It was . . . a video rental store.

Ah, InMotion, my darling. My beacon of glowing screen-induced bliss.

I entered that store armed with plastic and a strong desire to find the best electronic babysitter Visa could buy. I knew what I was buying. So did those franchise owners: sleep. For the jacked-up price $7.99, I was purchasing 127 minutes of blissful, uninterrupted sleep. Actually, $7.99 was a bargain, all things considered.

I returned to our post provisioned with two DVDs of the family entertainment variety.

"Kids. Welcome to Ft. Richter, where the chip bag runneth over and the videos don't stop. We are going to hunker down here for awhile."

"How long will that be?"

"Awhile."

I have no idea what animated, virtual sleep potion I returned with, but as I popped the DVD into my laptop, I doled out the following set of sitting orders:

1. "Under no circumstances are you to leave this fort."

2. "Don't wake me unless: a.) movie is over, b.) four-
   year-old decides to fraternize with the enemy . . .
   er, other travelers, or c.) they call our flight."

Then I lay down as a wall between my kids and any pass-
ersby and succumbed—most likely with a blankie stolen from
one of my offspring.

How many movies did the inhabitants of Ft. Richter watch
that Christmas of 2012? Don't remember. What I do recall is
that when we arrived safely in Columbus several hours later,
the troops rested, regrouped, and had one heck of a holiday.

PART II: FT. RICHTER, 2020

It's been over eight years since the kids and I weathered the
storm in Ft. Richter. That storm was invisible to us, much like
the unseen agents that are once again forcing us all to change
our plans. It's March 2020.

My "kids," ages twenty, eighteen, sixteen, and twelve, are all
hunkered down—including one dispatched to a fort far away up
North, where they have recently risen from the rank of high school
senior to a new title known as "essential employee." Imagine that,
my sixteen-year-old frontline worker, holding out hope to the
masses in the form of Hungry Howie's pizza. I don't know what
foods you all deem essential during this time, but pizza definitely
heads up my list. The only difference is that, living in an early epicenter of the coronavirus, this mama doesn't want to order food
out during the lockdown. Them germs apparently last for days and
probably know how to jump for miles. The Southern contingency
will make our own pizza, thank you very much.

Here in Ft. Richter 2.0, we, once again, have no idea what

the duration of our hunkering will be. Like before, the off-spring engage in electronic distractions, this time of their own choosing. And I let them. Of course we interact, but during the day, I work. I just quit my full-time university job because, ironically, I want to travel more. Or, I did. I miss that high school senior too much and was planning to embrace the life of a digital nomad. Best laid plans, right?

But I do have a remote gig (three of them, actually), and from these online endeavors, I'm attempting to piece together what we need to provision this new fort. In between work and worrying about a certain global situation, I emerge at turns to say hello, check in on the daily to-dos I have assigned each member of the Fort. In an effort to remind us all that Mom is making the money to float our Fort, I have taped a notecard up on my "office" door that reads, "I love you. I am working. Mom."

Did I say office? I meant back deck.

Since we are squeezing four people into a two-bedroom shotgun, I have extended my office space to said deck. As an acquaintance pointed out online, March 2020 in New Orleans is "obnoxiously beautiful." Hence, my outdoor office, which gives me the benefit of being in nature (and away from other respi-rating humans) while working and of allowing my recently-re-turned-to-the nest older kids to have a semblance of privacy.

Lately in my office, I've been learning how to adjust my old afghan in the sycamore branches over my head to keep from getting a sunburn. Man, sunburn on top of lung failure would really suck. Meanwhile, in that office, I trade off hats between several remote jobs—including job hunting, because I still want that sweet high-paying gig known as *a single job*.

Recently, I also took a provocative selfie in my outdoor office for none other than Mister Linen. We went on exactly one date—and what a date it was—before lockdown hit. Under an old oak tree in City Park we sat sipping rose and nibbling on gourmet cheeses. It was all very romantic—the type of date where you relax into conversation with your intellectual equal. It sure is nice when that equal also turns out to be an excellent kisser.

A week after that date, I received the call from Isaiah that LSU was shutting down. I arrived to a campus over which a pall had settled. None of the students spoke. They sat in little bunches on stairs or on worn down couches seeking solace in their phones. The local schools closed a week later. And one week after that, Ada's restaurant in North Carolina closed.

And that's how we've all ended up in my two-bedroom shotgun with the new outdoor deck office, where, among other things, I chicken out of sending said provocative text. Instead, I google pandemic mortality numbers and load up the virtual grocery cart with our weekly provisions.

Speaking of provisions, Ada has taken on the meal planning. Yes, yes, yes! We have been delivered from mom's mess-hall reminiscent one-dish wonders. Now, thanks to Ada, we eat pesto-stuffed peppers and chili-garlic stir-fry. Lunch is grab and go. Everyone is pitching in at the Fort, though. Isaiah takes my youngest on walks where they stay waaaay away from any other people. He also doles out chore reminders and heads up after school homework check-ins. My A-student sixth grader is currently rocking a D in English, and I am concerned. Ability is not a problem. Completing assignments in this world of Zoom-mediated synchronous learning *is*. I wonder, should sixth graders really be soldiering on while we are in the middle of figuring out what the upshot of this insidious disease is going to be?

The city is grieving or, rather, needs to be. We have already lost Ellis Marsalis. A dear friend my age has been to the ER several times with breathing problems. But we have no funerals, no second-lines. Rats are roaming the Quarter in droves. Amongst all this chaos, could it be enough for us to simply adjust for a minute?

Gate Zero Ft. Richter was a playful attempt to handle an uncomfortable but totally normal life inconvenience. The new Ft. Richter is different. What we are experiencing is not actually unprecedented. Plagues have come and gone for millenia. But parenting during a plague, now, *that* feels unprecedented. The ground is as slippery as my freshly disinfected kitchen floor. We go on with our routines, trying to establish some sense of normalcy. But this experience isn't normal.

Two of my kids have already launched. They are used to having freedom. Now they are restricted in ways that I know must be painful for them, the momentum of their young adulthoods stalled. Two weeks into lockdown, we were all "Your grandparents stood for you on the front lines; you can sit down for them." And it's true. Right now, the sacrifice we are being asked for pales in comparison to those who actually fought on the front lines. Staying home in our fort is the best way to fight this particular battle, but the family reunion feel of this time is already beginning to wear off.

So, when I'm not trying to strong-arm some semblance of normalcy, I worry. And I have been surprised to find that a new wave of missing Elijah is cresting. It's been nineteen years since he passed. By now, I know that I will always be grieving Elijah. What surprises me is that I miss him so much right now. I miss him for myself, but I miss him for the kids too—mostly Isaiah. I think this kid could sure use a big brother right now.

I imagine an alternate world where Elijah lives. For some reason, twenty-two-year-old Elijah is in a band. He's just a little further down the line than his younger bro, who I suspect is not doing as well as I'd like to think, and knows how to buddy up to him. I feel like all the kids would benefit from someone older who, compared to me, is just a *leetle* less prone to knowing in their bones how precarious life actually is. Of course, I probably wouldn't be that mom if Elijah had lived. It's all a fairy tale that my psyche invents to deal with the ache that has reopened in this hard time. I wonder why, in the absence of a tactical manual, I am reaching for the life I wanted my son to have.

In place of a manual and in the continued absence of young adult Elijah, I have been turning to poetry for some succor. Kahlil Gibran's "On Children" has been a breath of fresh air. Coincidentally, I first heard of it in 2012 as I strove to parent in new ways and finally grieve the loss of my son.

> And a woman who held a babe against her bosom said,
> Speak to us of Children.
> And he said:
> Your children are not your children.
> They are the sons and daughters of life's longing for itself.
> They come through you but not from you,
> And though they are with you yet they belong not to you.
> You may give them your love but not your thoughts,
> For they have their own thoughts.
> You may house their bodies but not their souls,
> For their souls dwell in the house of tomorrow, which you cannot visit, not even in your dreams.
> You may strive to be like them, but seek not to make them like you.
> For life goes not backward nor tarries with yesterday.
> You are the bows from which your children as living arrows are sent forth.
> The archer sees the mark upon the path of the infinite, and He bends you with His might that His arrows may go swift and far.
> Let your bending in the archer's hand be for gladness;
> For even as He loves the arrow that flies, so He loves also the bow that is stable.[6]

I am not finding as much comfort in the poem these days. Where once I was just oh so "yeah, man" to this poem, now I find myself talking back.

You may give them your love but not your thoughts . . .

Come on, man, can't I just give them a few thoughts? How about this one? "You just touched your face for the twelfth time in ten minutes."

What about this thought, Khalil? Can I pretty please give

them this one? "I think watching *Bob's Burgers* while eating yet another burger is not only meta, it's downright *healthy*."

. . . for they have their own thoughts.

Pretty sure their thoughts are not helping them out too much right now, Khalil. Thoughts I have overheard recently: "I feel like a highschool housewife" (Ada). "Ah, the sweet sound of Mom bleaching the doorknobs again as I drift off to sleep" (Marci). "What kind of name is effing Hezekiah He?" (Isaiah). Okay, that one is just funny.

I'm just saying that I think maybe a few of my thoughts could help. And this thought is definitely not related to my need to pretend I can control things—especially things related to things that could hurt my kids.

But, back to the dispatch from our little Fort.

My youngest is responsible for the daily disinfecting of doorknobs, light switches, faucet handles, beetles. Okay, maybe not the beetles—if they wash their little beetle feet before they come inside. To these duties, I have added the rank of Sign Maker-in-Chief. As a result, reminders about our new routines adorn various posts. Isaiah calls this nagging; I like to call it . . . nagging. However, the new signs seem to be working, and my son told me so yesterday. (Yes, you told me that, Isaiah.)

These signs are excellently rendered using Sharpie on 4x6" cards. My favorite one is taped above the toilet: "Hello. I am a paper towel. My one purpose in life is to help you turn off the faucet. Please help me fulfill my life's purpose, and use me." Other aptly placed signs include, "Wash your hands before preparing food. Wash your hands before unloading the dishwasher." Are we sensing a theme yet, class? As commander-in-chief of Fort Richter, I'm about to order up a sign that says, "Just fucking wash your hands into perpetuity as if you have just been party to your husband murdering the king and you are overwrought with guilt and the metaphorical blood on your hands. I want to hear you intoning 'Come out, out, damned spot!' when I walk by the bathroom, okay? It should sound like twenty seconds of a noble having a sleepwalking, psychotic episode in there."

This unprecedented domestic situation has had an odd effect on me—probably several odd effects, truth be told.

One of the strangest is a sense of déja vu coupled with a complete and utter lack of certitude as we hunker in uncharted territory. The current need for exactitude and discipline reminds me of my early days of parenting; our regimens also remind me of the many ways that I have, quite simply, loosened up since then. Now, with everyone home literally all the time, the dishes must be done twice a day, and the countertops cleaned with bleach. Full stop. No disclaimers. The pandemic is here, and doesn't care if I have become a hippie.

This return to "ten-hut" parenting feels foreign to me because I actually hate telling people what to do. I understand that it is necessary to lead the efforts here at the new Ft. Richter, to combat the sheer uncertainty of this phase of the pandemic. But that doesn't mean I have to like it. I tried to be collaborative at the outset, appreciating that my older kids are adults, but—revelation here—living in a constant state of fight-or-flight panic about whether or not I could contract this disease and leave my kids without a mom does not engender a spirit of collaborative problem-solving. I feel a whole lot more like Captain Von Trapp than the free-spirited nun who sang her way into his heart.

Maybe I should add whistles to my Instacart order.

I would much rather be like Maria. And I was heading there in my parenting—until now. After I ceased fundamentling the hell out of my mothering, I leaned more into my natural parenting proclivities. Or perhaps those proclivities were just beginning to emerge alongside the woman I was becoming as I bushwhacked my way out of the jungle of mind-stifling beliefs. Who is to say?

My hard exit from fundamentalism happened in tandem with my divorce, and I have never heard of a divorce that doesn't alter those involved. In the wake of this change, some people switch from drinking beer to red wine; others take up new hobbies—like jet-skiing, salsa dancing, or getting over gas-lighting (hey, everyone needs a hobby). Divorce, like any great leaving, is a disruption that simultaneously harms and heals. It's like my chiropractor said one day when I told him about my change of marital status: "I'm sorry ... [crack] ... and congratu-lations." I didn't get it at the time because in my world, divorce was basically the worst thing that you could ever go through. You would be better off dead than divorced. But he was right. Even as I mourned the family I had tried to create, I was begin-ning to heal some very old wounds.

[Brief aside: This is not a book about my marriage—or my divorce. Another person holds half of that story, and it's private. I will only say that for seventeen years, two good people who were basically children when they married did their very best to forge a life in the wake of one of the hardest things two par-ents can experience, the death of their baby. To that marriage I brought many expectations about what it meant to be a wife. I also laid many unfair expectations on my husband about what it meant to be a husband. I am sorry for that.

I recognize that all that I did as a twenty-one-year-old came from a place of living in a way that aligned with my val-ues at the time. I was the one who insisted on writing submis-sion into my marriage. I literally contracted to place my hus-band in a place of authority that no young'un in his twenties should have foisted upon him. It all seems very odd to me now, because in a way I *led* our family into me taking a submissive role. Did I do it because I thought I was following a heav-enly mandate? Absolutely. Was it paradoxical and fucked up? More absolutely. But I have come to view the girl who made that decision with kindness. Give or take a few thousand Bible studies, I don't think my ex and I are so different from many couples who married young and, once they grew into them-selves more, found that the marriage would not contain the people they had become, or wanted to become.]

Regardless of the way the phenomena came to be, my

marriage was steeped in fundamentalism. Ergo (yes, ergo!), the twin leavings from fundy-Jesus and from my union wrought massive changes in me. Those shifts did not occur overnight. At the beginning, they involved the absence of certain activities, like attending church five days a week or daily devotionals. But mostly they involved the setting aside of certitude. My mind opened up to explore a central research question: "If this whole shebang does not work as I was taught, then what do I make of this world?" In other words, I know what I no longer believe, but what *do* I think?

Taking up this whopper of an epistemological undertaking as I chased down forty was daunting. But it was also intoxicating. For the first time in my adult life, I felt like my mind had been released from a cage. I was ready to roam the forest of ideas. I was free.

When I was a fundamentalist, I had a tacit agreement with the church. I would only read books that aligned with the American Evangelical worldview. It is much easier to "take every thought captive to Christ" if you are only reading thinkers who have done a lot of that heavy lifting for you. What people may not realize is that in Christian bookstores of old, the shelves were filled with writers who tackled a wide range of topics through a Scripture-as-literal lens. One of those topics was parenting. Two of those authors, Michael and Debi Pearl, created an authoritarian parenting empire around the notion that we are to "train up a child in the way they should go" (Proverbs 22:6). The Pearls focused on the training part of the equation:

> "Never reward delayed obedience by reversing the sentence. And, unless all else fails, don't drag him to the place of cleansing. Part of his training is to come submissively. However, if you are just beginning to institute training on an already rebellious child, who runs from discipline and is too incoherent to listen, then use whatever force is necessary to bring him to bay. If you have to

sit on him to spank him then do not hesitate. And hold him there until he is surrendered. Prove that you are bigger, tougher, more patiently enduring and are unmoved by his wailing. Defeat him totally. Accept no conditions for surrender. No compromise. You are to rule over him as a benevolent sovereign. Your word is final."[7]

Please join me in a collective moment of picking our jaws up off the ground.

In regards to a child, are we really supposed to "defeat him totally"? Are we *really* supposed to "rule over him as a benevolent sovereign"? If raising the next generation of unquestioning, emotionally repressed soldiers is the goal, then regularly beating a child into abject submission sounds like a means to this end.

Keep in mind that this type of thinking was sanctioned by the very mainline Evangelical church my family attended at the time. Somewhere around 2005, my Sunday night study group read it, along with another little gem of propaganda called *Created To Be His Help Meet*. That book reinforced the notion that women were created for men. I'm pretty sure you can figure out what follows.

My group absolutely tore up those two texts. No one ever questioned whether or not we *should* spank. Instead, a group of dear people whom I know loved their kids deeply sat around our house and examined the finer points of whether or not to use a glue stick or a switch—but never the hand, because you wouldn't want your child to associate spankings with, of all things, *you*.

Enacting this "training" galled me. Even at the time, it felt wrong, but I was amygdala-deep in this theology that foregrounded submission to biblical lines of "authority." Those lines were clearly drawn in a single direction from child to parent and from mother to husband. Even though I hated the spankings that I administered, I thought that they were a necessary part of my parenting duties. When pitted against the possibility that my kid could end up an enemy of God, learning early obedience seemed a small price to pay. I thought I was showing my kids love, helping them grow into the kind of people who would escape the fires of hell. In fact, I was a tool of an Evangelical fundamentalist regime.

Reckoning with the fact that I was raised in a high-control group, enacting the rhetoric even as I was journaling "Do Hindus really have to go to hell?", has been painful. I left fundy Jesus for my own sanity, and I am still reckoning with the moral injury of how I used to parent.

Let me be very clear here: Fundy parenting hurts kids. Full stop.

Perhaps one of the greatest harms of one-size-fits-all, discipline-focused parenting is this: In trying to train up our children, we miss out on the absolute wonder of their existence. Like any system that disenfranchises, individual differences are not lauded. The gifts of a child are strip-mined so that they can be put to best use for the cause. And when fundamentalism and capitalism procreate, their lovechild is a person-sized widget in the Christian-making factory that is American Evangelical Christianity.

When I ceased to be a fundy, the spankings also ceased. Immediately. So did attempts to evangelize my kids. On the other hand, post-fundy me didn't try to convert my kids to whatever the hell I was becoming, either. It was already a shock for my kids to see me behaving in ways that were so different from the mother that they had known. And they were in the middle of having their family of origin altered. We were all grieving. The last thing they needed in those early days was for me to come in with some new dogma. The kids needed safety, structure, and an unwavering promise that whatever happened to our family, whatever fresh uncertainties we were facing, I was going to be on the scene.

On my own time, I enjoyed a romp through new thinkers who had previously been off-limits—short list of them here maybe?—but I didn't share those explorations. While a huge first step in reparenting my children was simply to remove the expectation that they were put here to create more Christians, I didn't tell them not to be Christians. I never sat my kids down and said, "I don't believe in original sin any more, and neither should you." (So yeah, Khalil, I did all right with letting my kids' thoughts be their thoughts until words like "unprecedented" and "vector for disease" came on the scene.)

It was a very strange time. I was both giddy and gutted, floundering and free. Again, a field manual would have been really helpful. I found none. At first, I went a little hippie. Okay, I went a lot hippie I went so hippie that Navis and I used to have a bit called "me and my pagan mom." If we were walking home from the grocery with our dinner fixin's swinging from our arms, little Navis would say, "Today, me and pagan mom went to the grocery store. We bought eggs and cheese; we did not buy incense." In this period of newbie post-fundy parenting, I remember talks with my kids along the lines of, "Look, I know that your dad and I are in different places, but we both love you. Our homes are different, but here are some things that are still the same: Homework still happens. Chores still happen. Bedtime is a thing. Respect is important."

Important, yes, but also under review. Like damn near every idea I previously held, I was retooling the notion of respect. Respect in my fundamentalist past had flowed mostly in one direction: up. It moved from kids to parents to Christ. Respect in my new home ran bidirectional. I did not force my kids to respect me just because I was ovulating when I got laid. Last time I checked, none of them had asked to be born. If anyone owed something in this situation, it was me. During this period of parenting, I was learning the art of respecting the wisdom that my children had.

In my previous life, I might have been prone to whip out a little "Foolishness is bound in the heart of a child; but the rod of correction shall drive it far from him" (Proverbs 22:15). It is upon Proverbs like that one that the Pearls built their abusive approach to discipline. Now, I can say to the former fundy me, "I see your puny Proverb and raise you the words of a major prophet: 'And a little child shall lead them'" (Isaiah 11:6). Not good enough? Taken out of context? Then let's settle this once and for all with the words of Jesus himself. When I was a kid I learned that if words were written in red in the gospels then Jesus said them, and we need to pay extra special attention to them. Rather than beating supposed foolishness out of kids' hearts, let's perhaps remember that Jesus already did this argument and he won because, well, he's Jesus. Jesus invented the callout.

Here's what Jesus had to say about grownups and entering the kingdom of heaven:

> "Verily I say unto you, Except ye be converted, and become as little children, ye shall not enter into the kingdom of heaven.
>
> Whosoever therefore shall humble himself as this little child, the same is greatest in the kingdom of heaven." (Matthew 18:3–4)

Bam. Bible drop. Jesus himself implied that kids are not harbingers of foolishness. They are the wise ones here.

Aside: If the old Proverb and Jesus's words seem to be contradictory, then you can either contort your mind to try to make them square, you can use the tried and true "But that was the Old Testament" argument, or you can just let the contradiction be and remind yourself that the humans who wrote the Bible were just as much of a mess as you, me, and our whole conundrum of a species.

Once I lost the overlay of the fundamentalist narrative, I started to fall in love with each of my kids. I mean it. I had been so afraid to fall in love with them, fearing that the other shoe would drop. Funny how when you stop trying to control your kids, you can start to see each facet of their individuality as something to nurture—not train. The result of this new perspective was a small simple word with huge implications: awe. When I laid down the dogma, I picked up wonder for the world. My kids were no exception. I wanted to make up for lost time.

And, lest this all sound super evolved and nuanced, let me balance out the picture a bit.

I was in awe—and I was effing tired. Let's just say that fatigue and losing the fear of the Lord meant that the house was not pristine. Perfection was not only unattainable; it began to be distasteful. So the dishes might not get done tonight. Who cares? We are playing a game, we are connecting. We are approaching something like happiness. There will always be dishes and laundry to be done. But these human moments are fleeting.

That approach worked well sans pandemic, when no one was posting videos about how to bleach all of your groceries. The trick during this new period of regimentation is to remember that while the need for structure has re-emerged with a hell of a potential wallop if we misstep, these stringent measures actually are working toward a visible outcome. We are washing virus off our hands, not sinstains off our souls. Enough said.

Our present reality is stressful. But it's also relatively peaceful. We have had very few arguments. They really are older and able to handle themselves, no drill sergeant required. From inside the new Ft. Richter, laughter, strange words, and new activities abound. In addition to being very good at entertaining themselves on their asses much of the day, I have found that my children each possess or are obtaining new talents at a rapid rate.

Example 1: A couple of days ago, Isaiah informed me that he is learning to draw boobs. He found a YouTube tutorial about drawing anime boobs of all sizes. Yesterday, he showed me his work. And I have to hand it to him: the kid's got talent. Today he told me he is setting up his Fiverr account. I wonder if these two bits of information are somehow connected? I kinda hope so.

Example 2: Last week, Ada furiously deconstructed three pairs of jeans and sewed *the most amazing* circle skirt without a pattern. I have no such gifts; to me her feat seems like pure magic. My contribution to the cause came in the form of discarded denim legs. Lately, I have taken to cutting off the legs of my winter jeans because business wear on the top and cut-offs on the bottom is my new uniform. One can hide a *lot* with clients via Zoom. They are just lucky I put on pants.

My youngest remains undauntable. Her only complaint is that she simply can't stand the little spots that bleach solution leaves on door handles and she WILL wipe them off. Yes, dear. Noted.

In addition to exploring new talents, my kids and I sure are making some precious new memories. Last night, Ada asked me for a gin lemon drop. This is the one cocktail that I have a natural inclination towards making. Thanks to my bartending buddy Jeff, I am now the proud owner of a little bartending set. Jeff and I were going to trade bartending for piano lessons until quarantine got in the way. The upshot is that I now hold hostage two jiggers, a cocktail shaker, a long-handled twirly spoon thingy, and a Hawthorne strainer. Poor Jeff. It probably wouldn't be kind of me to send him a picture of his set with a text that says, "Quarantined is for keeps," right?

Last night, using my newly acquired set of tools, I made us each a drink. I made this drink much in the way that I rock climb. That is to say, it ain't pretty, people—it does not look graceful or sexy like those mixologists who pirouette their ways through precise measurements and drunk patrons whilst somehow making you feel like you are the only person in the room—but I do get to the top. Ada kept telling me to apply heat to the shaker in order open it. This made no sense to me. Blunt force trauma, however, did.

The endeavor's saving grace was that I produced two perfectly executed sugar rims. Those rims were delicate, reminiscent of freshly fallen snow on a Vermont mountain peak. Were he with us, I'm quite sure John Denver would have written a hit about those freshly frosted, sublime rims.

As Ada and I clinked our martini glasses, something inside of us clicked. The day's stresses melted. We both felt the shift and grinned. Isn't this the charm of happy hour? Weary workers flip the switch and begin to unwind.

"Mom, this is the happiest I've been all day."

"Me too, honey."

I am grateful that there's still room for the rigor and the relaxation, the sour and the sweet—and now, unlike in the original Ft. Richter, also the boozy.

Ada asked for another and I said, "You're going to have to use that Seagram's shit. This Japanese gin is expensive."

"Deal."

Later, she called from the bathroom, "It's okay if you remind me to wash my hands, Mom. I'm tipsy." Then she danced out, sporting her wet fingers for me to praise. Instead of gold stars on a chart, my eldest got another drink. Put this moment on my parenting resume. Another New Orleanian drinker is born.

Isaiah, on the other hand, doesn't like anything like a good drink. At eighteen, he hates beer. Last night, I was finally able to categorize his desire.

"So basically, you just want Kool-Aid infused with some sort of booze."

"Yes, that's basically it."

Ada and I came upon the idea of zesting the last of the lemons into a simple syrup in order to need less actual juice. This is a pandemic-infused idea, because when I searched for lemons at Rouses online, the website basically said, "Lemons no longer exist. Nor do limes. Nor does lemon concentrate. May we suggest purchasing some lemon-scented furniture polish? Just drink straight gin and then take a whiff." I ordered three cans.

As the evening went on, my two began to bake. I retired to the office with my second lemon drop, and I absolutely used the good gin. Mama gotta have some perks, y'all. I listened to those two laugh while Ada shook up a third drink. That girl has had exactly three hangovers in her life. Guess we'll see what the backside of last night holds.

She has yet to emerge. I, on the other hand, awake reasonably refreshed. I make my way to the kitchen to find a wee Marci wrapped up in her fuzzy blanket. Okay, that's not true. Marci is not wee. She is sprouting up and resides in that liminal space where minds are very aware of grown-up things but still retain their innocence. I love this age. This blanket-wearing thing is new. I really think she is subconsciously comforting herself by self-swaddling. I also think we should all follow suit and bring back the Snuggie. I hug her and make a cup of coffee in my little coffee press that my friend gave me for Christmas.

I rarely used it prior to the pandemic. Preferring to drop Marci off at school and work from a coffee shop where I could type in the company of other remote workers and wonder if the old man who always graced the corner was really God, I left the press in the cupboard for special occasions. Guess worldwide mayhem fits the bill. In the midst of the bedlam, that little press and I have become buddies. It's also beautiful, and I have always been drawn to beauty. These times are nothing if they are not a beacon to sit and recognize the small wonders all around us.

To the beauty of my little coffee press's clean lines, I add the privilege of watching my sycamore tree bud. Just as the heat has arrived, this kind tree has unfurled her tender leaves and offers me shade for the better part of the day. I like to think she remembers that Jonah needed shade as he reckoned with the Lord over the Ninevites, so many of whom could not yet tell their left hands from their right. I need the shade too. I am cocooned in the inner sanctum of my little outpost.

At the rear of Ft. Richter, I sit under the sycamore's shade. I sit and sip my brew out of a clay mug etched with an oak leaf on one side. The mug was also a gift from a dear friend— a friend who lives a few blocks away from me and is having a hell of a time recovering from Covid right now.

I sit alone, yet surrounded by gifts—gifts of nature, gifts of friendship, the gift of relative quiet before the day begins barrel down. Ft. Richter has been reborn. And this time we, like so many, actually, like everyone, exist in a holding pattern. No need to stretch my frame out on the floor to shield the brood from foot traffic. My job is to sit here, legs tucked criss-cross applesauce, and take the very best care of myself that I can. If we are going to make it through this, I need to create a fort within a Fort. I need to fortify myself with kindness.

A few days ago, I had the strongest sense that I wouldn't make it, that dying was a forgone conclusion. I told my friend Abram about this wave of knowing and the fear that I was receiving some sort of message from the universe to prepare for my death. Abram replied very simply: "I think you need to tell yourself a better story." So today, I cradle my cup, caress my fears, and find that a few tears begin to fall.

I remember when Elijah died that I went into shock. Thank God. I remember thinking that I had to be ensconced in some sort of cloud because I could not have borne the full force of the loss. Our bodies protect us in this way. While I have certainly been feeling triggered and have had to beat back the old trauma intersecting with a new threat, this new situation does not yet rival the feelings of new grief—again, thank God. I consider it a gift that I can just sit in quiet and feel the tenderness course down my cheeks. I can't help it, and don't want to. These tears are appropriate. They are self-care.

Would the old me have known to nurture myself in this way? Would I have tried to find solace in the Psalmist? Would I have seen the pandemic as judgment and spent nights in "spiritual warfare" to try and protect my children? Would I have seen it as a sign of the end times, raising my eyes for the return of Christ? Perhaps I would have doubled-down on my efforts to evangelize, knowing that many would be headed to Judgment Day earlier than expected.

I don't know. We can never know where our lives would have ended up without certain sorrows. These sorrows act as points of initiation into maturity.

I have always been wired to be sensitive. Like, I was the kid who would give a firefly a funeral. Fundamentalism offered me a sort of protection against the problem of pain: nothing could truly be that painful if everything was in God's hands. Or if it was painful, at least we could trust that God had some mysterious purpose in play. Yeah . . . no. It was an attempt to take a spiritual bypass around one of the actual fundamentals of human existence: sorrow. I tried to shelter in its certitude, and for a while it worked. Until Elijah, I could handwave away the problem of pain. After Elijah's death, no such sleight of hand was possible.

Prior to his loss, I framed my sensitivity as some sort of spiritual gift, like prophecy or mercy. I see things differently now. I know now that, wielded well, this sensitivity enables me to tune into others and offer a space of empathetic non-judgment—a fortress against the harshness and uncertainty of the outer world. But I have to find ways to shelter myself. These days, my sensitivity is in full-on overdrive. The weight of being in an early epicenter of the pandemic, the real and imagined losses threaten to undo me. I hate that I have practice in living with really hard things—but that practice of living with grief, knowing that I have found a way to live in the wake of my son's death, has provided me with the sense that I can do some really hard things.

So, today, I offer my sensitivity the sanctuary of this sycamore. I retreat to the outer recesses of my Fort and into the sanctuary of my heart. I trust that my heart is good and that while I am not doing this pandemic parenting thing perfectly, I am doing what I can.

One of my favorite authors, Nora McInerny, talked about trying to get an A in grief after she lost her husband, her father, and her pregnancy all within the span of six weeks. I have gravitated toward authors like Nora, who have lost much and have accepted the hardship with one hand and cling to joy with the other. I think of Nora this morning and realize that I have been trying to get an A in pandemic management. I think I have felt like nothing less than an A will do. I don't know what will become of this collective situation, but I do know that giving myself the grace to say, "You are doing your best, little mama, and that is all you can do," is about the healthiest thing I've done in a while.

Out of that place of quiet, I am able to move into action. I reach out to my little cadre of friends. They asked me how I am really doing, and I actually tell them. I am ensconced in this fort, but simply reaching out and hearing "You are doing a good job" from those who know me well is what my soul needed to be fortified.

Maybe I don't have a video store nearby, and I don't know when our plane will take off, but I am, for the time being, sane enough, stoked on just enough caffeine. I am well rested. I am teaching— doc students, gifted middle schoolers from around the world. I already love them. Hell, I get to write. Do these things "make up" for the hellscape of the invisible threat? Of course not. But I have learned that there is no balancing of this type of scale. In fact, this scale is another made-up way that we try to uncomplicate the painful parts of life. Let's just put it down and let two things be true at once: This time hurts. I hurt. My kids hurt. The tears are very close behind the eyes at all times. So is the comfort.

So, it's time to close this missive and get to work, even though writing feels like the real work right now.

I'll simply sign it,

Under the sycamore on the outskirts of Ft. Richter

The Good, the Bad, and the Birthdays (Sing the Damn Song)

In January 2017, if you had been a fly on the wall in my little New Orleans home, you would have lighted upon a quintet of people surrounding a birthday cake. You would have heard us singing the Happy Birthday song with much gusto. You would have seen the birthday girl, a golden-haired seventeen-year-old, slice the chocolate layer cake, doling it out to her family members like she knew the drill, and you would think, *What a happy little cadre of birthday celebrants.* And you would be right—mostly.

To fully understand this scene, you have to know something about my fertility, so here goes. As a fecund fundy, I birthed three of my five children in January, and their birthdays fall within nine calendar days of each other. Apparently, as that fertile bearer of arrows, I mean humans, I had a penchant for certain, um, *activities* to occur during the month of May.

To this overshare of information about my fertility, I add a very important fact that undergirds the above scene: I am a birthday person.

I *love* my birthday. I love other people's birthdays. It is well known that many a relationship upheaval has ensued simply because the individuals involved are fundamentally mismatched. I am not talking about mismatched libidos, or politics, or (gasp) astrological signs. You wanna see a relationship take a mighty blow? Watch a birthday person mate for "life" with someone who would prefer to pass the day doing, well, exactly what they do any other day, and you will finally learn the meaning of the words "irreconcilable differences." This part of relationship compatibility is so important that one's status vis-à-vis birthday personhood should be information we learn on the very first date.

For all you online daters who text into infinity before even confirming that you are talking to an actual human, ask the chatbot what they think about birthdays. Go ahead. I dare you. For us old-school folks who jump into that first cocktail date with gusto, let us ditch the cat person/dog person line of inquiry for a minute. Instead, picture this first date: You notice that your potential *whatever* (bang, queer platonic partner, polycule addition, or lifelong monogamous mate) is looking pretty damn sexy from behind their bourbon. It's time to take the next step.

> You: I really like you, and I think this could really go somewhere, but before we take this further, I just have a very important question to ask. Are you . . . a birthday person?
>
> Sexy date from behind their bourbon: A what?
>
> You: Check, please.
>
> Boom. Bullet dodged.

Look, some people simply are not birthday people, and I don't want to date those people. Non-birthday people don't understand that for 364 days a year, we all pretend that we don't want everything to be all about us. We lean into our altruism. But for 1/365th of the year, every human should have a day that is one-trillion billion percent all about them. Only them. A birthday person understands that on your birthday, you should wake to the sounds of birds serenading you with the very joy of your existence. Small forest creatures should make your bed. Relatives with whom you have a blood feud over your long-deceased Aunt Bessie's broach should deposit large sums of money in your bank account—unless you're a member of the asshole-for-life club, like a cult leader or a corrupt politician.

In which case, you should wake up on your birthday to a house with no heat. Did I mention that in this scenario you live in Antarctica and your birthday is January 6th? On *your* birthday, you should be unable to reach a repair human, and when you reach that repair human, you should be given a repair window of between the hours of 8 a.m. and never. And that repair human should charge you double for your job and not actually fix the problem and gaslight you into thinking your heater is not actually broken. They should shadily mumble something about "backordered parts." When they leave your frigid house, they should turn around and smirk, revealing that they are in fact Krampus sub-contracting out as a birthday imp.

Perhaps cult leaders and corrupt politicians and other assholes who make everything about them every day of the year should have a *reverse* birthday. What's that, you say?

A reverse birthday is a lot like reverse Christmas Eve. On regular Christmas Eve, families often open a single gift—a gift that isn't the crème de la crème of Christmas gifts, but one that shows you have put a little love and thought into the process (so yeah, socks). A couple of years ago, I woke up on Christmas Eve morning ready to do what I do every Christmas Eve morning: read stupid shit on the internet. But alas, this Christmas Eve, the elves had come overnight and tinkered with said laptop. There was no booting. No warm light of the laptop's glow. Just a coal-black screen. As I stared into the void, I coined the term reverse Christmas Eve. On this Christmas Eve, instead of receiving a gift, I would get the pleasure of forking out a large sum of money for a new Macbook. Excellent.

What the heck does reverse Christmas Eve have to do with grief or birthdays or anything? I guess it's just that we as humans bring expectations to certain annual events, and I have expectations about birthdays. Namely: we effing celebrate them. Even if we are feeling tired or antagonized or otherwise, er, less than festive.

This particular birthday in late January was no different. It was Ada's special day. However, by this point in 2017, we had already *laissez les bon temps rouler*'d our way through Christmas, New Years, Twelfth Night, Epiphany, Navis's birthday, Elijah's birthday (okay, mostly me on that one), and the first weeks of the Mardi Gras season. In New Orleans, you don't stare down a stark house devoid of decorations on Boxing Day and start waiting for St. Patrick's Day. Nope. You roll right on into the next wave of celebration. Red and green are replaced with that Mardi Gras trifecta of green, purple, and gold.

So, by this point, we were valiantly trying to keep the parade rolling, but we needed one of those Mardi Gras tractors to give our little family float a lift.

In addition to the back-to-back celebrations, all of us were in that part of the school year where we had, as the poem goes, many miles to go before we could sleep. I was in my third year of a full-time doctoral program. My three high schoolers wore the haggard look of kids keeping up with a conveyor belt of AP coursework. Like many of their peers, they could enter college with 5,937 hours of maybe transferrable AP credit . . . and an ulcer.

Despite the tired, I was happy to bake—birthday person, remember? So, I sifted and beat that batter with the tenderest of care. I imbued it with maternal blessings for Ada's next year of life, wishing her success on her ACT and college admission essay. Each stroke of the whisk sent me into nostalgia for the little girl of days gone by.

Yeah . . . nope.

What actually happened is that I threw a box cake together and prayed it would be prettier than Isaiah's second birthday cake, which looked exactly like two pieces of crap. I am not being hyperbolic. I had tried to make that boy a little matchbox car cake, but the wheels fell off and we were left with little choc-olate, um, *logs*— but it's okay, because during the divorce I made him an Angry Birds diorama of a cake replete with an actual catapult from which we shot little molded marzipan birds. So he's fine. You're fine, Isaiah. *Right?????*

But, back to Ada. Who knew that Betty Crocker and I would be in cahoots to make her seventeenth birthday cake one of her absolute best?

In making Ada's cake, I was attempting to follow in my family's footsteps where home-cookin' equals love, especially on birthdays. In my family of origin, whether money was in short supply or falling from the sky, we found a way to cel-ebrate. Most years, my mom baked me a lemon bundt cake. Notably, it did not come from a box. That cake was so moist and lemony that I was tempted to squeeze it into a glass and drink it. (Oh No. Is this why I like lemon drops so much? Therapist and Mister Linen, help!)

So, when the moment arrived, I lit Ada's very respectable looking (if not from-scratch) chocolate layer cake. By respectable, I mean the cake was round. Like a good little layer cake, it sat there poised, hoisting seventeen candles as beacons of celebra-tion. I mention this cake's beacon-like quality because two years prior, Ada's cake fell. The middle resembled one of those sink-holes in Florida that swallow up entire tour buses of retirees. Only a can of icing could hide what lay in the depths of that cake. Thus, I was pretty pleased to invite my offspring to this year's beacon.

The scene set, together we launched into the world's most awkward celebratory ditty. Singing "Happy Birthday" is a pre-carious endeavor under the best of circumstances. That careen-ing melody is like riding in caravan of drunk thieves trying to steer their wagons across a high mountain pass. The first *Happy birthday to you* is safe enough. The notes, literally steps apart, are easy to maneuver. Same with the second *Happy birthday to you.* The caravan stays on the mountainside. But that third *Happy BIRTHday dear [insert loved one's name here]*—that octave leap between the words "happy" and "birthday" is enough to jetti-son even a sober caravan off the mountainside into the cloudy abyss. "But—it's—my . . . birthdaaaaaaaaaay!" they would cry as they descended to their deaths. The song should come with a warning label: Do not drink and sing.

I have no idea what possessed songwriter sisters Mildred and Patty Smith Hill in 1893 to unleash such a song on, wait for it . . . kindergartners. That's right, *kindergarteners*. This dynamic songwriting duo of school principal and teacher originally entrusted the tune to small children, who, research shows, have a difficult time differentiating between their speaking and sing-ing voices.

Handing this tune over to kindergarteners is the musical equivalent of handing a five-year-old Evel Knievel's stunt bike and telling him to have fun jumping the Grand Canyon. Had these sisters ever heard a five-year-old sing? Close your eyes and imagine the worst children's concert you've ever attended. Forget for a moment that the kids are cute. Everything is bigger when you are a kid, including an octave, so imagine those kids on infinite loop craning and stretching their vocal chords to reach that final *Happy BIRTHday*. Do this, and you will have come up with a damn good purgatory scenario. Add this soundscape to the cult-leader's reverse birthday surprise, and the scales of justice would finally be set aright.

Now, unlike the poor octave-addled children, my kids actu-ally can sing. All of them could float an octave before they could tie their shoes. These kids can handle harmonies in a way that has made me fantasize about going on the road as the Von Richter Family Singers. Our repertoire would roam from the bas-tions of musical theater such as *The Sound of Music*'s "The Lonely Goatherd" to every song in Hozier's catalog—a cappella.

Yeah. They are that good.

So, imagine my surprise when Ada's illuminated cake was greeted by the most lackluster version of "Happy Birthday" ever to grace the planet. If you had been a fly on the wall, ignorant of the signification of a candle-studded cake, you would have thought that we were mourning our beloved family guinea pig. You might also have thought that to honor little Kipper's passing, these humans engaged in the strangest of ceremonies. Sidenote: we really did have a guinea pig named Kipper, which my youngest used to sit near (okay, on) and comfort with the words "It's okay, Pipper." Dear "Pipper" survived, but an eavesdropping alien would think our dearly departed had languished like a heroine in an English novel who died of consumption. Such were the sounds of the dirge that drifted across my kitchen that fateful January day.

That's when I lost my birthday celebratory shit. Calling a halt to the whole shebang, I uttered these words: "Sing the damn song."

Yep. That's what you would have heard, and I have heard it many times because, of course, it is captured on video. Who says you can't force a little joie de vivre on occasion. Am I right?

Well, they did, and thirty seconds later, the birthday train was back on track. We landed that effing octave like a young Mary Lou Retton vaulting to victory at the 1984 Olympics. We ate that very regular-but-imbued-with-love-and-a bit-of-Betty-Crocker bliss cake. All's well that's micromanaged well, right?

The above meandering tale illustrates that, even if my kids' mom is a little birthday-neurotic, this particular birthday was, give or take a few expletives, fairly normal. But there is another layer of this onion to peel, and it involves, of course, grief. It also involves sex advice columnist Dan Savage.

Ever since I broke faith with fundamentalist notions of sexual fidelity, I have been unable to squelch my curiosity about how people who aren't raised in purity culture do love and marriage. I have found Dan to be a trusty guide. Dan started his advice column in 1991 on a lark. His first letter-writers were staffers who addressed him "Hey, [slur]." Dan, a married "monogamish" gay man, did not intend to become a guru for all the straights like me who come to him with all manner of complaints. Originally intended as a joke, that column has laughed him into a tenure of more than thirty years of offering sex and relationship advice.

When I listen to Dan talking about "the price of admission" to relationships, or extolling a caller who seems surprised to find her boyfriend sexting someone else when he told her, *at the beginning,* "I have cheated on every partner I've ever had," or advising yet another querent to "dump the motherfucker already," I imagine him sitting at Ann Landers' desk, which he purchased at auction, and speaking straight to my straight, late-to-the-game, sexually liberated heart. I imagine many people feel the same. When it comes to sex and love, people are inherently curious critters. The labels of Savage's listeners range from cishet, libido-stoked divorcees like me to kink-curious, solo-poly, demisexual fin-doms—and everything in between. Savage's success demonstrates that whatever the label, people want to know how to make love and sex work. And Savage answers us all.

Prior to listening to Savage, my sex education was, shall we say, *limited.* I learned that men in the Old Testament *knew* their wives. It's actually a lovely metaphor, but I didn't get it. From my parents, I learned about the mechanics of sex in the same way I found out about Santa Claus's true identity: "We noticed that you have been asking a few questions lately." Actually, point to my parents for talking to me about sex at all. As a result of their tutelage, I understood that "knowing" someone meant that tab A went into slot B. I wasn't quite sure what slot B was, but my curiosity was momentarily sated.

Over the years, I had attended a few church-sanctioned marriage seminars that likened male sexuality to a light switch and female sexuality to a Goldberg machine on steroids. Men were simple. Women were complicated. We had all sorts of buttons and gizmos and levers, and they needed to be recalibrated every day—sort of like what Navis dials into the espresso machine at the coffee shop each morning. You just never know what button or dial or lever a woman needs pulled and how that relates to whether or not the man has learned to do the little things, like take out the trash or process an emotion that involves oxytocin. Newsflash: it *does relate*.

In these seminars, I learnt that men could be in the middle of a fight with their beloved—then suddenly notice the delicate curve of her neck peeking out from behind her loose-fitting turtleneck and want to "know" her—badly. I guess this version of sexuality allowed for angry makeup sex, something I have never been interested in. Also, men were like toasters who were constantly "popping up." Women, on the other hand, were like crock pots—"slow to warm up, but, boy, once you got them going . . ." Mind you, you have to put all the right ingredients in and wait about fourteen hours, but brotha, you were going to have one heck of a holy dish.

It was all very . . . odd. The upshot of this "education" was that I brought even my married sex life under the purview of my fundamentalist ways. I believed Jesus was literally everywhere, bedroom included. My early forays into partnered sex were actually not partnered. Nope: they were freaking spiritual ménages à trois. I am quite sure I fucked up quite a fuckable moment early in my marriage by insisting that we slow down and "invite Jesus into the bedroom." I wanted every time I let my husband "know" me to literally be a sacrament.

I am pretty sure that doing it under Jesus's invisible yet watchful eye was not the intended takeaway. All of my Catholic friends who are still reading this book can enlighten me on that. I mean, what was I expecting Jesus to *do* exactly? Each time I was getting known, was he going to nod in silent approval that I had waited until my wedding night to have sex? Was he going to offer us a way to be even *more* pure?

There was absolutely nothing tantric about the hyper-spiritualized sex of my early marriage. The above behavior is merely one example of, say it with me, kids: a high-control group influencing even the most intimate aspects of a member's life. So, yes, fundamentalism got in bed with my early sex life. And our love child was one cantankerous, sanctimonious little SOB.

Inviting fundy-Jesus into the sheets was built upon four tenets of fundamentalist sex education:

1. Just don't (do it) until your wedding night.

2. If you were born with a uterus, it belongs to your husband or, if you're not yet married, your future husband.

3. For people in possession of a uterus, offer your husband sex every night, even if you have the flu or a pinched nerve or are just plain tired. If you don't, you are setting up prime "lustful eye" conditions. If your husband has a wandering eye, it's your fault, so offer him the goods every day lest he stray. But don't offer it in any direct, playful, or seductive way. Never say things like, "I would love for you to [insert desire here]." Instead, slip into your nightie, turn to your husband, and say, "Is there anything I can do for you?" He'll take it from there.

4. Don't be gay.

As you can see, I had a lot of catching up to do.

In midlife, I turned to the *Savage Lovecast* to learn all the new words (and *boy*, did I). I also rubbernecked into the carnage of strangers' imploding relationships, gleaning what I could so that I could try to not repeat their mistakes. Much of my early listening involved picking my jaw off the floor with a "He wants her to do *what????*" I also felt better about my own mistakes because, after all, I hadn't done *that*.

What began as patching up my knowledge holes about sex and love grew into actual tools I could use to help my relationships succeed. Did I just say "succeed"? From Dan Savage,

I learned that not every relationship that dissolves is a failure. The end of a relationship is painful, but there are no relationship skywriting planes waiting to spell out the words "Failure" over every split. Reframings like this have convinced me that the reason for Dan Savage's three decades of wild success is simple: He's really, really good at what he does.

Savage is much more than some keen-witted, one-liner spouter. He is a deep thinker, and I find his incisiveness to apply to much more than sex and love (and ultimately, isn't it all about sex and love of some variety?). Put simply, Dan Savage is effing *wise*. Savage doesn't work from a one-size-fits-all rule book. He infuses his advice with ethics, honesty, fidelity, and a fair amount of pragmatism.

So, what does all this have to do with birthdays and "Sing the damn song"?

Well, I don't remember the particular caller or their quandary, but I do remember that Dan began his response with these words: "Isn't that just like life to serve up goodness and hardship right next to each other?" (That's a paraphrase—sorry, folks, I'm about four hundred episodes into the *Savage Lovecast*, so that's the best I can do.)

For some of y'all, this general idea is a no-brainer:

"Take the good with the bad."

"The rain falls on the just and the unjust."

Anyone who pays attention to how an actual day unfolds will find this wisdom intuitive. But I was born an idealist who came to be well versed in the art of spiritual bypassing. Spiritual bypassing is exactly what it sounds like. Instead of reckoning with the hard reality of a lost job or loved one, we simply opt out, using spirituality to bypass (repress) the hard emotions. Some of us bypass in small ways, with thought-terminating clichés like "I'm sure it's for the best." Is it? Really? You're sure?

As an Evangelical, I climbed into my Mack Truck at an early age and barrelled down the bypass, emboldening myself with these words: "All things work together for good to those who love God and are called according to His purpose" (Romans 8:28). I spent half a lifetime under that anthem of spiritual bypass. All things means *all* things, right? Chronic illness? Working for good. Natural disaster. Good. Death of my baby boy? Working for my good.

Are you freaking kidding me?

And here's another newsflash: Just because you leave fundamentalism doesn't mean that you shake off the programming in a flash. Vestiges of magical thinking remain *to this day*. When things are going relatively well, I probably make too much of the smooth sailing. And when Gigi gets into an accident while we are cruising along with our cappuccinos on Thanksgiving morning, I am very likely to feel like the eye of some deity has personally targeted li'l ole me. I'm not saying this line of thinking makes any kind of sense. I bought an old car. Have I had a little bit of bad luck with said car? Okay, a lot of bad luck—but in my saner moments, when I am not whining to the car gods about this problem child of a vehicle, I can recognize the fact that I am just a single mom with an old car doin' her best.

It took a gay man with a sex advice column to finally get me to understand that I can't just cordon off the good from the hard and enter into a Promised Land flowing with milk and "No. Effing. Problems." I need this reminder, and when the good in life bumps up against the hard things that feel very high stakes, the statement can feel grounding. It can prod me toward accepting life as it *is*, not how my highly imaginative, post-fundy brain can want it to be.

But the way birthdays hit when they belong to a deceased loved one? Well, that's a reality I have been wrangling with for the better part of twenty-three years. Grief takes on so many shapes in our lives. When grief and birthdays intersect, it can give rise to an uncontainable landscape of emotions. But grief is *not* an emotion. If anything, it is a force unmatched in its intensity.

I've come to develop a bit of what I call a dark romance with grief. I have traced her curves, outlined her edges even as she has winnowed me into an entirely different shape. Sorrow and rage, joy and despair make up her voluptuous curves. If you enter into a dark romance with grief, she will unmake and remake you. Your life may look so radically different by the time she's reshaped you that everyone from your priest to your postal worker will hardly recognize you. Grief does a number on the life we thought we were going to have—just like love.

Fair enough.

But can we also talk for a moment about how absolutely freaking weird grief is? Maybe "weird" is a stand-in word for "Hanging on for dear life to the last vestige of physical connection with the beloved." Here's what I mean: Whatever your metaphysical beliefs—whether you think we are just spiritual beings having an earthly experience, or think that when you die, nothing remains but a corpse that is pushing up daisies—can we agree on one thing? Whatever love is, love is shown in the body. We may think of love as some mystical union, a divine force, or simply a concept. But a concept doesn't have feet.

You know what does, though? That's right. A body.

We love through our bodies. We love with our hands, mouths, and ears. Our mouths whisper an "I love you." Our vocal cords vibrate with *Hush little baby, don't you cry*. Our fingers sweep a curl off our lover's cheek. We put our own cheek to their chest and listen to the beat of their heart. Hell, our own heartbeat and breathing match theirs as we lie body to body. We use our wrists to whisk children's birthday cakes into shape and hope that they turn out better than that piece of crap cake from years gone by. Our eyes analyze FAFSA websites and wedding registries. It's all pretty fucking corporeal.

Some of what our bodies do, we enjoy greatly. And some of it is simply, as Dan Savage would say, the "price of admission" to be in relationship with our chosen human. If we are doing the work of loving well, we are using both brain and heart to learn our human and offer up our bodies to loving them. Nowhere do we become more artful in loving than in parenting. I say this because if there is one relationship in which the duty flows in one direction, it is parenting.

I chose to have five children. When I had them, I signed up to artfully *learn them.* I tried to study them and understand how to show them love in ways that actually feel like love—*to them.* This is why I believe that if we have to constantly tell someone, "You know I love you, but . . .", we need to go back to the drawing board and ask why we would need this disclaimer. Knowing that you are loved is not an intellectual knowing; it's a visceral one. Just like we give love in our bodies, we feel it there. Our hearts, bellies, and nether regions are well equipped to know what love feels like.

When the giver of love is attuned to the heart of the recipient and is willing to change the ways that they love, magic ensues. When we say that relationships take work, this is what I think we mean. The more aligned our overtures of love are to the body of the beloved, the more they feel loved. And the more those overtures are reciprocated, the closer the hearts grow. There is a saying in education: "Teach the students you actually have, not the ones you wish you had." The same is true in the parent-child relationship. We love the kids we *actually have*, not some Betty Crocker projection of our psyches. The beauty of this arrangement is that our kids will *show* us who they are if we let them.

Great. Awesome. Parenting solved!

But what happens to a body that is used to loving another human in very particular ways when those avenues of loving become unavailable? Well, we act weird. Our bodies still sense opportunities to give love, but the body we want to give it to is buried, in my case, under a crepe myrtle tree far away. No wonder I visited Elijah's grave so much after he left. No wonder

I wrote a song, "Empty Place," so laden with images of bodily longing for my baby:

There's an empty place at my table
where your winsome smile used to be
and true blue eyes filled with summer skies
left an empty place inside of me

You were all of springtime come calling
Your lips were roses in full bloom
but you left winter in your wake
Now a cold wind blows inside of me

Loving you was easy
It's just been so hard to watch you leave
The hardest part of letting go
is dreaming these barren dreams

So I'm living here with all this longing
I'm living in the in-between
and aching arms reach out to hold you
find a gaping hole inside of me

The song is longing embodied. Of course I miss Elijah's ways. But the absence of his grin, the feel of his sweaty little fingers, the outline of his tiny frame as I nestled against him on the couch is the pain to which this song attends. My ears craved the sound of Elijah's voice asking "house house?" (roughhouse). Only his voice could have assuaged the assault on my senses, which strained with unmitigated desire to love.

So, the weirdness ensued. I would hear a child who sounded like Elijah. For a moment, my body would respond with an urge to go to my child, only to be reminded that no corporeal being called Elijah exists. No wonder the idea that we will actually *see* our loved ones again is so much more comforting than some cosmic sense that we are all "returning to stardust." Big whoop. My body doesn't want stardust. It wants a little hand to hold, and it won't ever have it.

But we have to make do, so, in the absence of the actual body of our beloved, we cling to stand-ins. I still have one of Elijah's baby blankets, which has long since stopped smelling like him. Still, this blanket is something Elijah's body touched. When I want to feel close to Elijah, I take out that blanket that used to swaddle him and hold it to my heart. I talk to him and let the tears come. Anyone who doesn't understand this type of holding would walk in on a grown-ass woman holding a Pooh blankie and have a few questions. Rightly so. Cause it's weird, y'all.

After a while, the bereaved are able to keep most of our weirdness out of other people's way. It's a good thing, I guess, because our weirdness makes everyone else feel weird too.

Even though he didn't say, "I've got a case of the grief-weirds," C. S. Lewis knew exactly what I am talking about. Lewis, well-known writer of *The Chronicles of Narnia* and several theological works, married in midlife. His wife, Joy Davidson, was his intellectual equal and playmate. He described her mind as "lithe and quick and muscular as a leopard. Passion, tenderness and pain were all equally unable to disarm it. It scented the first whiff of cant or slush; then sprang, and knocked you over before you knew what was happening."[8]

When his wife died of cancer a scant four years into the marriage, Lewis was utterly devastated. And of course, being C. S. Lewis, he chronicled something stranger than the land of Narnia: the inner landscape of his loss. In *A Grief Observed*, Lewis bush-whacked his way through the land of his own unrelenting heart-ache, commenting on the uncomfortable weirdness that grief begets not just in the bereaved but in those who encounter them:

> "An odd byproduct of my loss is that I'm aware of being an embarrassment to everyone I meet. At work, at the club, in the street, I see people, as they approach

me, trying to make up their minds whether they'll 'say something about it' or not. I hate it if they do, and if they don't. Some funk it altogether. R. has been avoiding me for a week. I like best the well brought-up young men, almost boys, who walk up to me as if I were a dentist, turn very red, get it over, and then edge away to the bar as quickly as they decently can."[9]

When people are in the early throes of the grief weirds, we often want to isolate ourselves with our little Squishmellow Griefys. We know that we aren't normal. Our world has stopped, but other people's lives keep moving forward. Love is always in motion, and when we lose someone, our love for them becomes frozen in time. No wonder Lewis ended the above passage with this line: "Perhaps the bereaved ought to be isolated in special settlements like lepers." Sign me up, bro.

In lieu of griefer colonies, the grieving attend support groups; we tire out friends with our retellings of broken hearts. Some of us hit the bars or the books especially hard. Grief can make us feel so out of kilter with the kinetics of the world. Everyone is bustling about, acting so damn normal. We are anything but.

When you are in grief, you see your loved one everywhere. Lewis puts this idea poignantly: "Her absence is like the sky, spread over everything." Damn straight. At first, I saw Elijah everywhere. Nowhere was safe from this presence of his absence. He seemed to be in the sky, the streets, the grocery store, the kitchen. Psychologists call these places grief triggers. I agree with the term because they invoke a type of psychic violence on their victim. The bereaved are in a double bind because they desperately want to remember everything, but every memory is frozen in time.

So, we create little shrines in our homes, sanctuaries where we can try to feel close to the one we lost. The intimate space of connection that we so carefully built becomes a dusty homage to what was. My grandmother's shrine was the bedroom she and my grandpa occupied for over half a century. My grand-parents lived in an era when couples commonly slept in separate beds. I love this about them. They had sixty years and ten kids under their belts. They didn't need a marriage bed to prove a damn thing. They had a life. After he died, my grandma kept their room in the exact state in which he had left it, kept my Papa's bed made, his baseball cap hanging on the poster. His shirts remained neatly hung as if awaiting his return.

I think what my grandmother did is more socially acceptable than other forms of grief enshrinement. My grandmother married my Papa when she was fifteen. That is the same age that my youngest child is now. My grandmother grew up and grew old with my Papa. I don't think anyone expected her to get over it. When she died a few years after he did, none of us were surprised that the room was still unchanged.

I, on the other hand, was not in my seventies when I lost Elijah. I was young—twenty-seven. There was no parallel version of involuting and enshrining myself in his room and waiting out the rest of my days. Nothing reminds you that life is moving forward like a passel of toddlers, am I right? Enshrinement wasn't an option. But neither was living in a state of grief that C. S. Lewis likened to getting the same leg amputated every day.[10]

Put differently, if getting a pack of kindergarteners to land an octave is awkward AF, try showing up for life when you are pretty sure that part of your own body went into the ground with your beloved. Talk about singing the damn song. My children required me to show up for the song even as I could come nowhere close to landing the octave. Whatever squawking I was doing, metaphorically speaking, made kindergartners look like Pavarotti. That's because when grief rips you open, you are aren't *carrying* grief. You are *in* grief.

Healing is when the script finally flips, when grief is, instead, in you. When it pervades your song instead of squelching it. Over the long haul, I have grown around my grief. It's not that the grief shrunk. But there is an expansiveness around it that allows me to carry it. It hurts like a phantom limb that longs to be sedated. Healing isn't so much hurting less but a recognition that whatever doesn't kill you *makes* you. Period.

But first, it has to unmake you, and that process is more akin to living with a roiling pot of lava in your belly than anything resembling a five-year plan. Resistance truly is futile.

The sense that I am immersed in grief has muted over the years; I no longer see Elijah everywhere. But to this day, I can't see a butterfly without thinking of him. Elijah, every bit a rowdy little boy, had a contemplative side. He loved exploring nature, and one of my last memories of him is playing outside with a water rocket that hooked up to our garden hose. Elijah delighted in the butterflies drawn to its glistening, airborne stream.

Elijah could attend to things in an uncanny way for a child so young. His early attempts at scribbles lasted for hours. It's as if he were trying to unlock the secret of crayons, moving them round and round to decipher how the wax transferred onto the page. Once, when we were driving home, Elijah looked up from his carseat and noticed, I think for the first time, a perfectly pregnant full moon.

From the backseat, I heard a soft, "Moon? Oh please."

I really think Elijah thought I might stop the car, pluck the moon from the sky and hand it to him. And if I could have, the earth would have been missing a moon that night. That's how much parents want to give our kids all the good things, moon included.

Elijah had two birthdays on this planet, and of course, being a birthday person, I wanted to make them special. On his first birthday, we sang that damn song with much silliness and aplomb and plopped down one of my few actually (as opposed to relatively) good-looking birthday cakes in front of our toddler. Up to this point, Elijah hadn't eaten so much as a piece of candy, but the kid got the idea. He didn't know what the day was about, but he did know what to do with cake. After he baptized himself in that chocolate, nothing but a bath would do.

But after Elijah died, the question of what to do with his birthday became another grief burden. And I gotta be honest: since then, we have had some pretty weird birthdays. At first, we picnicked at the cemetery where Elijah is laid to rest. For years, my ex and I packed up our little ones and laid out a spread near his tombstone. We sang the song and ate his favorite foods. We downed many a Goldfish cracker in Elijah's honor, wondering if it was rude to let the little ones turn his grave into a jungle gym. Once we moved away from where his grave lay, we put on slideshows at home—a smaller, family-only version of yearly memorial.

Over the years, these attempts to party wore thin. Sure, celebrating Elijah's birthday in some way is important. But these days, it's mostly me and Elijah out on the bayou where I live. I sit with my son near the water. I take out my phone and write:

Today, I remember Elijah, sitting in the stones, sifting them through his chubby fingers. Fascinated by rocks. A perfect toddler.

Today, I remember Elijah in Europe. Paris. The Louvre. At Pompeii hating the sunscreen on his head. Eating gelato in front of ancient frescoes.

Today, I remember Elijah. Shooting off the water rocket. Staring at butterflies in the sky. Full of wonder and life.

God, I love that kid. Happy birthday, buddy. Mommy loves you.

On Elijah's day, I hold space, letting the bitter and the sweet coexist. I trust that this old grief is working its way through me, winnowing out a softer, kinder version of myself. And if that was all that January 20th was, a quiet remembrance of the little boy who lived, it would be enough to illustrate Savage's thesis.

Certainly the birthday of a dead child can remind us that hardship and joy abutt—but that's not where Savage's truism ends.

Remember that golden-haired girl and the respectable cake and singing the damn song?

Ada was born exactly two years and one day after Elijah's second birthday. The batter from his birthday cake had not dried when Ada decided her day had come. I think this fact proves that Ada is a birthday person. She was kind enough to allow her big brother his day, but dammit, she wasn't gonna share her own. The first labor pangs hit around two in the morning. Two hours later, on her *own* birthday, thank you very much, Ada arrived.

Poor Ada, though. If you think it's tough to plan a birthday for a kid unfortunate enough to be born around Christmas, try watching your mother navigate the emotional whiplash of planning back-to-back birthdays—one of which amounts to a memorial service for a brother you don't remember and the other a celebration of your own life. And try doing that for about eighteen years in a row. Ada, if you are reading this, I'm sorry. You got the raw end of the birthday deal here, honey.

For years, these days felt like inverses of each other to me. When I contemplate Ada's new year, my feelings of hope and anticipation are the antithesis of the unfulfilled longing I have for my son. Every birthday is a reminder of how old he would be. Every birthday marks another milestone not met, another barren dream that remains unfulfilled. My two oldest kids feel linked, Elijah and Ada siblings who actually touched each other, knew each other as kin, even if one was a toddler and one was an infant. Perhaps they even knew each other in deeper, visceral ways for that fact. So I can't help but meaning-make with their birthdays in ways that I don't with my other children's. I hope this is not hard on Ada, because I want her day to be her day and not overshadowed by the one preceding it. But in my heart, I know that some residual melancholy inevitably bleeds over.

The good and the hard are holding hands. Dan Savage is

right again.

Regardless of my attempts to patch together my heart, there is no way that my kids didn't grow up in the shadow of my eldest's passing, because the mother that they have has been unmade and remade into someone who is, in some ways, unrecognizable to my former self. I don't know if this is a good or bad thing. But it does make me think, on this eve of Elijah's birthday, that if my son has a legacy, it is this new creature I have become.

Our children are so stitched to the fabric of our souls that sometimes, even in the wake of death, it can difficult to know where their souls end and ours begin. This is the great mystery of mothering to me. The love is so intense, the desire to nurture and protect so woven into my DNA, that I still labor to simply let my children continue to grow and be the people that they are meant to be. Yes, Khalil Gibran, my children are not my children, but damn, have you ever nursed a baby, let alone five of them, for years on end?

That I was going to be rendered powerless in the face of my grief for a time was an unalterable fact, but the choices I made while trying to put myself back together are choices that I hope Elijah would be proud of. I've tried to let this loss soften me. I've tried to become a mother who trusts her children's hearts. I strive to be an example of how even though life will serve you up sorrows that you don't think you can live through, you can.

I will always be proud to have carried and given birth to Elijah. On his day, I remember this simple fact: He lived! Elijah lived! And I got to be the mother who witnessed his little life. What an honor. I will always be sorry that he is not on this earth still and that I don't get to learn from him the kind of lessons that each of my remaining children teach me. I don't know how to not regret his loss, but I do know that I can let it exist alongside the deep joys of knowing my other children. I can let it lie in the sod, a little seed that gives rise to trees of compassion, of care and tenderness for those who are hurting, which is basically everyone, everywhere at some point in their life. I can move between sorrow and joy without fear that either will be my only state.

This is what two decades of birthdays without Elijah have taught me. This is why Ada's days, these days, are much less tinged with sorrow. My hands cannot touch my son, but my misty eyes remind me that I am lucky to be Elijah's mother— on the day he was born and on every other.

Turns out, I can sing the damn song after all.

Fundamomalist: Part 1

Being a mother is exhausting. Being a fundamentalist is equally tiring. Merge the two into a Fundamomalist and you get a whole other level of tired.

This tiredness is not born so much from the myriad tasks that are tacked onto an average day. I imagine that families who are really into club soccer or dance, say, give up their free time to these endeavors much in the way that our family's weeks once involved Sunday morning church, Sunday evening Bible studies, and our daily dose of Scripture. As a stay-a-home Fundamomalist, I did all the regular things that moms of many kids do: cooked a multitude of meals, cleaned many a mess, and intermittently homeschooled my kids when the perils of public school encroached upon their young psyches.

By "perils," I mean the one time a young Isaiah had to wear a neon orange amoeba suit and roll around on stage representing the beginning of life on the planet. I was incensed that this theory was being foisted upon my kids by those ultimate purveyors of propaganda known as, you guessed it . . . *secular humanists*. Back in my fundy days, calling someone a secular humanist was pretty much the fundamentalist equivalent of calling someone a racist or a fascist. There was no worse type of subversive than this human . . . ist.

After the Great Neon Amoeba Incident of 2010, I yanked those kids outta school faster than you can say "Big Bang." I saw the school's agenda as directly counter to what I was attempting to do. And what was this all-encompassing task of mine? Let's look to the Bible for the answer to that question. And let's do it with the King James version because it just sounds so damn good. According to the Psalmist:

> "Lo, children are an heritage of the LORD: And the fruit of the womb is his reward. As arrows are in the hand of a mighty man; So are children of the youth. Happy is the man that hath his quiver full of them: They shall not be ashamed, but they shall speak with the enemies in the gate." (Psalm 127:3-5)

First, let's notice how fun it is to say "*an* heritage from the Lord." Now, consider this verse that has been used by many a fundamentalist group to get women to birth a lot of babies. Do I like all my babies? Absofuckinglutely. Would I have had five kids if this and other verses hadn't informed my childbearing decisions? Maybe not.

While I think the Psalmist was basically saying, "Hey, when you have enemies, it's good to have a lotta kinfolk around you to help," this verse has been utilized to create a network of fundamentalist groups who want to birth, train, and deploy literal apologist soldiers in God's army. This is exactly what I was trying to do with my kids—in addition to singing them lullabies and washing another round of finger paint off their hands. As a Fundamomalist, it was my objective to raise up those kids to be soldiers in God's army, arrows in a quiver who are in need of sharpening so that they can go out and make, you guessed it again, *more* fundamentalists. Capri Sun, anyone?

As a pastor's kid, I was commandeered for the army early. And even though I wish I hadn't been raised a fundamentalist, I understand that my parents were acting out of their own integrity. Their choices were not born of moral turpitude but out of their very deeply held beliefs, which led them to a sense of higher calling. And that calling required them to pass onto their kids some very specific and totalizing ways. Fundamentalist Christianity works for them. And I wouldn't wish them to let go of it, especially now, when they have devoted their whole lives to that faith with absolute fidelity.

I can hold respect for my parents while also being glad that that faith, taken to its logical extreme, ironically turned me into a woman who stopped herself from heading down the same path. It's almost a "hate the sin love the sinner" situation, but in reverse. My parents are no more the sum of their beliefs than I was when I was a George Bush (Sr. *and* Jr.) voting, abortion-hating, right-wing Evangelical. I was that woman. And I came to be that woman because I was programmed in a high-control group by people who were actually doing their best. Was it controlling as fuck? You betcha. Was it done with malice? Absolutely not.

There is no way to talk about how I became and then unbecame that woman without also talking about baby fundy me. Here she is: Welcome Desiree, the sweet, little honey-haired arrow in training, to the scene. That little girl was a daddy's girl, the youngest arrow by a long shot in his quiver. And he doted on that girl. My dad made me a swing in the front yard and a whole-ass jungle gym in my brother's room. He taught me to bait a fishing hook and clean a mess o' fish. On our many long road trips, he made up songs to help pass the miles. Wherever my dad was, I was close to follow. When we were sent North by the Baptists to save the Catholics, my dad began building a church from the foundation up. For real.

When that church was being erected, my daddy brought me along to help. "Helping" looked a lot like me swimming in the baptistry and roller-skating in the sanctuary before the carpet was laid. During the week, he oversaw the concrete being poured and nailed the support beams in place. My dad used his time spent sawing and hammering to build out his sermons. Then, on weekends, he transformed from carpenter to exegetical Evangelist.

It always began the same way: "Turn in your Bibles" to whatever the passage of the week was. He would read the passage, provide some context, and begin making his points. "So, what Paul was saying in this passage is that the gospel is for everyone, and this was a big deal for some churches who thought that Jesus had only come to rescue Jews. As the Apostle to the Gentiles, Paul made it his mission to expand the reach of the gospel."

The sermon would start out like a book club. However, somewhere near the end of the message, the Spirit would come over my dad. He would look across the pulpit like you were the only one in the room. You could not escape the gaze. Nor did you want to. Fire flew from his lips as he spoke in a frenzy:

"The Lord is here right now! And He is calling on you! You *shall* know the truth, and the truth shall set you free. Whosoever shall call upon the name of the Lord shall be saved. You can be *free* from your sin. You can be *free* from your addiction. You don't need those cigarettes. You don't need that beer. You don't need your drugs. You can be free from all of it. But you have to call on Him. Jesus is patiently waiting for you, patiently waiting. He's saying, 'Oh sinner. Come home. Come home. Come home!"

The altar call was soon to follow, which is when attendees are invited to step forward and forge a brand-new commitment to Jesus before the witnessing of the entire church. It was during one such call that I, at around five years of age, walked into the waiting arms of my father to get saved. I believed all of it: my own sin weighing upon my child's heart like lead, the regret that my sin had cost Jesus his life, the relief that I wasn't going to hell anymore. I was forgiven.

My father had both set up the need for salvation and delivered it to me. As a result, my faith was mired in my love for my dad. When I went door to door with him and passed out fliers promoting Vacation Bible School, I did so as a young convert—a soldier in the Lord's army. I remember those fliers, which featured a garish-looking, mimeographed clown holding balloons that kids could color and trade in for a treat on the first night of Vacation Bible School. At age eight, I stuffed mailboxes as a devotee to what I thought was *the* answer to the world's ills. And, most of all, I did all this as my father's daughter.

Sidestepping for a moment the fact that clowns are creepy AF and that somewhere in northeastern Ohio, a middle-aged mom is working through her religious trauma about Buddy the Bible Clown, allow me to share a bit about what Vacation Bible School actually *is*. Think a much milder version of *Jesus Camp*—shorter in duration and with a lot of cookies. Baptists are very good at snacks. We know that a good helping of Chips Ahoy! makes the gospel go down easy. Think "Hell is real; have a cookie."

When I was a child, Vacation Bible School, or VBS, as the initiated call it, was actually amazingly fun, a relief from the tedium of summers. My dad, the amazing fire and brimstone preacher, was also a hell of a VBS putter-onner. Every summer for one week, my dad put on puppet shows, led us in rousing renditions of "I'm in the Lord's Army," and served up the gospel in ways that were very relatable to kids.

The VBS of my youth was akin to a humble traveling caravan putting on little sideshows. Today, it has evolved into something to which P. T. Barnum would aspire. When I attended, we used to do Kool-Aid shots whilst watching the story of Noah's Ark play out a flannel graph. At the last VBS my kids attended, circa 2010, they auditioned for lead roles in a full-on musical, eventually performing for an audience of no less than three hundred people. Those kids choreographed for Christ. I was proud.

The point of these events is, of course, to evangelize the wee ones in ways that are geared toward their young psyches. I have a lot of feelings about this now, but like many people born into fundamentalist groups, I didn't question it. Jesus is just what we did.

If a kid cuts her teeth on VBS, Sunday morning church, Sunday night church, Wednesday night prayer meeting, choir practice, Thursday night visitation, and morning Bible studies; and if a kid buys into the beliefs wholeheartedly; and if a kid loves her daddy, that kid is very likely going to start evangelizing very young. I know I did. I punctuated lazy afternoons looking in the ditch for tadpoles that were sprouting limbs with periods of passing out tracts to anyone who would take one. I was about six at the time. As much as this type of street-witnessing remained a staple of evangelism, as I grew, I embraced another type of witnessing, a little thing called "relational evangelism." Relational evangelism is exactly what it sounds like. You become friends with people, form connections, and then insert your gospel pitch into the relationship.

So when I say that fundamentalism affects every relationship, I mean *every* relationship. When you are a fundamentalist, you are a fundamentalist first. Even your relationship with yourself is seen through the lens of Christian first, human, *ehhhhhh*, kinda sometime? I would argue that Christian fundamentalism encourages you to have *no* relationship with yourself whatsoever. Your job is to, as the apostle Paul put it, "crucify the flesh with its passions and desires" (Galatians 5:24).

In case you have forgotten, crucifixion is an excruciatingly tortuous process whereby the death is exacted over a period of days. Paul's metaphor holds up because it turns out that the desires of the flesh are pretty darn pesky and keep cropping up. Quelling them requires nothing short of violence to oneself. I think Paul knew that and picked exactly the right word to describe the psychological torture involved in attempting to divorce your mind from your body. Epistemological hand shown, y'all.

In addition to lopping off parts of yourself, as a fundy, you are moving through the social world applying norms that are basically one-on-one marketing strategies. In every friendship, you are looking for an opportunity to connect. Then, you wait for a chance to dispense a little Pez-sized gospel about how "God loves you and has a wonderful plan for your life."

One of my favorite childhood friendships was with a little girl I met at school. April was also a fundamentalist. Only, while I was a Bible-totin' Southern Baptist, April came from a *Watchtower*-reading family of Jehovah's Witnesses. What ensued was a sort of friendly matching of wits between the kids of two fundy families. While April and I were getting along just fine, both sets of parents believed that the other was going to hell.

So, our parents—through us—tried to help us deconvert from our particular brand of fundy. It was like an elaborate chess match being played vicariously through us. April would share her latest copy of the *Watchtower*. My dad would slide *Steps to Peace with God* into my hands as I left the house. April would say something like, "We just want you to see the light." I would take this intel back to my dad, who would counter with, "Tell her that you are in the light and you are walking in it every day."

Y'all, at the time that all this back and forth was going down, April and I were, like, exactly eight years old. No lie. But I loved my daddy, and April didn't seem too worried about any of it, so we just kinda muddled through and swung from tree branches like the little tomboys we were. We were both believers, but we were innocent of the implications of our beliefs. We never popped each other's respective belief bubbles, and for that I am grateful.

Though the friendship remained fairly unsullied from the attempts of our parents, it did serve as a sort of precedent. Friendships, like all other aspects of life, were either places where you and another fundamentalist Christian grew your faith together or where you attempted to bring another human into the fundy fold. No relationship was just a regular ole "Hey, I like you. Wanna be friends?" There was always an implicit "Wanna be friends so that we can Jesus it up together?"

Fast forward through years of training in how to win the lost, two summers as a missionary helping to run those VBS baby Jesus Camps, marrying, and becoming a mother.

Being the fecund fundy that I was, I gave birth to five kids in pretty close succession. Of course I was going to look for opportunities to convert my kids. And, here's the really fun part. As a fundy parent, you need to get on with that converting before your child reaches the age of accountability. What's this magical age, you ask? Hint: not the age at which you get assigned an accountant to help you learn to manage your allowance. It's way better than that. The age of accountability is when you gain the mental and spiritual maturity to actually sin, to really *know* that you are sinning—like sin-sin, in a way that might make your mama blush.

The upshot of this is that once you reach the age of accountability, there is no going back. Your sins are forever on the slate, and if you die without accepting Jesus, you are going to the bad place. I don't mean The Bad Place with Ted Danson in it. I mean the bad place where the "worm dieth not, and the fire is not quenched" (Mark 9:44). It is paramount that, once you reach the age of accountability, you pray the prayer and get yourself saved as soon as possible in order to avoid the fire and the worms. Oh, and the isolation. Did I mention that in hell you are utterly isolated (except for the worms, so that's a small comfort, I guess)?

Given that the age of accountability is, to understate it, very important, it would be nice to know when this age is about to happen. Like, it would be nice to plan for it, right? "Heyyyy, little one, you know you are about a week out from the age of accountability, so if there's anything real bad you want to do, like rob a bank or peek at something untoward online, now would be a good time." I mean, I had five kids, so some way of keeping track would have been a real big help to me. I could have scheduled in my kids' salvation opportunities: soccer practice, spelling bee, save from damnation.

But no such luck, and here's why: the age of accountability is completely different for each person. That's right. It's completely variable, and there's no letter that arrives in your chimney Hogwarts-style that says, "Congratulations, you are now going to hell if you sin. Good luck." Nope. The age of accountability is just something you kinda figure out. There are signs, like if your kid steals from the cookie jar and lies about it and then looks real sheepish, they might be getting close to the age of accountability. (Never mind the fact that my puppy will exhibit this exact behavior when he pees in the wrong place.)

Naturally, as a good fundamentalist mom, I wanted to get all my kids saved before they reached the age, so whenever a quiet moment occurred, usually about once every eight months as they were recovering from a stomach flu, I would take advantage of this "teachable moment" and dive in. Keeping things short and sweet, I would share the bullet-pointed version of the gospel. Please remember that you have to get people lost before you can get 'em saved—so you have to follow a little logic train that goes something like this: "Have you ever done anything wrong?"

Usually the answer to this was yes, because as a fundy mom, I was very good at letting my kids know when they had sinned and fallen short of the glory of God. Whacking your brother with a Lego? Falling short. Hoarding food up in your room for your secret food club? Falling short. Lying? Short. Not sharing? Waaaaay short. Not sharing with me, your giver of life? Way, way, short, shortie.

The kid I was talking to this day was Ada. She was somewhere in the kindergarten–first-grade range and had recently learned to read, so it seemed like I could share the gospel with a little literacy scaffolding. We flopped down on the giant bed next to our fish tank. (The fish were stolen from our previous residence, but that's something I am accountable for. Don't worry about it.) We went through the whole drill, Ada dutifully listening as I explained how we are all sinners, and it only takes one sin to become a sinner. We all rightfully deserve to be punished for our sin, but God has made a way for us. If we accept God's free gift of salvation, God will forgive our sins and let us into heaven when we die.

All was going well until I completely flubbed the deal. Every good salesman (er, I mean evangelist) knows that you don't ask the proselyte if they have questions. No. You close the damn (I mean dang) deal. *You* go for the ask. So what I should have said was, "Would you like to pray to receive Jesus into your heart?"

Praying the prayer is how the deal is sealed. If you pray that prayer even one time and really mean it, then you are set for all eternity. Saved. It's a done deal.

But instead of asking Ada if she wanted to pray the prayer, what I actually said was, "Do you have any questions?"

To this query, Ada responded, her eyes fixed on the five stolen koi in our tank: "Yes. Do fish have eyelids?"

There it is. Inquiry as the death of evangelism. What did this question mean? Had Ada not reached the age of account-ability? Had she reached it but was deflecting with this fish-eye-lid question? All I knew was that my teachable moment had passed. I would have to wait for the next stomach flu and sol-dier on. (The answer, by the way, is no.)

Tone shift, y'all. While the above story is a lighthearted ren-dering of the grueling existence I now call fundamomalism, there is a much darker side to this way of parenting. When Elijah died, we took a sick comfort in the fact that at least he hadn't reached the age of accountability, so we knew where he was: in heaven. I know that the bereaved grasp for any salve to soothe our hearts. But finding relief in the fact that your child didn't live long enough to go to hell is one pretty effed-up balm.

This age of accountability mindfuck is wonderful grist for subverting and converting children and royally fucking up their childhoods. I used to think my kids got a lesser version of the disease, but maybe not.

During quarantine, three of my kids ended up in my bed-room reminiscing about their upbringings. Among other things, I learned that my children used to play a lovely little game called Salem Witch Trial. I think you get the gist of the game if you know anything about witch trials—specifically, the end of witch trials. Turns out that while I was inside nursing the baby or whipping up some ants on a log, my three eldest would take turns being either the inquisitor or the witch. Ironically, being the witch was the coveted role of the game, so they would fight over who was going to be on trial next. I'm pretty sure if I had poked my head out at the opportune moment, I would have heard my kids squabbling, "But it's my time to burn!"

In the middle of this little quarantine-induced nostalgia fest, Ada dropped a bit of knowledge about how her younger self had grappled with the age of accountability rhetoric we then embraced. She began with something like, "I hope this is not too heavy, Mom" (thereby ensuring that it probably would be). Turns out that Ada had experienced cracks in our beliefs when she was very little. She wasn't sure if she believed the gospel. But she knew that if she didn't, and she was wrong, she would end up in hell if she died after the age of accountability. So, little Ada's logic went like this: "I don't want my parents to go through the pain of losing another child. But I don't want to put them through the pain of knowing that I am languishing in hell." Utilizing this lesser of two evils logic, little Ada wondered if it would be better if she died before she reached the age of accountability.

Unfortunately, I think if she was tying this sort of logic knot at around age seven, the jig was already up. Sorry, little Ada. You were accountable for something or other that you did at that age, just as I was apparently mature enough at around age five to know that failing to flush the toilet was pretty much a mortal sin.

But let's unpack this for a moment. My seven-year-old child spent time contemplating whether or not it would hypothetically be harder on her parents for her to actually die young or for us to live with the fact that our unbelieving daughter was languishing in eternal torment. Are we all agreed that this is a pretty fucked up thing for a kid to wrestle with? This moral conundrum existed alongside Ada twirling around in her princess dress and arguing over who deserved more M&M's at dinner (falling short!).

I think that one of the worst things Fundamomalist me did was to lay the framework for these types of musings to fester. Even as I sought to inoculate my children against the perils of public school, I infected them with beliefs that were far more psychologically damaging. "Evil-lution" ain't got nothing on "It might be better for your bereaved parents if you are dead instead of damned." I have had to reckon with the fact that I stole part of my children's innocence—even as I sought to safeguard it. My motives were pure, but I was safeguarding them from the wrong things. As a result, I implanted into their minds the same ideas that have caused me so much pain.

As a Fundamomalist, I taught my children not to trust their hearts, that no mistake is minor or simply human. Instead, I was several miles down the road of teaching them to believe that the inclinations of their hearts are "only evil all the time."

Wow. Really?

I am reminded of my father's retort when my mom would complain, "You *always* [insert problematic behavior here]."

"Honey, we both know I am not that consistent."

Having lived with my heart for about fifty years now, I have to concur with my daddy. I am a lot of things, and on my worst days, when I am drawing myself up to my full 5'7" frame and letting the Priceline rep who won't refund my car rental know that their policy is "abhorrent" and "puts low-income single parents at risk," I wouldn't want the full measure of my life to be judged by that snapshot of myself. (Also, if the lady who had to listen to me deliver this diatribe last Saturday is reading this, lemme buy you a drink at Pal's to make up for my assholery.) I am complex. So is every human. Fundamentalism's fuckery does not allow for this complexity, instead employing a one-size-fits-all approach to humanity's darker sides.

Why don't we talk more about the abhorrent practice of impregnating children's souls with the belief that they are literally evil? I don't think I am overstating what my upbringing taught me. I can chapter and verse this idea. In fact, I think I will: "The heart is deceitful above all things, and desperately wicked" (Jeremiah 17:9–10).

As I read that verse now, I just want to say to Jeremiah,

"Dude, who hurt you?" But as a child, I took the idea that I was evil deep into my heart. How could anything other than self-loathing spring from such a harmful belief? The basic question of whether or not I am a good person still rares up even though, intellectually, I don't believe that people are born evil, are all one thing, or are incapable of change. And unfortunately, believing that you are forgiven of your sins, accepting the "free" gift of salvation, does absolutely nothing to erase the belief that you are fundamentally evil. If you really believe it—I mean *really*—then the effects of this mindfuckery are incredibly traumatic.

Undoing the work of my rearing through the way I parent my own children has been one of the strangest longstanding efforts I've ever undertaken. It lies alongside the very long work of living with the grief of losing Elijah, and it is definitely informed by it. I feel fairly certain that my ties to fundamentalism via my great love for the people who had taught it to me would have remained in place if Elijah had not died. They might have even remained if he had not died in such a traumatic and tragic way. Under different circumstances, I might have had a schema compelling me to trust that some greater plan was involved. If Elijah had suffered an illness, for instance, I think my faith would have found a way through.

But Elijah didn't die like that. His death coupled with the way that he died created an extreme rupture in my psyche. Mourning Elijah was not clean pain. The pain was compounded by an extreme version of that uncomfortable mental state that psychologist Leon Festinger first named cognitive dissonance. This dissonance can come from acting in ways contrary to our beliefs (done that one) or from holding two seemingly contradictory beliefs. When the beliefs meet in our mind, they square off with each other. The result is a sense of mental disequilibrium.

According to Festinger, brains don't like this state, so they try very hard to resolve them. Sometimes, this involves one belief bowing to the other in a "Ya, you got me, bro" kinda way. Other times, we handwave away the disparity and file it under ideas like "paradox." If one is mystically bent, a nice little thought-terminating cliché can do the trick: "It's just one of God's mysteries, honey."

In my case, the two beliefs that created disequilibrium were a.) God is loving and has a wonderful plan for my life and b.) God is a betrayer who allowed me to be an unwitting instrument of my son's death.

Disequilibrium, my ass. My brain contained razor blades.

I would try to lean hard into God's goodness: *Maybe God has a purpose in this I just can't understand. Maybe Elijah would have grown up to be an unbeliever, so God was protecting him. Or maybe he would have grown very ill and suffered greatly, so God took him swiftly. Maybe there's some lesson in all of this for me. What if God is going to use this accident to bring glory to Himself? God is testing me, like Job, to see if I will renounce my faith. God knows that I will emerge triumphant and be a better witness.*

These thoughts are utter insanity to me now, but they are evidence of how, even in my bereaved state, fundamentalism trumped my own humanity. I was bereaved. I needed to be spending the better part of a year letting grief move through me. Instead, I remained a faithful Fundamomalist. I was forced to sift through the rubble of my baby's room with the cold comfort of verses like "All things work together for good for those who love God and are called according to his purpose." But none of what had happened to Elijah felt good. If we were to think of God as Father, then weren't we to use this blueprint to examine his actions?

This type of musing would send me careening over the dissonance cliff into the opposite set of thoughts: *What kind of capricious, narcissistic deity needs to let a mom bury her baby in order to gain glory for Himself? This is not the action of a loving parent. I know, because I am a parent. I have loved God since I was five years old. I have tried my best to serve Him. I gave Him everything, and this is what He allowed.*

I lost about twelve years trying to square these dissonant

thoughts, to balance the bitterness and the bargaining. During that time, I continued to lead small groups at church, play in the worship band, parent, start a nonprofit in my dead son's name, and move away from the Mobius strip in my mind surrounding Elijah's death. I needed to blame someone, and when I was focusing on the God is good side of the coin, that someone was easy to pinpoint: me.

I was evil. Primed with mental scaffolding that predisposed me toward hating my heart, I landed in the slough of repressed sorrow. Each thought about the unfairness of Elijah's passing and my part in it as a prime actor dovetailed with my grief in ways that made me want to leave the planet. Ten years into this dark age, the agony faded into a dullness of spirit that I can only describe as wraithlike. I was among the living, but I was not alive. Unable to physically put myself in a grave for fear of what this would do to my living children, I succumbed to a state of subsistence that was equally as unfair to my family as it was to me.

Even in the midst of the darkness, my remaining kids tethered me to whimsy and called me to play. But I was enacting play because I knew my kids needed it, not because I felt playful. I suppose it was therapeutic. But even my kids could not save me from my stupor. And asking them to would have been laying too heavy a burden on them.

I wish I could trace a clear line of healing from the wraithlike state to the one where I almost feel *too* alive. But I do know one thing about my healing: it began with a quickening.

That quickening followed on the heels of my final prayer as card-carrying, Evangelical Christian. It was a simple prayer, and as earnest as the one I uttered in the arms of my dad when I was five: "God, if you are there, please, please show me. I have been seeking you my whole life, and I am open to you if you want to come find me, but I just can't do this anymore." That was it. With that prayer, I foisted the responsibility back into the hands of the Almighty.

And with that surrender, the dissonance resolved. I felt peace. The knots in my mind began to loosen. I didn't have to try to make the pieces fit anymore. I had fought this place for so long because I inherently felt its repercussions. In the wake of this quiet moment, I would be leaving, breaking the heart ties that had forged me, breaking my parents' hearts, giving the people who'd once known me best cause to wonder if I had gone insane. But in that moment, I felt a unison with myself that I have since become as fierce about protecting as I am my children.

But the prayer itself, humble and pleading, was not the quickening. When I quickened back to life, the first thing I felt was unmitigated, white-hot rage. Why had I been raised in such a way that I believed strength meant submission? Why was a bright-hearted girl tamed by a faith that made her unable to listen to her intuition and tell her husband, "No chance in hell we are building this bed"?

Women in high-control groups that tell them to quell their intuitions—tell them that men are always more rational and to be deferred to—become unwitting agents of harm. When we talk about patriarchy hurting women, this is part of what we mean. I felt uncomfortable speaking up about my concerns because of the contract that fundamentalism caused me to forge with my then husband. If there is a burden of guilt to be laid anywhere, it is on this system of belief that hijacked my agency as a parent.

It is not my ex-husband's fault that I didn't speak. My quickening began not with my prayer but with mis-aimed rage at my ex, and I still face fallout from choices I made during that time. These choices were the result of over a decade's worth of involuted grief shooting to the surface. I'm not proud of them, but I know they were necessary. I firmly believe that quickening into anger was the first step toward coming to terms with my own brokenheartedness. I could not have let those tears lay me low—low enough to truly begin to heal—without the quickening of my rage.

And this, people, is why we should not be afraid of our own anger. Maybe don't be Desi circa 2012 taking an oozie to every belief I ever held and hurting a lot of people in the process. But maybe do ask of your rage, "What are you trying to camouflage?" The hotter the rage, the deeper the hurt.

Ten years out from the quickening, the rage has passed. I feel quickened to beauty, to lust, to loyalty, to tenderness. Instead of crucifying the flesh, I caress it. I am quickened to the rotundness of my own life experiences. Each anniversary of Elijah's passing, I face the agony of his loss anew. Each year, I am reminded that I dream barren dreams for Elijah.

But this agony coexists with the creative adventure of bearing witness to what each of my living children are accomplishing. Being quickened means moving into each experience through the lens of embodiment. It means letting some chords remain unresolved and knowing that this, too, can be beautiful. But mostly, it means I am developing the capacity to hold grief in one hand and awe in the other.

Grief Zero

The bereaved are among us. They walk in our midst every day, people whose arms ache to hold their lost loves. The bereaved shroud ourselves in work—putting a pin in our sorrow so we can function. In an effort to be kind, we lie, engage in the Great American pastime of grief denial. But what else are we to do? In the US, if you lose a family member, you *might* get three days off of work. Let that sink in: seventy-two hours to get that whole grief thing on lock and hop back to it.

Because grief is not productive and the economy must roll on, right?

Apparently, if Christ can be resurrected in three days, the rest of us can at least be ready to return to our cubicles. Yet three days is barely enough time to begin making funeral arrangements, let alone ready your grieving self to contribute to late-stage capitalism.

Here's what three days out from Elijah's death looked like for me. I was choking down protein bars so I could nurse my eight-month-old. They tasted like sand. (Oh wait, they still do.) Three days after Elijah died, I kept vigil over his ashes while my husband scoured the cemeteries for his final resting place. Three days out, and we were trying to decide if Elijah would be laid to rest in "babyland" or in an adult-sized plot. Neither seemed to fit. Tell me, where is the proper place to bury a two-year-old?

Three days out, I vacillated between manic hyper-spirituality and that gift to the early bereaved nervous system: shock. Sleep was fitful at best, interrupted by intrusive thoughts about Elijah's last moments on earth. Did he suffer? Did he call for me? How could I have slept through my own child's passing, blissfully unaware of the events transpiring two rooms down? Each morning I would awake with lead in my bones. For a few moments, I would be blessed with not remembering why that was . . . and then I would remember. My baby was gone, and his absence had carved out a crater in my body.

As surely as being pregnant with Elijah had rounded me out, his loss hollowed me lean. I was a gutted, gaunt creature who surely looked like I belonged in the sanatorium. I probably did. My insides felt fileted, which I know is a physical impossibility. My whole body felt like a phantom limb. Elijah had lived in every cell, and now my nuclei were collapsing. The DNA of my psyche unwound. Being alone was unbearable, but when I wasn't, I doubled down on efforts to make sure Elijah's death was "bringing glory to God."

Precedent did exist for me to just sit and feel my grief. The Bible is replete with examples of people in mourning: "Have mercy upon me, O LORD," the Psalmist cried out, "for I am weak: O LORD, heal me; for my bones are vexed . . . I am weary with my groaning; all the night make I my bed to swim; I water my couch with my tears" (Psalms 6:2, 6).

Sounds about right.

If that passage isn't evidence that some sort of mourning roadmap is present in Scripture, try on this passage from none other than that bastion of biblical woe, the Book of Job: "May the day of my birth perish, and the night it was said, 'A boy is born!' That day—may it turn to darkness; may God above not care about it; may no light shine upon it" (Job 3:3–4).

Just in case the details are fuzzy, here's a quick recap of what led up to Job basically saying "I wish I had never been born." Job's tale of woe begins . . . in heaven, where God brings up to Satan just how awesome Job is and is like, "Have a go at Job, Lucifer. You won't break him."

Lucifer says, "Wanna bet?", and then masterminds one man's shittiest day ever. Job's tragedy comes in the form of four verbal battering rams that deliver their blows in the span of moments. Whoever wrote Job's story makes sure we know that hardly had one messenger bearing news more devastating than the one before him finished speaking when the next arrives.

Job is basically just having a day; and then: ". . . there came a messenger unto Job, and said, The oxen were plowing, and the asses feeding beside them. And the Sabeans fell upon them, and took them away; yea, they have slain the servants with the edge of the sword; and I only am escaped alone to tell thee" (Job 1:14–15).

I imagine Job thinking something like, *Okay, not great, but I still have the sheep.*

Yeah, think again, buddy. Because: "While he was yet speaking, there came also another, and said, 'The fire of God is fallen from heaven, and hath burned up the sheep, and the servants, and consumed them; and I only am escaped alone to tell thee'" (Job 1:16).

Well, this one seems a bit more personal. I mean, fuck the Sabeans, but the fire of God? Okay, that's oddly specific. At least I still have the camels.

At this point, all readers highly recommend that Job exit this conversation and run for the hills. He doesn't. In fact, while *that messenger was still speaking:* "There came also another, and said, 'The Chaldeans made out three bands, and fell upon the camels, and have carried them away, yea, and slain the servants with the edge of the sword; and I only am escaped alone to tell thee'" (Job 1:17).

I imagine Job beginning to sway a bit with the import of it all, tallying up the losses: *Asses, sheep, servants, camels—all gone. But I still have my family.*

Job, you really shouldn't have said that, because:

"*While he was yet speaking,* there came also another, and said, 'Thy sons and thy daughters were eating and drinking wine in their eldest brother's house. And, behold, there came a great wind from the wilderness, and smote the four corners of the house, and it fell upon the young men, and they are dead; and I only am escaped alone to tell thee.'" (Job 1:18–19)

At this point, it might be worth noting that Job had ten children: seven sons and three daughters.

After this news, Job does what any human who has just received such a harrowing blow would do. He falls to the ground. Well, first he stands up. That's a no-go. *Then* he falls to the ground.

Honestly, if I had been Job, the rest of the book would not have been written. The Book of Desi would have ended right there with, "She fell to the ground, and there she lays to this day. The birds came and perched in her hair, and a monument was raised over her, and people come by whenever they feel like their lives are particularly shitty so that they could say, 'At least we don't have Desi's life.'"

But that's not what Job does. The text says that Job falls to the ground and, get this . . . worships. At least, that's how the King James translators chose to render the Hebrew word "avodah."

According the translation: "Then Job arose, and rent his mantle, and shaved his head, and fell down upon the ground, and worshiped and said, 'Naked came I out of my mother's womb, and naked shall I return thither: the LORD gave, and the LORD hath taken away; blessed be the name of the LORD'" (Job 1:20–21).

I recently found out that *avodah* can also be translated as "work," and while I'm sure biblical scholars have done their due diligence, that word just seems to fit better. To me, Job was working pretty damn hard to make some meaning out of the four-fold destruction that had visited his home. Job's worship seems to be more of a submission. Really, the whole theme of the book can be found right there in Job's initial utterance:

"The LORD giveth *and* the LORD taketh away" (emphasis mine). There's an implied (and later explicated) acceptance of God's positionality as, well, God.

However, Job's initial take soon gives way to a different sentiment. At the beginning of chapter two, there is a whole other round of God talking to Satan and bringing Job to Satan's attention *again*. Like really, is there no one else in all of the ancient land who could have been considered? How about Ehud the tentmaker, or Abijah the vineyard tender? Weren't they pretty cool guys? Isn't Job busy at this point, shaving his head and worshiping? As essayist Martin Shaw recently wrote, "Turns out you might not want to be getting God's attention."[11] But God's attention Job has, so after this second round of "being considered," Scripture says: "So went Satan forth from the presence of the LORD, and smote Job with sore boils from the sole of his foot unto his crown" (Job 2:7).

The whole point of these boils is to afflict Job with something so physically uncomfortable that he can't do the work of tending to both his body and his heartache. Had those boils happened in isolation, certainly Job would have been upset, but I imagine the ancients were a little better at putting up with little inconveniences like boils or crops failing or cholera than we are. But in this post-catastrophic state, Job sits in the ashes and seems to be reduced to scraping his boils.

Enter the wife, who gets a bad rap but to whom I totally relate. Basically, her grief (which is completely sidestepped in the entire book) expresses as anger, and she says:

"'Dost thou still retain thine integrity? Curse God, and die'" (Job 2:9).

Like, Job. Give *up* already.

I'm pretty sure that Job is not the kind of man who would ask for directions in traffic, because he stubbornly refuses and decides that, while he won't curse God, a little cursing actually *is* in order:

That's when we find Job saying, "Why died I not from the

womb? Why did I not give up the ghost when I came out of the belly? [. . .] Let them curse it that curse the day, who are ready to raise up their mourning" (Job 3:11, 8).

Can we blame the guy?

* * *

Poet John O'Donohue spoke of thresholds, moments when the world immutably changes. According to O'Donohue, "A threshold is a frontier that divides two different territories, rhythms, atmospheres."[12]

You meet someone and feel in your bones that this could be your person. You get the acceptance letter. You get the rejection letter. A phone call comes after your evening meal, and suddenly you are thrust into the reality of flying across the country to bury your father, or packing up the house of thirty years and downsizing. Life was one thing, and now it's another. The rhythms in our hearts are altered, the atmospheric pressure plummets, we are airlifted into uncharted territory with a dull machete and maybe a first aid kit.

Maybe.

Job's stream of messengers ushered him over a threshold. A cry from the back of the house when Elijah was found carried me over mine.

I call it Grief Zero.

Bones shift in the skin. Jolts of nausea and a jaw-clenching new reality come to roost in the body. The nervous system stews in stress hormones, increasing risks of arrhythmia, even cardiac arrest. Some people's hearts literally break—usually women, it seems, who can suffer weakening of their left ventricle. It's called broken heart syndrome. Some people die from it. At Grief Zero, the throat constricts. Legs and chest are lead. The physiologic effects of grief are well described, yet remain poorly understood.

I know I had them all the day Grief Zero hit. The day is

chiseled into my synapses as surely as Christ's lifeless arm was wrought in stone in Michelangelo's *Pietà*. The years have not lessened the memory, only made it possible for me to revisit it with something akin to self-compassion. I recall that day not as someone who is dissociating and numb but as a woman who has since traveled far from that twenty-eight-year-old mother who woke up to a sunny Sunday morning. I remember Elijah, excited to sleep in his new bed the night before. Trusting as I sang his blessing song:

> *The Lord bless you and keep you*
> *The Lord make his face shine upon you*
> *And give you peace, and give you peace, forever*

It is the same song Elijah heard every night of his life. It was his bedtime ritual. It was a song that asked God to watch over my boy and bless him as he rested. It was his lullaby.

I remember checking on Elijah later that evening, around midnight—seeing him nestled in his Winnie-the-Pooh blanket. He looked cherubic, like toddlers do when they are recharging their little batteries, getting ready to spend the next day runnin' around the yard chasing butterflies or dancing down the hallway. Elijah's energy was boundless. He didn't just walk, he danced his way through the world.

That late night check where I assured myself that Elijah was resting safe and well is my last memory of Elijah alive.

It was not I who found Elijah, and that is a small mercy for which I will always be grateful. I was in the front of the house when I heard the cry from his room. And that one "Noooo!" contained the unthinkable but absolutely knowable horror that Elijah's body was all that remained.

As I lay eyes on my lifeless son being carried to our living room, I followed in Job's suit and went down. From my knees, I cried out. Like Job, my submission took the form of a prayer.

"Thank you, God, for Elijah. Thank you for his life."

For all my claim of remembering, I don't remember the rest of the prayer, but it was something along the lines of giving God glory and returning Elijah to his maker. It was some sort of acceptance and gratitude for what we had shared with Elijah.

I do remember that even as the authorities asked us to perform CPR, we knew the efforts would be fruitless. Words like "mottled" and "rigor mortis" were being applied to my baby's arms. There was no doubt that no life was left in Elijah. So I sat on my couch and I cradled him—much like Mary holds Christ in the *Pietà*. His full weight in my arms, I repeated, "I'm sorry. I'm so, so sorry." In these last moments, I traced his frame. Kept his head steady. I just let the full weight of my boy rest in my arms one final time, and I tried to begin saying goodbye—a task I won't complete until my own final breaths.

This was Grief Zero. Holding my mottled baby whom I sang to hours before. Feeling coldness consume his frame. I hoped he hadn't thrashed, that his passing had been easy. Most of all, I hoped he hadn't called out for his mama. I couldn't bear the thought of Elijah wanting his mom and dying alone, so I hoped that angels had ushered him over his own threshold. Grief Zero was not so much new territory as it was a portal into a black hole of the soul that no clinical language can adequately describe.

Ironically, as I was home holding my baby's body the last time, our congregation was in worship a few miles away, completely unaware of our loss.

Elijah had slipped away while I slept; as we sat in horror, our church family sang of God's glory. And this is the parallel nature of our existence, isn't it? While one mother labors and delivers a stillborn child, another welcomes a healthy child into the world. One son visits a father who has no recollection of all the years they spent fishing together. Another decides that estrangement is the only option to heal from her childhood abuse. Thresholds are appearing at this very moment. We are all living a hair's breadth away from the edge of Grief Zero.

We did reach one of the senior pastors, who came over

immediately. This man embodied all the good parts of being a pastor. He didn't say much; he just sat with us, and when the authorities arrived, he stayed as we shared the details. Of course this death was an accident, and it was treated as such. The police stayed for an hour or so, and then the coroner came. The gentleness with which we were treated still moves me. If someone is stepping over a harrowing threshold, gently, gently, hold them up. For they have no strength to stand.

Elijah's body was taken, and we were left with a burgeoning house of friends and family arriving. At Grief Zero, there is a swirl of activity, but at the epicenter is only coldness. The soul is at absolute zero. I'm sure scientists can name the chemical reactions occurring when a soul is at absolute zero, but who cares? No drug can fix the rending. No muscle relaxer can help a mother so deeply bonded to her son understand that he simply . . . isn't. This is a lesson that can only be learnt over a lifetime. I'm still learning it, and I am grateful I didn't know then all that this lesson would entail. It was better to hold the last things Elijah touched and let absolute zero take hold.

Only I didn't. At least not for long. In the early days after Grief Zero, I turned into a hyper-manic witnessing machine. Perhaps a biblical blueprint existed for me to shave my head and sit in sackcloth, but it was a blueprint co-opted by fundamentalism. So, instead of fully leaning into my grief, I got to work.

Amidst a cascade of casseroles and condolences, I started to turn Elijah's death into a witnessing point. One conversation with a former music professor still stands out. When asked how I was doing, I sidestepped the question completely, instead telling her that God was going to work good out of Elijah's death.

Her reply floored me: "My God doesn't use the death of little babies to get glory."

That conversation might have been the moment that, confronted with the reality of unimaginable torment, I took spiritual bypassing to a whole new level. And I did it in the way only a lifelong fundamentalist can. People tried to steer me towards resources that would help me heal. My husband's boss sent us Rabbi Kushner's *When Bad Things Happen to Good People*. I read three paragraphs and put it down on principle. The very the premise was flawed: *None of us are good, Rabbi. Did you even read the Torah?* Kushner was grappling with the problem of pain through a lens that seemed to me nonsensical, so I set the work aside and retrenched in my efforts. Incidentally, I recently returned to Kushner's text and found myself nodding vigorously in agreement with every word.

I sidestepped so much grief work with my dogmatic assertion that God was in control. Even fundamentalist friends encouraged me to just be a grieving mom. One friend who had lost a sister said, "It's like you have giant barrels of bitter sorrow on your shoulders. There is nothing to do but drink them down."

Uh. No, dude.

I couldn't hear any of it, and for over a decade, I doubled down on my efforts to turn Elijah's death into something good.

Job had been tested and found faithful, after all.

If God wouldn't make this death matter, I would. Elijah had been God's. I was God's, and as his vessel, I would find a way. Souls would be won.

I don't want to paint a picture of a woman who never cried, who stoically soldiered on in the wake of her son's loss. It's not so much that I denied the pain as that I tried to alchemize it too soon.

In the early days, people gathered around us in incredible outpouring of grace. In those moments, I remembered why a church family is called a family. Ours rallied to our aid. The day we found Elijah, our worship leader came and set up his keyboard in Elijah's room. A small group of friends flew in from far and wide. After Elijah's funeral, a few of our closest took us to a bed and breakfast on the beach. We sat quietly and talked of Elijah, eating chocolate and listening to the waves. A dear friend brought oil and massaged my taut body. The tears came.

I wonder now what would have happened if we had all been allowed to stay at the beach for about three years. Perhaps I would have found a way to heal sooner, would have come to understand the relationship between space and stillness and healing, versus rushing immediately to some kind of accomplishment. But as the bereaved know, the world can't stay stopped forever. Friends had to fly home. Church members cared, but after a few weeks, they too needed to be less present. My husband had to return to work. All of these things are normal, and I fault not the world for having to keep spinning on its axis Or maybe I do. If we didn't fear grief so much, if we had wizened grief guides in place, if we had ways to put slings on our broken hearts, perhaps we could learn that grief has gifts to offer us. But no, efficiency takes all.

Though others' worlds moved on, I was still at absolute zero. The days were a strange mix of normal routines—caring for my baby daughter, who seemed mercilessly unscathed and cheery, while avoiding Elijah's room. Friends had helped us disassemble the bed, and Elijah's room became a study. The absence of his bed was a blessing, but walking past Elijah's room became unbearable. I was living in the belly of the beast, swinging between crying jags and cooking dinner. And in the midst of it all, I felt this intense pressure to make Elijah's death mean something. It had to mean something big. So, after the casseroles cleared, I began to armor up and get about the business of bringing glory to God.

I also turned the intensity inward. If I was being tested, it was my job to figure out what the test was and pass it with flying colors. Had I loved Elijah too much? Had I made him an idol? If so, I didn't want to make that same mistake with Ada. God might have to take her, too. And what was I to do about having future kids? I believed that I was to take all the kids God would give me, so I decided not to delay pregnancy. Three months after Elijah died, I conceived, so pregnancy hormones were added to the griefstew. In addition to witnessing and turning over every possible meaning stone to make sure I hadn't caused God's anger, my womb now swelled with new life, even as my cells were heavy with the absence of my baby boy.

All of my efforts were directed at remaining faithful. I thought that if I could be faithful enough, worship enough, lead enough people to Christ, then somehow Elijah's death would not have been in vain. In the early years after Elijah's loss, I didn't entertain doubt for long. Like Job, I worshiped; I worked. The modern-day equivalent included playing keys in our church's praise band. I helped lead small groups in our church. Eventually I signed up to volunteer for Franklin Graham.

Franklin Graham is evangelist Billy Graham's son. He conducted a crusade in our little town, and I went all in, starting with attending a citywide training so that I could work on the floor when the altar call came.

On the big night, I remember standing in a sea of new converts on the stadium floor, feeling so incredibly empty. I looked over and caught the eye of my then pastor. His face was aglow with big "I just led a person in the sinner's prayer" energy. Mine was awash with disappointment. I had spent weeks praying for the citywide revival, inviting friends, hosting a very poorly attended picnic, and now here I stood with not a single soul who wanted to pray with me. I had gutted out a pregnancy amid soul-shattering sorrow, and months later, here I stood, alone in a crowd with nary a convert to my name.

In contrast, my pastor looked positively beatific. He lifted his face and worshiped. "I am just basking in the glow," he gushed.

Brother, what glow?

At this point, I still didn't really question the underpinnings of my faith. I just figured I was going about the whole thing wrong. I felt the disappointment keenly, and I do remember being like, "God, what do you want from me?" But I soldiered on. One does not simply walk away from an entire fever dream of a belief system that was emblazoned into the psyche from the cradle. And one usually doesn't know that one day, one is going to. This is why the argument that if someone deconstructs their faith, they must have "never really believed it," doesn't hold water. I lived my faith every day, even in the face of the hardest loss. And I held onto it like a rope cast over the edge of a lifeboat. Albeit one that was lined with razor blades.

*   *   *

In the early years of Elijah's loss, the pain of being in my body was another reason that I tried to close the wound by working for the Lord. My body was where Elijah had lived. My body had held his limp frame. My eyes had seen him carted away in the back of a pickup truck swaddled in his Pooh blanket. My mouth had spouted words of comfort to the children who stood in front of his open casket: "The body is a tent. Elijah is alive; he's with the Lord now."

My ears still echoed with the sound of my mother's shrieks when she was told that her grandbaby was gone. My hands couldn't be trusted—they had hammered and drilled the wooden bedframe where my son had breathed his last. My heart must have been dull to the Lord, or I would have heard him warning me not to leave my son alone. My body housed a monster of a mother, yet this mother was still tasked with "working out [her] salvation with fear and trembling." The body was definitely no place to be.

Books felt safer. Books moved me out of my body and into my brain. I had turned to books when I first found out I was going to be a mother. I read them all, hoping to prepare for the intense caregiving that early parenting is. But I could find no book for a mother who had unwittingly built the bed that claimed her son's life. So, I floundered through the heroes of the faith. So many were the texts I waded through that I can't recall them all, but I do remember fumbling through a few Christian mystics.

From St. John of the Cross: "In the dark night of the soul, bright flows the river of God."

The thought is akin to the Psalmist's declaration that "The LORD is close to the brokenhearted and saves those who are crushed in spirit" (Psalm 34:18). These thoughts were comforting. I might be brokenhearted, but God was near. I wanted God's nearness, but I think I wanted Elijah's more. I was frustrated because it seemed that, like the Lord, the books gave, and the books took away. Verses like the above brought me a measure of comfort, but they were followed up by lines that only reopened the wound: "The righteous person may have many troubles, but the LORD delivers him from them all; he protects all his bones, not one of them will be broken" (Psalm 34:19–20).

And therein lies the problem. What about Elijah's bones? What about his protection? Surely Elijah and all the little ones who we lose are righteous, are they not?

Even Job's story proved problematic in the end. His book's middle chapters can be summed up by a seemingly endless and very poetic back and forth that goes something like this:

Job's friends: You must have fucked up pretty bad for this to happen.

Job: I sure as fuck did not.

Job's friends: Yeah, you did.

Job: Did not.

Job's friends: Did too.

God: Hey, I am really big and mighty, and I created all this, so everyone shut your damn mouths and worship me. And also, piss off, Job's friends. You are wrong. Job is my favorite.

Job: Okayyyyyyyyy.

It takes the writer of Job about 280 chapters to get to that point (okay, forty-one chapters). Then we get the ending, which must have been written by a man trafficking in some early form of Mesopotamian stoicism. The end of Job reads like that old joke about country music backmasking: "What do you get if you play a country song backwards? You get your wife back, your truck back, and your dog back." Ta-da!

It's all so very neat: Job has passed the test, didn't forsake God, and for his trouble, God not only speaks up and basically says, "Stop bullying my boy Job, he's cool"—Job also gets all of his money returned and a whole new crop of kids, to boot!

"So the LORD blessed the latter end of Job more than his beginning: for he had fourteen thousand sheep, and six thousand camels, and a thousand yoke of oxen, and a thousand she-asses."

Awesome. Does he also get all those servants back, too?

"He also had seven sons and three daughters."

Wow. What a synchronicity. What an effing *manifestation*. The exact same number and gender of the kids he lost. It's *almost* like the humans are literally replaced! So cool.

"And he called the name of the first, Jemima; and the name of the second, Kezia; and the name of the third, Kerenhappuch. And in all the land were no women found so fair as the daughters of Job: and their father gave them inheritance among their brethren."

Oh, good. At least they were pretty. It would have been such a shame if Job's replacement daughters were ugly. But also, score one for early feminism with that inheritance.

"After this lived Job an hundred and forty years, and saw his sons, and his sons' sons, even four generations. So Job died, being old and full of days" (Job 42:12–17).

Neat.

Shortsighted.

Actually, infuriating.

If I could teleport back to when that ending was written, I would snatch that scroll out of the author's hands, rip off last section, force-feed that tripe back to the author, and write an ending that goes something more like this:

"And Job died too the day that whirlwind took his family. He just didn't know it yet. His new wife and kids were very precious to him, but Job remained brokenhearted for the rest of his life. At night, after Job kissed the sparkly new family, he would slip out of his tent and wander the hills all 'Long Black Veil'-like and send up a wail for the life he had lost. Job 1.0 was definitely demolished. Job 2.0 moved through the world with as much ease as he could muster, but he did so with one eye half-cocked and his hand on his holster."

I mean no disrespect for the tale of Job. I understand that this work of antiquity is grappling with the hardest of human questions: the problem of pain. I just happen to think that this verse more adequately wrangles the beast:

> "In Rama was there a voice heard, lamentation, and weeping, and great mourning, Rachel weeping *for* her children, and would not be comforted, because they are not." (Matthew 2:13–18)

This is the single verse in the Bible that even comes close to adequately describing Grief Zero. What we need in Grief Zero is not to be placated. We deserve sackcloth. Ashes and ruination are our right. When we downplay the horror of Grief Zero, we turn the knife in the wound. What the newly bereaved don't need are platitudes. Damn them all. What we do need is to be allowed to descend—deeply and, with no promise of re-emergence—into the pit.

Only, we don't need to do it alone.

We need grief warriors who are grizzled and who have walked through Hades to come and sit with us. We need, as I wrote in a song by the same name, people to lend us their hearts. Our ventricles and our vision have failed. As my song says:

> *Don't bring me a platitude on a platter of gold*
> *no need to remind me it's all for my good*

And don't testify here; this isn't the time
Can't bear to hear how your heart's on a mountain with views
so sublime
Come with compassion. Come with your tears.
Come with your mind full of peace and wrestle these fears
Come close beside me, here in the dark
Wait in the ashes, and lend me your heart

Few but worth their weight in gold are the warriors who can lend their hearts to the bereaved. I call them ash warriors. These souls will sit in the soot with you and allow the outward environment to mirror the devastation of your heart. I know that instead of trying to heal up, I needed to be as hurt as I was for as long as I needed. Maybe that's not what others need. Maybe this view of grief is somehow decadent, but I believe it actually hearkens back to an ancient liturgy. We have lost sight of these ancient ways, and yet, they may be our salvation.

Frances Weller speaks of these ancient rituals. Weller is a psychologist, a self-described soul activist, and community advocate. He is also a grief tender. In contrast to running from grief, Weller advocates the opposite. He says we need to develop a lifelong apprenticeship with sorrow. This apprenticeship rests upon the immutable fact that "everything you love, you will lose."[13] With lead-in material like that, I imagine Weller is super popular at parties.

Weller calls us back to the ancient, reminding us that grief has always been communal.[14] He says that "subconsciously, we are awaiting the presence of others, before we can feel safe enough to drop to our knees on the holy ground of sorrow."[15]

The holy ground of sorrow?

Am I the only one reading those lines who is floored by this concept? I have thought of many things as holy in my life, but sorrow is not one of them. I am a good American who has learned to do all sorts of things with sorrow. I can numb it, run from it, pop a pill for it, call it a case of the blues, but drop to my knees and call it holy? That's a new one for me.

Or was that what Job and I did when we dropped to our knees?

Weller argues that we are wired with the ancient ways; hence, our subconscious waits for someone to show up. The problem is that we have privatized grief, shamed our sorrow, and in the name of "giving people dignity," we have relegated them to "recycling their grief," in Weller's words.[16] We tell people that they need to do grief-work, when in reality, they need to let their grief work through them as leaven. And we need to let them do it in the presence of people who can act as a container for grief's wildness. Containing grief is not comfort. We may need but a handful of people to attend to our sorrow, but need them we do. Weller says that we should set aside time with a few trusted souls to share our grief. In those moments, simply say, "Tell me of your sorrow, and I will tell you mine."

We don't work out our grief any more than we can actually work out our salvation. We simply succumb to sorrow in the safety of a few souls who can sit with us.

Job's friends actually did a pretty good job of this near the beginning of his sorrow. They sat for a good solid seven days. If they had been able to continue in that vein, Job would have been better for it. But good ole Bildad, Eliphaz, and Zophar just couldn't keep their mouths shut. Neither can most of us. Uncomfortable with silence, we speak too soon.

"I'm sorry for your loss."

Thanks?

"I can't imagine."

I'm pretty sure you can. We both know why you don't want to.

"He's in a better place."

Great, how soon can I join him?

I don't want to be overly hard on us puny humans. I point the finger at these platitudes . . . and I have used a few of them myself. The tendency to fix is ingrained. We hate to see sorrow, so we try to help move it along. Christ said blessed are those who mourn for they will be comforted. Problem is, we wanna just skate right past the mourning and slip into comfort. Can we just all agree for a moment that some things in life simply must be borne? That for some losses, deep mourning extends for little longer than the socially acceptable period of roughly five minutes? That nothing is wrong with an incredibly sad human?

Maybe their hearts aren't even broken. Maybe they are working exactly as they should when their owners bet everything on intimacy and have the rug ripped out. Maybe the magnitude of their love was so big, they are having to recalibrate their entire being around a void—their longing so intense that simply putting their feet on the ground and doing the laundry are laudable accomplishments. Maybe we should tell them every damn day, "Congratulations. You took another breath."

I don't have the answer for how to shift our consciousness around people living in Grief Zero. Weller offers a bit of a teaser, though: "We need to recover our right to ask for help in grief."[17]

I did the exact opposite. I comforted everyone but myself. In retrospect, this was an attempt to heal the moral injury of Elijah's death. I didn't think I deserved to be alive, let alone receive comfort. But once I decided to reach for forgiveness instead of redemption, I did begin to long for a bit of comfort. Or rather, I longed to mourn. I longed to go low and let grief have her way with me.

But where was I to go? I left my faith over a decade ago, and when I did, I cut ties with many of those who had known Elijah. The wound was so old yet so in need of debridement.

I couldn't afford a therapist. I found the next best thing: a really good bartender.

Mister Linen is one of those souls who is extremely practiced at listening to people. He is not a fixer. He has learned the fine art of just letting people effing be. I suppose it is a skill that comes with the territory, or his temperament, and from living in New Orleans for a really long time. I really don't know. But sometime in summer of 2021, I heard myself ask, "Can you hold me while I cry?" Such a simple gesture, probably enabled by a wee bit of gin.

Mister Linen of the sexy unbuttoned shirt, the country music connoisseur and preternaturally-gifted cocktail infusing genius, lay down on the floor, opened his arms, and let me crawl in.

The levy of loss broke.

Grief, long calcified, began to roil in my chest. My heart moved from absolute zero to red hot the way Gigi's temperature gauge skyrocketed on the way to Baton Rouge. Succumbing to the heat of my sorrow, I howled twenty years of loss into that man's chest. I gasped and thrashed, unleashing primal wails. Hot tears spilled out, a virtual Niagara's worth, breaking the dam behind my eyes. I wept for the boy who never outgrew his chubby phase, who would never ask for another moon, oh please, for the mother who didn't get to teach him to read, or drive, or send him off to college. I wept for all the ways Elijah's leaving buried me with him, for the thousand deaths I had wished for but that had never come.

It might have been fifteen minutes or five hours, but I unloaded loss upon loss into that man's arms. I cried for the concentric rings of grief that losing Elijah had wrought, for the mother I failed to be to my other kids because I could never be the lighthearted woman they deserved. I cried for my heart's inability to beat fully around the shrapnel of guilt lodged there since the day Elijah died. That night, I grieved for fucking up over and over while trying to carry the uncarry-able. I cried for the good girl I tried to be but who died the day her baby didn't wake up. For the hurt I have both clumsily held and wrought because I have not been whole for twenty years. For the friendships I scuttled because I didn't know how to carry the construct of an all-knowing good God in tandem with the image of my son's lifeless head lolling in my lap.

That night, twenty plus years of moment-by-moment missing of Elijah's cheeks and chin and grin converged.

Rivulets of rage and rawness pooled onto the chest of a man who had never met Elijah but instinctively knew to let me rail.

His levy held. In the presence of primal, gut-wrenching grief, Mister Linen remained mostly still. He surrounded my sorrow with silent steadiness. My frame shook against his solidness. His body became a wailing wall. Finally, the raw energy of my grief had a place to go. I had been sending it out to the sky hoping it would dissipate. It had not. My grief had not needed the vastness of the stars. It had needed this: the container of one man's arms. With every convulsion, his arms tightened—just a bit, just enough to remind me that this was not too much. Leave it to a playwright who cut his teeth on tragedy to take on the burden of mine for a bit. This holding was what I had needed and hadn't even known it, hadn't felt worthy of wanting.

After a time, I lay still, my cheek on his chest. I had found sacred ground.

Though I had released myself from the prison of understanding Elijah's death as some sort of cosmic plot point in the grand scheme of redemption, until this moment, I had not found the wherewithal to fall into the well and drink deep of the sorrow. I had been descending without a tether, drinking alone. As we know, drinking alone is never a good idea, whether it's a whiskey on the rocks or a chalice brimming with your own tears.

This single evening is exactly the kind of thing that Weller refers to when he speaks of shouldering grief in community. It was a turning point for me. The burden felt just a bit lighter. Another soul cared enough not just to listen but to witness the whirlwind in me. In case it wasn't clear, this cry-fest occurred two years ago. Elijah's death was over twenty. Grief is a long haul.

It is often said that there is no wrong way to grieve. I suppose that is true, with the caveat that we have to be actually allowing ourselves to grieve—fully, and at our own pace, and looking as messy as we need to in the process. Fundamentalist notions of what I was supposed to be doing to "serve God" in the midst of my sorrow interrupted my ability to adequately grieve. So did societal norms around feeling hardship. So did the need to keep several other humans alive. No shade, fellow humans. I like ya all a lot. But this suppression of grief alongside ill-conceived attempts to redeem Elijah's death wrought a different kind of destruction.

The day Elijah passed, I had set my little coracle of belief in a stream of meaning-making with his death. The more vigorously I paddled in the stream, the more the rapids turned my meaning-making oars into flotsam. Truthfully, my little boat called "Believe at all Costs" had already been battered. I had wavered in my worldview for years, ever since I was a late teen. I both wanted the Jesus story as I had been told it to be true while at the same time hating the implications of that story: the neverending evangelizing, the subjugation of people's identities, and, most of all, the idea that people would writhe in eternal flame for not being able to believe in Bible Belt Jesus.

Ultimately, Elijah's death caused me to pull on the thread of my doubts—or rather, I no longer had the energy to keep retying the knots that kept my faith from unraveling. And if some people's religious deconstruction is seemingly seamless, without much pain and with some sort of natural progression, mine was more akin to having a grenade explode in my gut every day—for about fifteen years. I knew the cost of leaving, so I wavered, but ultimately I could no longer say, like Job does, "The LORD giveth, and the LORD taketh away. Blessed be the name of the LORD" (Job 1:21).

Thus, I stepped over the threshold of my loss of faith. The upshot of that journey is that the woman I was before Elijah died is gone. I mean that as literally as possible. I had people say to me, "We don't know who you are anymore." Yeah. Me neither. It was death by a thousand gulps of grappling with a world that was not as I believed it to be. It was years of trying to close a psychic rift the size of a canyon with a band-aid.

So the tornado came again, only this time it didn't come for sheep or camels or my children—it came for me. And when it came, it dismantled my house of faith and my family. I cut ties with the community of friends who had brought those casseroles and cards and who had stood by me in the weeks after Elijah's death. Honesty requires me to own that I left them and not the other way around. The people I hurt on my journey to healing did not deserve to be left. And as much as I would like to say, "The grief made me do it," I didn't stop being a responsible agent just because my coracle capsized and I was a-flail in the whitewater of deconstruction. But it was a force, and I do feel like I drowned only to crawl out onto a bank as a naked, pulsing mass. The creature that was being reborn out of that river was feral. She chose self-protection over continuity. Creativity over community. Her own nature over nurture. Maybe she wasn't kind, but she was free.

I needed a clean break. And boy, did I break it good. I didn't want my grief, my true grief, witnessed by people who believed, as I no longer did, that God had been involved in Elijah's death. I needed to find alternative explanations that didn't involve God being a monster (or me being a monster) or Satan somehow stealing into my son's room and engineering his death. I needed to absorb the thresholds I had crossed, not gloss over them. From loved ones I needed grief-tending, not grief-mending.

When Weller refers to the ancient ways of grief, he doesn't speak in the abstract. Consider the sacred Scandinavian season of living in the ash. This tradition is exactly what it sounds like. For a year or more, the bereaved tended the fire of the long house. That was it. Those who had experienced great loss simply had to, quite literally, to keep the fire alive. In *The Wild Edge of Sorrow*, Weller describes the tradition thus:

> "This sacred season in the ashes was the ancient Scandinavian community's way of acknowledging that one of their people had entered a world parallel to but

separate from the daily life of gathering food, feeding children, and tending fields. Little was expected of them during this time, which often lasted a year or more. The individual's duty was to mourn, to live in the ashes of their loss, and to regard this time as holy. It was a brooding time, a deeply interior period of digesting and metabolizing the bitter tincture of loss."[18]

Once we cross over grief's threshold, our new psyches truly do exist in a parallel reality. We feel monumentally out of sorts because we *are*. Rituals and mourning periods give us the space we need to metabolize "the bitter tincture of loss" bit by bit. Compare this to the three days we *might* get before schlepping our altered beings back to that meeting where we discuss profit margins and "next steps." Who cares? Give me a fire to tend, a seed to nurture, a small creature to feed. That's about all the tending I need to do.

Such menial tasks can begin to move us from Grief Zero. Yet, the gap between what the sacred traditions offered and what the contemporarily bereaved are expected to endure is a vast chasm. As a rule, the bereaved get so little of what we need, is it any wonder that collectively we are so ill? How much dysfunction comes from the societal pressure to quickly return to a pace of life that was already unhealthy?

I can't say for sure, but I wonder if the lies we tell people out of kindness are merely a symptom of losing the ancient ways. After author Lidia Yugnavitch gave birth to her stillborn baby, she spent almost a year telling people that her baby girl was doing fine.[19] *Wild* author Cheryl Strayed returned to college the semester after her mother died from cancer. In Strayed's words:

"After her funeral, I immediately went back to school because she had begged me to do so. It was the beginning of a new quarter. In most of my classes, we were asked to introduce ourselves and say what we had done over the break. 'My name is Cheryl,' I said. 'I went to Mexico.' I lied not to protect myself, but because it would have been rude not to. To express loss on that level is to cross a boundary, to violate personal space, to impose emotion in a nonemotional place."[20]

And there it is. The return to regular life, creating a schism between what we are really feeling and what we say. In light of Yuknavitch and Strayed's stories, perhaps my fever dream of nearly nonstop witnessing for days after Elijah died is not so strange. Maybe that was just my particular expression of having lost touch with the ancient ways.

One thing that Job's author did get right was the sackcloth and ashes part. I just think that part should have gone on for about a year. Instead, we got ... what we got. The narrative lacks a sense of the long, soul-draining middle that Job certainly must have experienced before his miraculous restart. Perhaps that is the part of the story where Job should have been given a fire to tend.

The bereaved need to build little fire; instead, some of us build an empire.

Years out from trying and failing to build a legacy for Elijah on the back of a broken belief system, I finally settled down. Weller was right. Instead of trying to catalyze the grief too soon, I needed to lay low. Not long before I Mt. Vesuvisused all over Mister Linen's chest, I wrote these words:

"People in deep loss need, at minimum, six months or, better yet, a year to mourn. They need to be able to let their bodies fall apart and sit on the mossy banks of some cool stream. They need to be around the redwoods and rocky beaches and bayous. They need wine and tea and books and whatever music serves as a salve, be it Beethoven or Britney Spears (I can't imagine it, but hey, if Britney Spears is your grief guru, then go for it). They need something bigger than their grief, and the universe seems to be about the only thing that fits that bill. Yes, they need to move their bodies and find meaning that moves beyond the mayhem. Only then can they begin to move themselves into some sort of existence within society.

Maybe some of them need to be allowed to work. But I didn't. I still don't. I know with all my heart that what I need most now is a space where my physical needs would be met and I could tend to this grief wound that still has not been properly bound. This writing is part of the medicine because it's honest, but more than anything, I need to be allowed to *not* be okay for, at minimum, six months to a year. I know in my soul that, given that, I will be okay. And I actually am 'okay.' I'm not depressed or unable to step outside of my own pain for long enough to be aware of others. But I am not healed up enough yet to want to hold down a demanding job or get on the social justice train or do much of anything other than lead a quiet life of intimate exploration, to unleash my curiosity—but mostly I want to sit, sing a lullaby to both myself and Elijah, and finally, *finally* let the grief run its course.

I don't know if such a year is possible—let's call it a grief-battical—where I can know that everyone else will be okay for a minute if I finally take the time to just honor the cavern, honor the little boy, honor the life he lost, consider the man he would be, write sentimental songs about it, sit in a kayak at sunset and sing them to him. I just don't see how this can be wrong. Twenty years after losing Elijah, part of me wishes for a little house by the sea where I can sit and let the rhythms of the tide take me to my sorrow. Far from needing to rid myself of my grief, I need to behold it. I need seasons with it.

'How long will it hurt?'

'How long will your loved one be dead?'

Please, if there is a god still there, I would be so grateful if you would give me a moment to submerge back in that river and really surrender to it—not so that I can emerge a better, more productive version of myself, and not so that I can drum up more ways to reflect back to god the supposed glory of this loss."

I likely won't get that grief-battical. Neither will most of us, but I still wonder what would happen if we remembered the ancient ways.

Might I one day sit down by the sea and finally, *finally* honor the loss of one small boy?

Brokeass Bounty

Each year when I was little, my family would trek from Cleveland back to our homeland in South Alabama. My parents owned a station wagon, the kind adorned with wood paneling and an eight-track cassette player. Into that wagon, my parents jammed enough provisions to outfit a squad of soldiers. By provisions, I mean two-liter bottles of Coke that my mom would open somewhere near the Tennessee state line, fixin's for holiday pies, Christmas presents wrapped in dime-store paper.

My parents, roadtrippers extraordinaire, had all the gear packed the night before. All that remained was to wake up three sleepy kids and shuffle us to the wagon. My older siblings occupied the backseat, but as the baby by a long shot, I would lie down in the way back of that wagon. Sometime before the sun came up, my parents would dump me and a blanket into the flat bed, and south we'd roll. Thus, we would commence with a holiday spree that was two parts reckoning, one part repression, and all-around cacophony. By midday, we would have navigated most of the state where my father had been sent to save the Catholics.

My dad had been converted by an old pastor in our hometown, Brother James, and when I say that his conversion was life-changing, I am not overestimating. In the gospel of John, Jesus sees a new disciple heading his way, Nathanael. Jesus looks right into that guy's heart and exclaims: "Behold, a true

Israelite indeed in whom there is no guile" (John 1:47). That's my dad. I don't believe a lick of the gospel the way it was taught to me anymore . . . and I know that my dad believes it in his bones. For my dad, the gospel took hold deep and strong. And when he felt the call to preach, he followed it.

The story goes like this. One day, my mother and father were in church in our little South Alabama town. At the end of the service, Brother James gave an altar call. My dad was sing-ing in the choir, my mom sitting in the pews. My mom heard it first, the pricking to walk down the aisle. I felt it many times as a child, that little nudge in the heart, the Spirit mov-ing. My mom made her way down the aisle to Brother James where the following dialogue ensued.

"Brother James, I think I am being called to be a pastor's wife."

Problem was, my dad was just standing up there in the choir loft, singin' his heart out, seemingly oblivious to the call. How was my mom supposed to be a pastor's wife with no husband pastoring? Leave it to the Lord to shake his head and be like, "Hey, Holy Spirit, check this out. This dude is dense as the sed-iment on the bottom of the River Jordan. Go tap the lady. She's actually listening."

Brother James, ever the gentle shepherd, led my mom to a front row pew: "Well dear, just sit down here, and let's see what God does with this."

What God "did" next was apparently give my dad the memo. In between whatever verse of the invitation he was singing, my dad heard. He made his way down from the choir loft. Moments later, he and my mom were standing in front of the congrega-tion together.

Not too long after, our family set off for Ft. Worth for sem-inary. It was from Texas that we had been commissioned up to the shores of Lake Erie to start a Southern Baptist Church. Personally, I think my dad was way more stoked about this adventure than my mom. I think she had imagined being a pas-tor's wife in the South, like the Good Lord intended. We were

Southern Baptists, right? Apparently the Good Lord and the Southern Baptists missed that memo, instead deciding that many a Northern Catholic needed to trade rosaries for baptistries. Thus, in the fall of '77, my dad took a reconnaissance trip up North to spy out the land.

Like the scouts sent by Hezekiah to explore the land of Canaan in days of old, my dad returned to Texas claiming, with great gusto, "It's like the garden of Eden!" Problem was that, as the Good Lord would have it, by the time we made the move, it was January, and The Great Blizzard of '78 was roaring across the Ohio Valley. It's really called that—and for good reason. The Great Blizzard of '78 was such a cataclysmic weather event that it remains the standard by which all new blizzards are measured (sorry, new blizzards, you ain't got nothin' on this mother). The storm that battered the Great Lakes region roared for four days, clocking wind speeds of 111 miles an hour—the same as a category three hurricane. The storm eventually shut down the entire Ohio turnpike. Snowdrifts reached rooftops. Ohio was just . . . shut. Yet, somehow my family was caravanning across the state in the middle of this mess.

It was so bad that I imagine my as yet unborn grandchildren gathering round my rocker and begging, "Tell us again about the Great Blizzard, Gramma . . . please!"

I will put down my knitting, because I will definitely have taken up knitting by then. And gardening. And being rich. I will lean in and say, "Well, children, I was but a wee one not five years old when me mum set out 'cross the country. Our destination was a shitty little shire East of Cleveland. The winds howled. So did me mum, cursing the Baptists and rueing the day she agreed to leave the sweet red Alabama clay."

I'm pretty sure in this rendition, my mother will also have accomplished several heroic feats, like changing twelve flat tires and fighting off several trolls. Did I forget to mention that on my mother's maiden voyage to Ohio, she and my father, who was driving the U-Haul, became separated on the road? Well, they did—and in the days before GPS or cell phones, kids! I wonder if, at least for a moment, my mother considered making that separation permanent. It is no wonder that when we finally arrived East of Cleveland, a bedraggled and demoralized lot, my mother denounced the place with two sentences:

1. "If this is the garden of Eden, I know why Eve sinned."
2. "And I suppose they don't have Cokes here either."

My mom is a Southern Woman. And she was in her glory. Scarlett O'Hara could not have rivaled her in that moment. Whatever I think of her theology, I admire her pioneering spirit. I am sure that residing in what my mom called Yankee territory was a culture shock of monumental proportions. But my mom was sure of her call. She was in a foreign land, and to that land she brought the staples: grits, cornbread, drawl, and most of all, Bible Belt Jesus.

We may have lived in Ohio, but Alabama was home. My seven-year-old self felt it as surely as any soldier returning to American soil from overseas. The yearly road trip was as much a pilgrimage as a chance to gather round the piano and belt out "Jingle Bells" with three hundred of our closest kin. Alabama was our mecca.

So, each December, we rode across hill and dale, wagon packed to the gills back in the days before car seats were mandated. To help pass the time, sometimes my dad would sit me in his lap as he drove. He also welcomed my little stuffed animal, Joy the dog, to the driver's seat. We'd put Joy's little paws on the steering wheel, my dad hamming up what a great driver this little dog was. Was this safe? Absolutely not. But hey, Americans did a lot of dumb things in the eighties, like use copious amounts of Aqua Net, get on board with the Satanic panic, and elect Ronald Reagan as president. I'm not saying my front-seat joy ride was safe, but it sure was fun.

The trips were decidedly low-tech. Many years later, when my kids were little and I would trek them across the country, I took advantage of every form of electronic babysitter I could find. In attentive Darwinian fashion, I watched that technology evolve: Cassettes became vestigial organs replaced by CDs. A few years later, the CD player was joined by a DVD player that I slung between the captain's chairs of the minivan. I'm pretty sure I have heard Mary Poppins about 320 times and only seen it once. When I was a young'un, we passed the time by singing and listening to eight-tracks of Mahalia Jackson, whose powerful contralto voice scared the crap out of me. Of course, lots of things scared the crap of out that sensitive little seven-year-old—little things like:

- The green witch in *The Wizard of Oz* cackling her way across the sky
- That one Sunday school teacher who insisted that writing "Xmas" meant people were trying to "X" Christ out of Christmas
- The Rapture
- The guerilla warfare tactics of the Sandinista Popular Army in Nicaragua.

Fortunately, I wasn't too afraid of hell at that point. After all, I had prayed the prayer when I was five and *really* meant it.

I was a very normal child.

Returning to that red clay each year anchored me. I knew I was part of a lineage. That lineage was vast, making up in breadth what it lacked in depth. My dad's dad emigrated from Belgium at around the same age I was when my parents bundled me into the back of our station wagon. The family moved first to Canada, then the Dakotas, and somehow ended up in South Alabama. Apparently, when my young grandfather and his brother met two Southern sisters, they were smitten.

Somehow these two Belgian brothers did the most Alabama thing ever and married those girls. Gran was fifteen when she married, and out of that union, ten children were born. In a lovely little twist of fertility fate, the last two kids were twins.

The family stayed put for fifty years, living through the days when the rural poor kept Sears catalogs in the outhouse out back. That catalog was not there for the readin'. Enough said. Through the Great Depression and two World Wars, my grandparents stayed, embroidered as part of the rural poor who did the washing outside and rejoiced the day that the radio arrived.

My mom's mom, the one who made me eat the gumbo at midnight as soon as my family pulled up to her house, was leggy and lean. Even at eighty, those legs went on for miles. I knew that grandmother loved me. She put her love into that gumbo and force-fed it to you. My mom's mom was fierce. She too grew up in the South during a time when good girls *didn't* get pregnant. But she did, right before my grandfather was sent off to the Korean War. My grandmother failed to mention this little detail to my grandfather—a fact that resulted in my mom not meeting her birth father until she tracked him down in the eighties.

What I love about my maternal grandmother is that she made hard but necessary decisions about her life, including leaving four marriages and eventually settling down with the man I knew as Grandpa. By the time I knew my grandma, she embodied gumbo love, spunk, and a tongue-o'-nine-tails. She never wielded it in my direction, but others felt its barbs. If you got the tongue and the Bobbie look, look out. I've inherited that withering look, but I cannot summon it at will like she could.

In contrast, my dad's mom, my Gran, was soft. By the time I knew her, my grandmother was plump, and her raven hair was twined with gray. The sleeves of her pink muumuu stopped just short of her dimpled elbows. Gran was round in a way that made hugging her a haven. But it was her cheeks that I remember, soft and smelling always of old-timey Rose Milk lotion. This Gran was no Casper Milquetoast, but I never saw her riled up. If "Mother," my mom's mom, could castigate you with a look, Gran would just quietly go about her business and perhaps mutter a "Whatever flips your skirt tail up."

It was to Gran's tables that my family traversed each winter.

You read that right: It took two behemoth tables to hold enough holiday food for my Gran's diaspora, of which our little Northern brood was a part. One table inhabited the lion's share of the kitchen. It seems that it should have sagged under its load of chicken and dumplings, turkey, and a Lane cake infused with so much alcohol, my sister once said it should have a sign that warned, "Don't eat and drive." The house, on the other hand, did—sag, that is.

Many of my kin had stayed close to their roots. Others had dispersed to Tennessee, Florida, Oklahoma. The boys started businesses, the girls had babies—a hundred grandkids in all. It was to this lineage that I, the baby of the brood, returned each year. In Yankee land, I was just an awkward kid who worried about the apocalypse. But here, I was "Buddy's youngest." My dad was favored; so was I. Each year, I was thrust into a cacophony of kin, quietly navigating the grounds, taking in the older kids' antics and trying to avoid that uncle who would hunt me down wielding a battery-powered tape deck. The marching orders were always the same: "Sing for us, Desi." Sheepishly, I did, only to find myself facing another aunt or uncle who would literally pinch my cheeks and say things like, "My, how you've grown." The whole shebang was simultaneously grounding and overwhelming.

But back to the tables—or, rather, the respective rocking chairs that lived near them.

In the kitchen, a weathered rocker resided. As a child, it seemed that my grandmother lived in that chair, her throne for presiding over pies and family dramas. My Gran spent years of her life wielding a paring knife. Apples and sweet potatoes alike fell under her deft hand. That woman could peel a peach with the swiftness of a Navy SEAL. The peach never saw it coming.

Vegetables were no safer. My Gran deftly snapped beans into a colander, her snaps aligning with the rhythm of her chair. When Gran baked, she summoned Christmas into her domain. And her domain it was—as surely as the living room rocker was my Papa's. Behind that kitchen table, open shelves stood in resistance to their Bauhaus counterparts across the sea. These shelves were not showpieces; they were bulwarks. Bags of grits, old newspapers, and my grandmother's china didn't so much adorn them as stand guard against the hard times.

She never spoke of them to me, but in her house I heard those hard times whispering. How could there not have been? My Gran's body had gone through eleven pregnancies; one had ended in miscarriage. She had come of age during the Great Depression. She had lived through two world wars, Korea, and Vietnam. Her formal education ended at grade eight. What she lacked in book learning, she made up for with ingenuity and no small amount of work. I'm convinced she was a practical genius who, born in a different time, could have been a CEO. My dad says of his childhood: "We didn't know we were poor." I credit his praise to my grandmother's kindness and no-nonsense hard work through the hard times.

Out in the woods, my grandfather matched her work ethic stride for stride. The man had worked hard his whole life. When I knew my grandfather, he had already retired from hard labor. In his youth, however, he had made a living blowing up giant stumps out in the woods and hauling their remains to parts unknown. To many, those stumps were the useless remains of some forgotten tree. However, much like buffalo bones or whale blubber, those stumps could still yield fruit, or rather sap, that could be coaxed out through heat and turned into turpentine and then, as my father was fond of saying, into over a hundred different products. When my father was a child, he used to accompany my grandfather into the woods to harvest.

Those stumps and my grandmother's ability to stretch a meal made a livin' for those ten kids. No wonder near the end of his life, my Papa liked to spend long hours in the living room next to the second table.

This table did double duty when my dad was little. The top held the food, but the bottom became a fort of sorts for the younger kids. With so many children on hand, only the older ones got a dedicated place to sleep. The little ones scrambled each night for a bed, grabbing a blanket and, like me in the back of the wagon, burrowing beneath that table. By the time I knew the table, those days were long gone, and my grandpa would rock away, watching game shows and, I imagine, resting. The smell of his pipe mingled with whatever pie was baking. At Christmas, this second table carried the overflow of butter beans and cornbread from the kitchen.

We ate in shifts, situating ourselves wherever we were able. And at Christmas, this was a particularly hard undertaking with so many of us milling about. So, we rotated. Those tables seemed miraculous to me; the whole meal was some sort of loaves and fishes reenactment, and the cast was good. The miracle of the poor, rural South is that there is never enough money for the doctor or diapers or anything much at all. Yet our homespun holiday tables contain bounty of which King Solomon himself would be envious. It is still my favorite kind of fare: simple. Set out in the pot that cooked it. This kind of food adorns paper plates or rose-patterned china with equal amounts of ease.

Eating it was an intermittent, all-afternoon affair. You ate. You went outside and tried to figure out the Rubix cube of dislodging pomegranate seeds from their housing. You played fetch with the yard dog and shooed away one of your Gran's fifteen or so porch cats. You explored the back house full of junk treasures with your cousin Jimmy. Jimmy tells you to close your eyes because he has a surprise for you. You find out that the surprise is, *ewwww*, a kiss. On the lips. You realize that "kissin' cousins" is a real thing down here in these parts, but not for you, so you run back to the main house.

At this point, you take another spin around the tables and

notice that while the turkey has almost been picked clean, there is a fair amount of eatin' left on the chicken and dumplings. Plate in hand, you settle down in front of the Christmas tree that used to be the top of a giant pine tree in the backyard. The adults are ... somewhere, and much of the local tribe has left. Finally, the hoopla has died down and you can sit alone, mesmerized by large Christmas tree lights, the kind that were basically painted, oblong lightbulbs powered by a filament.

This type of hospitality still moves me. We live in a world where efficiency and notions of success spur us to hurry through our entire lives. The South of my youth knew that like life, good eatin' takes time. It was not prix fixe. We did not have courses. We had a baptism of food. My grandparents would have scoffed at small plates and the notion of slow food. The first would have been scorned for their impracticality, the second dismissed because "we are already doing that, Paris, and we do it under pecan trees that we shook to make this here pie."

Into this lineage, Elijah was born. This legacy was his birthright. As much as he was a child of the German side of his family, he had the blood of this Southern brood in him. By the time he was born, both sets of my grandparents were long gone. An aunt resided in the family home, but Elijah still visited that kitchen, sat at the table where my Papa used to pat my grandmother's bottom at meal times and wink. "It's the French in him," we would say. On the way to that kitchen, Elijah passed by the crepe myrtle I used to climb as a child. I would sit there, shooing away the black ants and eating bologna sandwiches.

Elijah never climbed that tree. Now, Elijah's ashes rest under a distant cousin of that tree in another Southern town. He does so not just as my child but as the great grandson of our Alabama tribe.

In life, Elijah tasted that bounty. He had a toddler-sized touchpoint with his Southern roots. He was too young to verbalize what I learned at that table, how the echoes of those long gone feasts resonated around that home. But I believe Elijah sensed these truths: Food is more than sustenance; it is the embodiment of a graceful gathering. Hospitality is not about heirloom china; it's about honoring the presence of beloveds, whether you are eating beanie weenies off a paper plate or sipping a Sazarac with Southern royalty.

Also: A graceful gathering is by no means quiet, or couth. The brokeass bounty of my youth invariably involved a set of chain-smoking, Yahtzee-rolling sisters who never learned that talking involves taking turns. Can you blame them? They grew up jockeying for position in a household of twelve. As a child, I would sit at the table beholding the brokeass bounty. Soon, The Sisters of the Virginia Slims would surround us, all three speaking at once, sharing anecdotes and antidotes to all manner of maladies.

The Sisters were strong, full of humor—even if some of them were in the middle of surviving domestic abuse of the "my man put one in me with a rifle" variety. One had been shot in the stomach by her first husband, divorced the bastard, and found love with a late-life sweetheart. Another told tales of my aunt who married a drunk. After he beat her one too many times, she waited for him to black out, tied him up, and gave him a taste of his own medicine. He never touched her again. Back in Ohio, I heard the stories of glory from the pulpit; at that table, I learned that life on earth sometimes requires fists and fast talkin' if you were gonna emerge from a marriage intact.

The Sisters had cared for my ailing grandparents, limiting my diabetic Papa's sugar intake, doing the washing, and generally making much of first my Papa and then my Gran before they passed. They swooped down in a dilapidated old chariot of a sedan after Elijah died. We sat on the same waterbed where I had slept the night Elijah passed. The same bed where two years prior, I had labored with Ada. Their eyes didn't look away from my rawness. Piercing my facade of bravery, they spoke with the authority of poor women who had weathered the worst.

Now, so had I. The problem is my living meant leaving, and not just leaving a hometown but leveling a whole life.

We have a saying in the South: "Don't get above your raising." It means, no matter what success you find in the world, don't be gettin' all uppity. Remember that red clay from whence you came. There's a country song about this, because, of course there is. The saying eschews snobbery; it embodies the tension that I think many of us who come from small towns or poverty feel when we behold a world beyond our upbringing. In my case, the tension comes from breaking faith with my faith. After all, at those tables, we didn't just learn the family lore or play poker with Papa; we talked of "what the Lord was doing in our lives." We prayed. Every meal, our congregation of kinfolk christened that mess o' beans by reciting two prayers: the twenty-third Psalm and Lord's prayer. Many a piping hot meal cooled whilst we prayed, "Though I walk through the valley of the shadow of death, I will fear no evil."

The seeds of my own faith were sown at that table, and it's a faith that I would choose . . . if I could only believe it. I didn't leave because I wanted to. I left because I literally lost my faith. I can't find it anywhere, at least not the version I so staunchly defended in my youth. If I could, I would walk around a big old table of faith and load up my plate with the good parts. If only Bible Belt Christianity was served buffet style on a big old oak table, you might find loading up on Jesus Loves Me casserole. I'll pass on the Eternal Damnation pie, thanks.

I suppose I do have that power, but it seems like exercising it would be a form of getting above my raising. It is also difficult to separate the spice of bigotry against those who think differently from the sauce of saving grace. And the truth is that all were not welcome at those tables. My grandparents were products of their time. They were poor Whitefolk raised in Confederate country. You can imagine some of their views. The raising one could say I've gotten above is a complicated one, and leaving it is not an all-or-nothing proposition. No matter what the song says, the last thing I have done is forget it. Leaving it was complicated, too.

In the end, my corporeal separation from my lineage was an indirect result of Elijah's loss. I cut physical ties with that lineage for reasons I don't entirely understand and can't completely justify. I would not have done so had I not lost Elijah. So carefully constructed were my thought castles before his death, I likely would have stayed in them. I think I instinctively knew what leaving would mean. Going nuclear on my life felt like the only option.

But when Grief Zero hit, the lineage was severed. Now the Alabama family tree is missing an appendage. The line of loss runs both forward and backward. I trace that line forward, mourning the life Elijah and I would have had if he had lived. But I also trace it backwards. He lost his life and, with it, the legacy of his complicated kin. He lost his chance to experience the bounty. I lost too. In the aftermath of Grief Zero, I lopped off the tree at its roots. I think I even blew up the stump. All I know is that my table is small.

I haven't been home in ages, but when I pass through Alabama, my heart still salutes the town of those tables. Maybe I blew up the stump of that tree, but the roots run deep. The tie still binds. I don't believe in Jesus, but I am still of my kin. What I lost in breadth, I have found with a small group of loyal friends. I make magic with a pot of black beans. I didn't break faith with the hospitality or generosity or even with faith itself. I lost faith in certitude. I will never cease to be that little girl who piled into the back of the station wagon to return to her roots. But I can never again be the faithful daughter who proudly wore the mantle of her faith.

What's thicker? The blood of Jesus or the red clay on which I was raised? Did I get above my raising? Or did I simply choose to live? Could I coexist with those of my kin who hold fast to Bible Belt Jesus?

The words of Jesus himself seem to hold the answer:

"Do not suppose that I have come to bring peace to the earth. I did not come to bring peace, but a sword. For I have come to turn

'a man against his father,

a daughter against her mother,

a daughter-in-law against her mother-in-law—

a man's enemies will be the members of his own household'" (Matthew 10:34–36).

The implication of this passage seems to be that the battle lines are drawn, and in case the idea wasn't stated strongly enough already, Jesus lands the final punch with these words:

"Anyone who loves their father or mother more than me is not worthy of me; anyone who loves their son or daughter more than me is not worthy of me" (Matthew 10:37).

To accept me fully as I am now would, I think, be asking my kin to deny what Christ himself demanded. The man was starting a movement, and he knew it. Total devotion was required. I don't think my discomfort is unwarranted given that Jesus also apparently said "He that is not with me is against me" (Matthew 12:30). I know that there are other ways to interpret Scripture, but at this point when someone says, "I believe in Jesus," I have to ask, "Which one?"

I'm not sure which Jesus is the real Jesus. For years, I was so wounded by fundamentalism that I couldn't even hear the Bible read aloud without having a panic attack. Given that I lay the blame for my son's death at the feet of a system that encouraged me to deny my own intuition and then try to turn Elijah's death into a mass-witnessing campaign, I think my wariness is warranted.

I've chosen not to become the prodigal daughter who returns home for the holidays. Do I do so out of cowardice or kindness? At best, I think I would be tolerated as a black sheep.

At worst, I might be cornered and get a real aggressive praying for. I'll pass, and pass the gin, please.

And yet, that brokeass bounty remains.

Of late, I feel very close to my Alabama ancestors. I feel the bounty they bestowed. It lives in me, and I carry that bounty forward. I won't be the matriarch of a hundred grandchildren, but I can reinvent the bounty in a thousand different ways. The bounty that I carry is the fortitude, the ability to make much with little. It's creativity. It's hard times wedded with generosity. It's the wholesomeness of a hundred fishing trips with Dad teaching me how to bait a hook. But more than anything, that bounty is the truth that in hard times, my kids will have a home to come back to. They have a mother who, while far from perfect, is present. I bring the essence of that bounty forward, for it is the bounty of the best parts of the human spirit.

Of late, I have questioned whether or not one can pass a sense of belonging on to a child minus a tie to a homeland. I have wondered, in breaking faith with my geography, if failing to give kids an annual pilgrimage to their roots has harmed them. I know that my family's blood runs through my kids' veins, but do they? Can I really deliver the essence of the bounty without the trappings of the jam-packed jalopy and tables that should buckle under the weight of their load?

The loss of what my living children didn't have, this sense of being smothered in love, of being both broke and bountiful, haunts me. My older kids have dispersed. I don't think they consider themselves of the South. There is no big family home to which they return year after year. I think the best I could do for them is stay in New Orleans. My grandmother married and stayed put. When I divorced, I did the same. I think of leaving, but something about the city still soothes me.

Meanwhile, technology has evolved way past that DVD sling in the minivan, and with it, we are beset with a great irony. That which promised to connect us has wrought division. It seems as if living on the Internet has uprooted us from parts of the past.

Becoming global denizens in the Digital Age is, as we say in the South, "great and all," but I wonder if these scraggly surface-level connections that exist in the terra nova of technology are taking a toll on our kids' psyches. I am not anti-technology, but I am pro-biophilia. We need actual nature to nurture our souls. So I do think that the connections we crave cannot be fully satisfied without inhabiting a sense of place. In my youth, I tasted that place. I think that in New Orleans, a city where outcasts have settled, my small family has put down some tender roots. Has it been enough for my kids to have some sense of lineage?

This is a question only my kids can answer. Their lineage hands them leanness in one hand and bounty in the other.

I am now old enough to be a grandmother. I am looking more and more like my mom's mom, while my youngest got my Gran's bones and laidback wit. Like my Gran's hair, my bounty is twined, not with gray but with longing. That longing runs through me just as surely as the gifts of my childhood. I said earlier that Elijah's death cut a swath of loss both ways. So it goes with the longing as well. I am nostalgic for the safety I felt barreling down the highway in the back of that station wagon. Yet I strain forward, charting out the new territory that each year of parenting brings. Some days, I orient to the past; others, I leap into the excitement of the new.

Perhaps rather than getting above my raising, I have just grown around it. I encompass my upbringing just like I do my grief. It doesn't matter what degrees I have gathered or what gains I have made: I am bound to that bounty. I am bound to the longing. I know it just as surely as I know that a mess of collards makes a meal fit for Southern royalty. I wonder if the family of my youth will one day find ourselves gathered around a far-off table, breaking bread and finding common ground over the bounty.

Fundamomalist: Part 2

Many of us are unwittingly handed scripts by our parents, whether we come from fundamentalist families or not. Whatever the script, it comes laden with expectations about how we are to human.

I recently had a conversation with a fellow parent who is a top-tier physician. When I asked them why they chose this field, they replied, "Because my dad told me to become a doctor." Now, as this fellow human showed no signs of abandoning ship to become a social media influencer or, worse, a poet, the script seemed to have worked out okay. Most of us wrestle to free ourselves from at least some aspect of the roles for which we never auditioned. But I'm not sure if we can ever completely free ourselves from the omniscient narrator in our head. We take up the mantle of our roles, knowing that as long as we stay on script, the people in our lives know what to expect.

We are all handed a script. If we are lucky, it goes something like this:

Heyyyy New Human! You Got This

Parent: Welcome! You are a brand-new human! I will do my very best to nurture you as you grow into the person you want to be. In addition to caring for your basic needs, I am going to be a safe place for you to explore your emotions, your interests, and your dreams. I am not here to control you, and my hopes for your future are in no way bound to my own unmet needs. Whatever you feel is okay. Your thoughts are precious to me. I am more concerned about your sense of psychological safety than I am about your gender, sexual, or political identity. You are you, and you are becoming you. Damn, I'm lucky to be along for the ride. (Also, you were born to a mom who says words like "damn" a lot. Don't worry about it.)

Improv for the next sixty years until Parent's deathbed scene.

Parent: Did I do all right?

Grown kid: Honestly, you fucked it up pretty good at times, but we doin' all right, ya know? You get some rest now, Ma.

Most of us are handed scripts with a lot more detail. Our little tots are swaddled in generational plot lines riddled with predetermined roles. Some of us get handed winners of scripts like "Don't Fuck It Up Like Your Big Brother" or "I Sacrificed My Dreams For You, Why Are You So Ungrateful?" My script was called "Fundy First, Human Maybe." My first role? Preacher's kid.

If lacking nuance, the fundy-first script of fundamentalism is incredibly detailed. It permeates every aspect of your life. It's sort of like how Mister Linen takes a bunch of plums and cooks them down real good. Then he strains off the juice and then sous vides the shit out of it for a real long time. What started out as a plum now exists as a concentrated little cordial infused with star anise, cardamom, and white pepper. Then this concentrated little cordial gets combined with all sorts of wonderful things, like gin, which becomes innervated by the infusion. Sometimes Mister Linen uses vodka, but that's a ridiculous choice because he should always use gin—specifically Bombay Sapphire.

Life as a fundamentalist is sort of like an infusion process, only your particular brand of fundamentalism is the spice, your brain is in the sous vide, and your life is the cocktail. I'd rather have one of Mister Linen's seventeen-dollars-a-glass affairs, thank you very much.

As a walking fundamentalist-infused cocktail, you believe that *everyone* should be guided by your particular belief system. For this reason, I'm pretty sure I was everyone's favorite party guest; I was just waiting for a moment to pepper the conversation with little nuggets about my beliefs—*and* . . . wait for it: assertions about how other people should believe them, too. Fortunately, I wasn't much of a drinker, because if there is one thing more annoying at a cocktail party than a fundamentalist scouting the bar for unsuspecting converts, it would have been me, Desi the Drunkamentalist. Picture Jesus and the angel Gabriel shaking their heads from their heavenly perch: "There goes Desi again—evangelizing under the influence. Didn't you get Michael to tell her that whiskey and witnessing don't mix?"

There is way too much alcohol in this essay, so let's move on.

Back to the fundamentalist script—it dictates every aspect of your life. And I do mean every. Fundamentalism controls how you behave in every situation, what information you may access, what thoughts you should gatekeep, even which emotions you are allowed to feel (hint: basically just the happy ones).

For the beliefs of the fundy script to take root, they are often nested in a group that, if not a cult exactly, certainly comes pretty damn close.

It all makes perfect sense.

A fundamentalist without a group of fellow believers is just a kook. Can you imagine some dude strolling up to you out of the blue and bellowing, "I am the last witness written about in Revelation. I am here to tell you that a UFO is waiting to transition you to life in space." You would tell the guy sod off. You would be right to do so.

However, what if you are just teensy bit extraterrestrially curious and run across these words on a flier? "If you have ever entertained the idea that there might be a real, physical level in space beyond the earth's confines, you will want to attend this meeting."[21] Well, hey, who hasn't ever "entertained the idea" of "a real, physical level in space" (whatever that means)? Why not check it out? Moreover, the same flier contains a lovely little disclaimer that clearly states: "This is not a religious or philosophical organization recruiting membership." Little tip: If an organization has to go out of its way to tell you it is clearly *not* a religion or a philosophical movement, run.

In this case, the flier was posted by a group known as Human Intentional Metamorphosis. Perhaps you know them by their other name: Heaven's Gate.

The group that became Heaven's Gate began in 1974, when Marshall Herff Applewhite and his partner Bonnie Lu Nettles posted fliers with those exact words in California and Oregon. Curious souls came together to meet other curious souls under the auspice of transcendence. The bonds of the followers were close. In the words of a former member, "I loved these people. . . . It meant everything to me."[22] All relational needs were being met inside the group. By the time the mass suicide occurred, Heaven's Gate bore the fullblown, telltale signs of a high-control group. Members cut ties with the outside world. They received new names and adhered to a strict code of celibacy, showering times. Some members were even castrated in order to control their sexual urges.

It's easy to judge members of high-control groups, thinking, *I would never sign up for that.* Of course not. But castration and suicide were not on the flier. In the words of former cult member Mark Vicente, "Nobody joins a cult. They join a good thing, and then they realize they were fucked."[23]

Vicente is right.

Some people are born into high-control groups, conditioned to their norms by parents and other important figures in their lives. Others edge toward them independently, thinking that something good is about to befall them, usually that some problem in their life is going to be solved. The bait-and-switch comes later. High-control groups do exactly what their name implies: regulate members' reality by stringently asserting their own scripts over any and all others.

Researcher and former Unification Church Moonie Dr. Steven Hassan has delineated how authoritarian groups maintain control over individuals by wielding undue influence over four main areas: behavior, information, thoughts, and emotions. Hassan's framework has a nifty name, the BITE model, and under each category, he offers a checklist of examples for readers to examine. It's sort of like one of those old *Cosmo* personality tests, only instead of exclaiming "See, I am an autumn after all!", readers can discover all the ways an authoritarian group has fucked them over.

Personally, I love to peruse this checklist with my morning coffee. Anyone sitting next to me in these times will hear me mutter things like, "Shit, guess I was raised in a cult."

Here's a breakdown of just a few BITE model examples paired with the ways that the Evangelical fundamentalism of my youth embodied elements of authoritarian control. But if you want to have a real nice time seeing if just maybe *you* were raised in a cult too, take a look at Dr. Hassan's website and mutter a few exclamations of your own.

BITE MODEL ELEMENT [24]	EVANGELICAL FUNDAMENTALISM OF MY YOUTH
BEHAVIOR CONTROL	
• Major time spent with group indoctrination and rituals and/or self-indoctrination, including the Internet • Instill dependency and obedience.	• Sunday morning church, Sunday night church, morning quiet times, Wednesday evening choir practice and prayer meetings, youth group and missions organizations, conferences, retreats, Thursday night witnessing, street witnessing, fundamentalist Christian school *• Children obey your parents; wives submit to your husbands. If you leave, or disobey even a little, God will punish you, and you might go to hell.

BITE MODEL ELEMENT	EVANGELICAL FUNDAMENTALISM OF MY YOUTH
INFORMATION CONTROL	
• Extensive use of cult-generated information and propaganda, including:newsletters, magazines, journals, audiotapes, videotapes, YouTube, movies and other media	• Too many pamphlets and Bible "study" guides and Sunday school books to name. My personal favorite piece of propaganda? The Left Behind series, which traumatized an entire generation of fundy kids. Come home and can't find Mom? It was probably the Rapture. Let's not forget Christian radio and good ole "Focus on the (White, patriarchal, heteronormative) Family."
THOUGHT CONTROL	
• Require members to internalize the group's doctrine as truth, which entails: a. The adoption of the group's "map of reality" as reality b. Instilling black-and-white thinking c. Deciding between good vs. evil d. Organizing people into us vs. them (insiders vs. outsiders) • Use of loaded language and clichés that constrict knowledge, stop critical thoughts, and reduce complexities into platitudinous buzz words • Labeling alternative belief systems as illegitimate, evil, or not useful	• Take these Bible truths into your heart. Meditate on them day and night. a. The Bible is the literal word of God; if another "truth" contradicts the Bible, it can't be true. b. If you are not for Jesus, you are against Him. c. The church is good. The world is evil. d. We have the truth; others are deluded, including other types of "Christians," every other religion, and especially those who are humanists. • "Let go and let God." "Know Jesus, know peace." "No Jesus, no peace." "God said it, I believe it, that settles it." "God always answers prayers: yes, no, or maybe." "If you don't feel close to God, guess who moved?" • Those are just a bunch of secular humanists who are blinded by Satan. Pray for them but don't listen to them. Buddhism is dangerous! Your life has no meaning without Jesus.

BITE MODEL ELEMENT	EVANGELICAL FUNDAMENTALISM OF MY YOUTH
EMOTIONAL CONTROL	
• Manipulate and narrow the range of feelings—some emotions and/or needs are deemed as evil, wrong or selfisht	• "Be joyful always, pray without ceasing for this is the will of God concerning you" (1 Thessalonians 5:17).
• Instill fear, such as fear of: a. Thinking independently b. The outside world c. Enemies d. Losing one's salvation e. Leaving or being shunned by the group f. Other's disapproval	• There is much to fear outside of the fold. a. "Take captive every thought, and make it obedient to Christ" (2 Corinthians 10:5). b. The world is waiting to corrupt you. You are "in the world, but not of it." "The whole world is under the control of the evil one" (1 John 5:19).
• Ritualistic and sometimes public confession of sins	c. Those [insert other group x] are going to try to corrupt you. d. If you leave, you might go to hell or at least be miserable without Jesus
• Phobia indoctrination: inculcating irrational fears about leaving the group or questioning the leader's authority	e. If you leave, you were never really saved anyway. You are now part of "the world" and not safe.
	• Accountability groups, small groups, public altar calls every Sunday morning and Sunday night; confessing sins in prayer groups
	• The pastor/husband is the God-appointed head of the church/home. You are stepping out from under God's "umbrella of protection" if you leave. Who knows what might happen?

I have not included all the elements of Hassan's BITE model above. Nor have I indicated the extent to which each of these elements were present in my upbringing and, later, in other fundamentalist churches I attended. The power of the model is its illumination of how the disparate elements of authoritarian control come together to suppress a person's freedom and natural inclinations. At every turn, the group has an answer for behaviors, information, thoughts, and emotions that could cause a member to disengage from the group. Paired with our natural need for emotional attachment, is it any wonder that children born into authoritarian groups often hold fast to those ideas, even, as I did, taking them to the next level? Hassan's model provides a bit of insight into how Fundamomalist was born. Is it any wonder that leaving took so damn long?

Let me be clear: Many follow Scripture and do so without becoming a part of a high-control group. But those who do can turn to the words of Christ to justify their behavior. There's a story in the gospels about crowds coming to follow Christ. In this story, Jesus did not say, "Y'all come. The more the merrier." Instead, he admonished people, saying:

> "Which of you, wishing to build a tower, does not first sit down and count the cost to see if he has the resources to complete it? Otherwise, if he lays the foundation and is unable to finish the work, everyone who sees it will ridicule him, saying, 'This man could not finish what he started to build.'" (Luke 14:28–30)

The tower to which Jesus refers is the work of following him. The cost for doing so was everything. One might think that with branding like this, Jesus would be destined to spend the rest of his days hanging out by the Sea of Galilee, mending fishing nets and whining, "But. I. Could. Have. Been. GREAT!"

Apparently, many did leave Jesus, but importantly, a small group of diehards known as the disciples remained. So, it seems that Jesus apparently knew a little bit about psychology. Telling people that what you are doing is *really special* but also *really hard* will turn some people away, but it will also serve to strengthen the core. And it did.

I am not saying that Jesus was authoritarian, but many authoritarian leaders have used similar rhetoric to strengthen groups of devotees. Jesus encouraged people to consider the cost of building a tower. Those in authoritarian groups know that demolishing one comes with its own price.

If you are thinking that fundamentalism only exists in offshoots of mainstream religious groups or spaces, guess again. Fundamentalists can be found on the far right and left, in wellness workshops and professional development trainings. Don't believe me? Peek under the hood of cults like NXIVM, the cult masquerading as a self-help program. You will likely find a smidge of fundamentalism if not more. On the surface, the beliefs of different groups vary widely. The tactics, however, are the same, and they are well worth examining because you don't need to be a full-blown Fundamomalist in the making to experience them. These dynamics can exist:

- In abusive relationships: "If you leave, no one will ever love you like me." (fear of leaving)

- In wellness spaces: "Growth is uncomfortable. You've got to push through." (thought-terminating cliché)

- In politically-infused, mudslinging monikers: "Libtard!" "Fascist!" (us vs. them mentality)

- In rigid parenting styles of families seeking to control children who don't follow the script they were assigned (let's just call that one fucked up and move one)

Here in New Orleans, we keep an eye on the tropics during hurricane season. As I write, there's a situation brewing in the Atlantic that lets me know evacuation could be imminent. Similarly, if you see the weather of rigid beliefs and authoritarian control swirling around the center of a charismatic leader who for "some reason" just can't handle being questioned, go ahead and gear up to watch the next cult docu series on HBO. It's coming.

While the dynamics of fundamentalist groups keep people entrenched in them, the beliefs themselves are also worth exploring. So is the question, "What actually *is* a fundamentalist, anyway?" The definition is in the word itself. Fundamentalists subscribe to a set of bedrock beliefs—ahem, the *fundamentals*. These beliefs are pretty much immutable. Scratch that. They are just immutable. Do not question them because they have already been settled, handed down from some leader who is mainlining Truth. *The* Truth, to be exact. To be a fundamentalist, you need a trove of these beliefs and a sense that these beliefs are the guide-post for *every* decision you make. And I do mean every.

Fundamentals differ from values, or key guiding principles, like kindness or equality. Whereas fundamentals snap to a very specific meaning grid, values are conceptual. They exist at the categorical level. Importantly, values, like all concepts that haven't been codified into a set of fundamentals, can be reasoned with. They can be contextualized and recontextualized. They can change and grow. You can have an adult conversation with a value, asking it questions like, "What does kindness look like today? Who is being treated well if I proceed on this course of action? How might I need to adjust course so that I am honor-ing the complexity of my values system? How have my values shifted over the years?"

We may hold our values very close, but we don't generally make people chant them at 3:00 a.m. or get a funny haircut because of them.

In contrast to concepts that we reason with, if you ques-tion the fundamentals, you will likely receive a good talking to by the gatekeeper of the beliefs. You will be question-shamed and told that you just need to take it to the Lord in prayer. Persist, and you will be branded a heretic.

And yet here is where I need to come in hard on the side of "People are complicated." My father, who is undoubtedly a fun-damentalist, actually did encourage me to question my beliefs. I am quite sure he doesn't like where I have landed, but even though my dad preached that Jesus is the one way to God, he knew that if I didn't come to faith through my own experience, then my faith was not really my faith. In his wonderful Alabama way, he would say, "If you can't question your faith, it's not worth a plug nickel."

Problem is, I couldn't really—question it deeply. I had counted that cost and was unwilling to pay it. Then Elijah died, and the only fundamental that mattered was his loss. That's the power of grief, and if there is a God we are all serving, it is the deity of love and love lost. Scripture says that God is love. Perhaps I agree after all.

As for the above definition of fundamentalism, I think it holds true across most forms. However, I am no expert. I can't speak with authority about fundamentalism writ large, but I can go on forever about my particular brand: American Evangelical Christianity, which bottle-fed Bible Belt Jesus to the masses. So let's talk about that script for a moment, shall we? Everyone loves a good listicle, so here we go.

THE NOT-SO-FUN FUNDAMENTALS OF AMERICAN FUNDAMENTALIST "CHRISTIANITY"

1. You are a sinner. You were born into sin, and you have a sin nature. The inclination of your heart is going to be to sin. Always keep in mind that your heart is desperately wicked. Got it? Good.

2. Your sin is an affront to a Holy God. Now, keep in mind that this God loves you very much, but he is simply unable to look upon evil. He is Almighty and can do anything, but he can't be in the presence of evil. This is apparently a level of multitasking to which the Almighty can't attend. Why? Well, he just can't, that's why. Doing so would go against his pure nature. God can create the world out of nothing in exactly seven literal days, calling forth sun and stars, separating sky from ocean, and mak-

ing all manner of critters and creatures who exist precariously on a planet perched just thus and so on her axis. But the one thing He cannot do, puny evil person, is look upon your sinfulness.

Who can you blame for this? Adam. Or Eve. Or the Serpent. It's not really clear, but somehow Eve was beguiled, and it's her fault even though she was deceived, and it's Adam's fault because he wasn't around to help her simply say no to that wily Serpent, and that Serpent was really Lucifer, who had been cursed because he had fought against God and lost his Morning Star status in heaven because apparently the other thing God cannot stand is to have his authority challenged.

So, there are two things that God can't do, and both of them are pretty big deals. And no, these are not narcissistic, weird behaviors because, after all, this is God we are talking about, and another thing He can't do is be wrong . . . ever.

Okay, now that we are clear that you are a sinner and that your sin is someone's fault from long ago, but also yours, let's talk about how God fixed the problem of your sin being an affront to him.

3. God killed his kid for you. Sort of. I mean, Jesus was technically a grown-up when it happened and knew that he was sent here to die for the sins of all humanity. So, there's that. Anyway, your sin is such an affront to God that the only way for Him to come near you again was to obtain a blood sacrifice.

Why does a blood sacrifice do the trick? Well, it certainly isn't because these fundamentals were born of a time when humans were a very young species that didn't have tools to make sense of many things in the world, like gravity or someone's brain not having enough serotonin or weather patterns that destroyed crops. It definitely was not young humanity doing their best to explain the wonderful and chaotic existence in which they fought for survival. It is most certainly ancient truth being handed down directly from God to all manner of prophets. These prophets were basically an ancient papyrus-wielding transcription service for God's truth. And when people translated these texts from Hebrew and Greek, they definitely did not have any political agenda whatsoever. Therefore, you can trust this truth.

God found a way to atone for your sin, and remember, even *one* sin makes you a sinner, and it's all written down in this book that isn't really a book, but a compilation of writings culled together over a couple of thousand years that a bunch of men decided in the year 325 is the truth. Speaking of truth ...

4. The Bible is the truth. Period. It's the literal truth except where it isn't literal, as in the case of obvious metaphors like "All men are grass" (Isaiah 40:6). And it is *definitely* a metaphor for Christ and the church when Solomon is talking about cupping his lover's breasts. But mostly, it's literal, and this book will hold the answers to your problems such as "Which ultra-conservative college where leaders have been embroiled in a sex scandal with the pool boy should I attend?" It can tell you who to marry and, more importantly, who not to marry: If you are going to be a deacon (this for the men only), you should be "the husband of but one wife." Whew. Glad to have *that* one settled.

5. Back to atonement. If you believe that God's son, Jesus, died for your sin, all you have to do is, well,

believe it. I mean, you also have to accept this gift in the form of praying the sinner's prayer. The sinner's prayer is basically where you admit to points one through three and ask Jesus to come into your heart and be your Lord and Savior. The Savior part makes sense, because saving your sorry ass is exactly why Jesus was born in the first place. But don't forget about the Lord part.

In order to be a fundamentalist Southern Baptist Evangelical Christian, you basically need to admit that you are not competent enough to have agency over your life. It's very much "Jesus, Take the Wheel" of *everything*. Stop pretending that you can make good decisions because you can't. Give over your agency to Jesus. Start running everything past him instead of your own reason, intuition, values, friends, or family. You are about to get one of those *Matrix* thingies in the back of your soul that mainlines Jesus's ways into you.

Now that you are all saved and have someone else at the helm of your life, you have two jobs: a.) work out your own salvation with fear and trembling ("Wait," you might protest, "I thought I just got saved?" You did, but now you have to get sanctified), and . . .

b.) bring others into the fold. Evangelize! You have the good news. (Well, some of it is good news—except for the part where you are such a horrible person that God had to kill his kid for you. Other than that, it's very good news.) Anyway, you have the good news, the key to solving humanity's most pressing problem. So, now that you are saved, it's time to pay it forward and get as many people on the glory train with you as possible. Other than not getting saved yourself, keeping your mouth shut about the gospel is probably the next worst thing you could do, other than voting Democrat.

7. Also, don't be gay.

If someone believes this list, fine. I am not here to disparage what brings people hope and helps them get through the day. We can disagree. Heck, I have a piece of wood in Gigi that I keep for the express purpose of knocking on whenever I compliment her. Whenever Gigi is doing well, I say things like, "Good job, girl; we've been two weeks without an extended vacation to the shop spa. Mama's gonna buy you a new seat cover." Then, I furiously look for the wood and knock. Someone could say that my belief is superstitious. They would be right, but somewhere in my soul, I believe that knocking on that wood keeps the dreaded engine knock at bay.

However, if my belief in wood knocking dictates a system of behaviors that I then want to cull in a credo, and if I want everyone to join the Sisterhood of the Wrangler Wood Knockers, and I can't shut up about the joys of knocking on wood, and especially if I make my single purpose in life to vote only for politicians who also believe in the powers of wood-knocking, you might want to avoid me at the gas pump. Similarly, if the above list is unquestionable, and if this list dictates every aspect of your life and instills bigotry into your social views, and if you believe that anyone who doesn't believe it is a heretic, I'm probably going to want to avoid you at, well, everywhere. Disagreement over belief systems is not the issue. Lack of civil discourse on both sides, however, *is*.

So, now that we are set on the fundamentals of my brand of the beast, I think it's important to touch on how weirdly comforting it is to have a few big beliefs about existence settled once and for all. In my former belief system, I "knew" about the nature of humanity, the causes of good and evil, and how to proceed with my life. It's like I had a placard nailed to my brain that set the trajectory of my life. I was in a lane. I knew what was in bounds for me: sex *after* marriage with my husband whenever he wanted to do it, voting Republican, going to church, strengthening my faith, winning souls—including those of my children. I'll say one thing for fundamentalism. It simplifies the world situation; anything you can't explain, you get to file underneath "God's mysteries" and move on with your day.

Of course the downsides are pretty big downers: loss of autonomy and critical thought, rigid gender roles, women's bodies ravaged from multiple back-to-back pregnancies. But it's the basics of the belief system itself that I find so harmful. Fundamentals like "You are totally depraved" are nothing less than soul strychnine. People who imbibe them in small doses, like most of my culturally Catholic friends, seem to do all right. Those who take a daily dose of the poison have a bit of a rougher go.

Fundamentalism didn't just give my life impetus; it provided me with a clearly laid out parenting trajectory. My parenting mission was simple: get my kids saved and on the path to winning souls. When I was raising my kids to be fundamentalists, I had no sense that teaching them they were evil could be traumatizing. Neither did my parents, I'm sure.

It's all rather logical, really. If you take as the starting point that we are all born damned, then your first priority becomes to get people un-damned by any means possible. What's a little *Left Behind* trauma compared to (gasp) actually being left behind in the Rapture? When you think that the natural end of every human being's script is a literal soul apocalypse, your life's mission becomes clear. And, if you aren't a hypocrite, you will get pretty dang fervent about fulfilling that mission.

My father spoke to this point from the pulpit. He used to tell this story of an atheist who said to a lukewarm Christian, "If I really believed what you say you believe, I would not sleep, I would barely eat. I would do *nothing* but travel the

earth and tell as many people as possible about this Jesus."
My dad is a *very* good preacher. And he didn't tell this story
to guilt people into evangelizing. He told it because he really
believes that it might help keep people from eternal torment.
My father is no grifter. Neither are many people you see holding megaphones on street corners, yelling at you while you
are just trying to buy tickets to see your stadium show. These
people are not trying to be unkind to you. You may think that
they are misguided. I do too, but they really believe that they
are in a life-or-death battle for your eternal destiny. What's a
little politeness when the stakes are so high?

While not everyone in God's army is born to be a preacher,
as Fundamomalist I believed we all had our parts to play in the
process. We all needed to adhere to the fundamentals, but I also
believed that we all had a special calling from God, a unique
way in which we were supposed to evangelize. I really hoped
my kids would receive their special calling from the Lord, get
assigned a special role in the fundy-first script. This calling
would utilize their Gifts of the Spirit (special name that some
Christians give to your personality traits). It would set them up
to make the most impact for Jesus. Now, what mother wouldn't
want her children to receive such a calling? Lord knows, I had
never figured out mine. Maybe my kids would fare better. As a
Fundamomalist, I sure would have loved it if some modern-day
prophet would ride up on his camel, pull out a horn of oil, and
deliver the calling.

Which kid would get their calling first? Let's just go with
Isaiah because his name alone is begging for it.

"And lo, God has given you a gregarious spirit. Because
you can make friends with a plastic rock at the Dollar Tree,
I say unto you that one day you will speak unto kings and
celebrities. Many of them also resemble rocks, so you are being
groomed to this work, my child. You will have a platform by
which to share with the nations. Now, go forth and build your
YouTube channel, my child. The time is nigh."

Or maybe Ada would get her calling first: "You will be a healer, and though you desire to draw bright geometric shapes for no particular reason, I say unto you that with each brushstroke, you shall expose the sins of the nations. Just don't say too much because, well, you have a uterus. Leave the real talking to your brother."

After delivering the calling, this modern-day prophet would ride off into the East, never to be seen again. We would all solemnly nod our heads. "Ahhh, so that's settled. Now we can *really* tailor your training. Off to social media influencer Bible school you go."

Don't get me wrong; I am not anti-calling. If you have one of them things, good on you. Callings are wonderful because they give you a point in a way that some of us flounder to find. It is much easier to know your calling and move steadily toward it than muck around with this process for the better part of forty years, during which you dream, you try, you fuck up, and you get real sad cause it didn't work out. You spend a few years numbing out and working on your mommy issues. You get a new dream and probably a boatload of school loans. You try again.

Callings aren't a cure-all, but callings, particularly religious ones, are particularly powerful. They take much of the guesswork out of life. Instead of asking "What should I do with my one precious life?", the question becomes *How?*: "How can I win as many souls as possible?" The hierarchies inherent in Evangelical fundamentalism, while constricting and patriarchal, provide structures that I found to be simultaneously comforting and confining while I dwelled in them. As a wife and mother, my job description was clear.

The paradox of fundamentalist calling is that committing your life to the cause makes you feel like you are taking responsibility for your life. You are stepping up! You have but to follow the Lord and rise to the occasion. In reality, fundamentalist callings cause us to sidestep the awesome responsibility called "Show up to your life with the cards you have been dealt and do your damn best."

Gawd. Sometimes I still hate that responsibility. That responsibility removes the spiritual safety net. There is no bypass for confusion. No "Jesus take the Wheel." Replacing epic purpose with puny old human-sized purpose allows for the possibility of failure from which recovery feels futile. Life gets messy and pretty much stays that way. One would think that without God in the equation, the stakes are lower. Maybe they are, but the responsibility feels awesome. There is no prophet coming to hand me a packaged purpose. No steed. It's just me and Gigi going off-roading on the occasional week that she's working.

As a Fundamomalist, I wanted my kids to find their callings—within the framework of fundamentalism and all its attendant rules, of course. But my expectations for my kids didn't just stem from my fundamentalism. The overarching goal of my parenting was to perpetuate my faith through my offspring, absolutely. But lest it sound like all we did was sit around and memorize Bible verses, I admit that I had dreams for my kids that were born as much from the middle class American mantra as they were from fundamentalism. That mantra goes like this: Study hard in school. Make good grades. Go to college, find a mate, land a dream job. Have a few babies for your mama. Of course, that secular mantra fell neatly under the umbrella of fundamentalism. That is, I expected God was gonna guide my kids into careers that would use their gifts well. And in using those gifts, my one-day grown kids would become powerful members of the Lord's Army.

I'm not sure why I assumed this, because if there's one thing that was clear about my kids from pretty much the moment they each arrived on the scene, it's that they were imbued with a sense of their own desire. Now, like a good Fundamomalist, I taught them to subject those desires to their higher calling, but the human spirit is pretty dang indelible. You can try to tame it, but it has a way of poking its head up through the maze of beliefs and restrictions and impositions to say, "Tame this, mothafucka."

Like I said, it is not just religious fundamentalists who latch onto ideas about how their kids' lives must progress. There is a fine line between equipping our children with the skills they need to pursue their dreams and imprinting our own dreams upon them. Having dreams for our kids is normal. When we impose very specific dreams onto their psyches and imbue those dreams with moral gravitas—aye, there's the rub. How could my own dreams for children, which were laden with fundamentalist notions of how to live, not have created the perfect conditions in which they might feel unworthy for something as benign as wanting to fuck around on the Internet for a minute?

Fundamentalism is a nifty little guilt incubator like that.

Even kids raised in the gentlest of parenting environments can feel like failures when they start moving away from societal scripts. Gentle homes like the one I am trying to create now can't completely counter other influences. How naive it is to think that I have the power to imbue my kids with all that they will need to navigate a world such as ours. I now parent from the stance of being both a powerful and frail force in my kids' lives. Fundamomalist was a hubristic gal. Midlife, tired, strapped-for-cash Mom is a lot more humble. She knows that societal expectations about what constitutes a "successful" life are as prevalent as fluoride in the tap water.

I feel for kids who are coming of age now. I especially feel for kids who sense that their true north runs counter to what society deems appropriate. Fundamomalist has been gone for a few years now. In her wake is a mom working from a different script. And I have come to the belief that my job is as much to help my children stubbornly cling to their internal compasses as it is to teach them how to do whatever it is we do nowadays instead of balancing a checkbook of fundamentalist dos and don'ts. I'm pretty sure it's just called "living." Bring on the next act.

Parenting and the Dreams of the Children: Or, How to try to (mostly) not let your PTSD Fuck up your Kids (too much)

When Elijah came on the scene, I promptly fell in love. Elijah stared straight ahead with gorgeous baby blues, alert and ready to take on whatever the next part of the journey entailed. The kid was present, seemingly unphased by having just barrelled through my private parts. Oh, I'm sorry, did I say private parts? Let me correct that: I mean my parts that had recently been inspected by at least ten complete strangers. Whatever the name for these parts, I think it's safe to say that, during and after childbirth, the word "private" no longer applies.

The whole process of a medicalized pregnancy, while understandable, is still strange to me. Someone gets laid. Okay, that part's normal. But pretty soon after that, it starts getting weird. A future birthgiver suspects pregnancy and purchases a stick to pee on. In my day, if two pink lines appeared, you waved the thing around near your partner, informing them as I did my then husband, "Hey, we don't need a divorce after all! I'm just pregnant!" I have a wonderful way of breaking big news like that.

After a future birth giver finds out that they have magic pee, they schedule a series of prenatal appointments. All of these appointments are meant to educate the new parent-to-be and ensure the safe arrival of the being who gave you magic pee. Throughout this period of time, future birth givers often read scads of books and try to figure out how the hell they are going to parent. We study parenting styles and engage with a myriad of questions: "Will I be authoritative (but not authoritarian) or gentle? Should I schedule feedings or just 'let the child lead'? And what the heck is hindmilk?"

All this self-education can lead first-time birth givers to make some very strong declarations about what we will or will not do in regards to our offspring. With the certitude of a researcher who has just read fifteen peer-reviewed studies decrying the horrors of pacifiers, we declare, "I will *never* give my child a pacifier." Fast forward to three months and you will find us crawling on all fours through Target like a crazed being, wondering if *this* pacifier might be the one that earns us an hour of shut-eye. An attendant kindly asks if we are interested in an orthodontic version of this little silicon nipple. Completely broken, we reply, "I don't care if it's magically bonded with the blood of baby unicorns. GIVE IT TO ME."

I have found that, in addition to providing the obvious reward of meeting our new humans, childbirth is an exquisite opportunity to extend our vocabularies. While laboring, birth givers get to learn *lots* of new ones. Hey, I love an impromptu vocab lesson as much as the next human, but I do question the wisdom of the timing of this particular one. I generally like to learn new words fully clothed and not feeling like a one-woman reenactment of Mt. Vesuvius about to erupt. Even stranger than the timing of this vocabulary lesson is the nature of the words: most of them have about six syllables, which seems pretty unnecessary, given that when birthgivers are hearing them, we are, at best, monosyllabic.

I have a favorite childbirth word: epidural.

I also have a least favorite: episiotomy.

In case you don't know what an episiotomy is, consider it

the lesser of two evils—a choice between the annihilation of a birth giver's nether regions and a need to do a little roadwork down there. I feel about episiotomies what I often feel about election time, when someone tells me that we have to choose between the narcissistic, fascist megalomaniac and the somewhat decrepit, ineffectual opponent. People who opt out of voting in this case might put out the "lesser of two evils" card in the same way that pseudo-intellectuals shout out, "Checkmate, atheist!" Turns out, however, that the lesser of two evils is in fact, *less evil*. Count me in for *less evil*, please. At least back in my birth-giving days, an episiotomy was considered less evil than the alternative. Future birth givers, consider the choice of whether or not to get one as practice for the myriad of imperfect parenting decisions you will have to make going forward.

Around the moment birth givers are about to push out those little bundles onto which we will one day project our own mommy issues, a doctor announces with no great aplomb that an episiotomy would be a good idea. In my case, that announcement came a few hours into labor, just as Elijah was crowning. Another new word! Incidentally, that's a pretty dumb word to explain that your offspring's giant noggin is hanging out around your vaginal opening. What is this effed up reference to royalty supposed to mean? Is your young prince, princess, or gender-fluid heir to the throne literally wearing your vagina as crown? Or is the idea more metaphorical?

Are our offspring in effect saying, "I am about to arrive. Get ready for me to take over *everything*. Even your most primal appetites for sleep, sex, or bodily sovereignty are about to bow to my whims. That vagina that used to enjoy a lover's caress? Yeah. I own that now. That's my super highway. Let's gooooooooooooo!"

As Elijah was about to exit the highway, my OB calmly announced, "Mrs. Birth Giver, we are going to need to make a small incision in your perineum [yet another polysyllabic word]. Otherwise, your baby's head is going to rip you a new one."

Okay, he didn't say "rip you a new one." I think he said something like "tear your perineum—by about an inch." Now, math is not my specialty, and I have the spatial skills of an inanimate object, but I knew where an inch-long tear would lead. Let's just leave it there and say that I agreed to said incision. Actually, I grunted. See? Grunts only take one syllable. One six-syllable incision and several pushes later, I held my son.

What an arrival. I already mentioned those cobblestoned, killer blues. As I locked eyes with my son and held him to my chest, oxytocin did its best. I was hooked. No shock there, because oxytocin is *the best drug* on the planet. Oxytocin is the engine that drives the love that makes the world go round. And when an infant is laid on a birth giver's chest, both baby and birth giver are bathed in it. Oxytocin is the real Big O, people. When I met Elijah, the axis of my very world shifted. It began to revolve around this little human. I barely noticed as the entourage around my now very publics began to pave over the roadwork. I was too busy meeting my boy.

And dreaming. I was a goddamn perinatal seer, peering into the future of swaddling, rocking, strolling, and snuggling that awaited. While I couldn't foresee all that this parenting gig would entail, I knew two things: 1.) It would require nothing less than a full on effort, and 2.) It was going to be damn fun. I started really dreaming that day, the most oxytocin-soaked dreams of a new mother in love. Gimme that shit over shrooms anyday.

Here's a truth about parenting: Little bundles come swaddled in big dreams. When a mother is handed a baby who blinks at her with her long-deceased Papa's eyes, she sees the past. She senses that this child has a place in her lineage—oldest, youngest, fingers shaped like her father's. She also sees the future. She doesn't know exactly what shape that future will take, but that future is bright, eclipsing her exhaustion, her episiotomy, even her own unhealed wounds. Climate change is momentarily forgotten. In the moment when we meet our new little human, the chance that they will grow up to be utterly unfulfilled and crippled with generational trauma is not exactly top of mind. No mother holds her newborn to her breast and croons, "Darling, I just hope that when you are grown you get to engage in endless hours of administrative BS for a boss who low-key harasses you and belittles your work. If you are lucky, your highest aspiration for each day will be seeing how fast you can hustle home to your Coors Light and watch whatever latest piece of *Star Wars* spinoff tripe has pushed George Lucas to an early grave."

No—a mother has the highest, shiniest hopes for her kid. She sees a ballerina, a scientist, a changemaker. How ironic that she does this when, at this phase of the game, the kid is basically a spit-up machine with lots of big feelings. No matter; the mother feels into the kid's potential, yearns to foster it. These dreams don't belong to the child; they are hitched to the heart of the mother, so she begins to sow the seeds for their fruition.

It's much like one of my favorite memes. Two friends are talking on New Year's Day, and one says, "I think this year is going to bring flowers."

"Really?" replies the other friend. "Why?"

Barely looking up from the dirt, the first friend says, "Because I am planting flowers."

This is what a mother does. A mother says, "I see potential in this baby," and plants and plants and plants and hopes that her labors will bring her child the ability to take over the tending of these dreams one day. Yet this way of mothering can easily tip from sowing seed and tending the garden of a child's heart into transgressing a child's spirit. It can get especially fucked up if the mother misses a crucial element: teaching the kid to dream a damn dream of their own. When that doesn't happen, the mother's own dreams may lead her to give and give and give, often to the point of sacrifice. Resentful of her ill-placed efforts, the kid rears up on their sixteenth birthday and yells, "But I never *asked* you to do that."

And the kid is right.

So, moms, dream on, and recognize that while we are caring for our free-spirited bundles of humanity, they are literally
one of our dreams come true—and, let us not make the mistake
of sacrificing other dreams in the name of being an altruistic
parent. Carl Jung spoke of this problem when he wrote that
"[t]he more 'impressive' the parents are, and the less they
accept their own problems (mostly on the excuse of 'sparing
the children'), the longer the children will have to suffer from
the unlived life of their parents and the more they will be
forced into fulfilling all the things the parents have repressed
and kept unconscious."[25] One of the best way to fuck up our
kids' lives is to ask them to somehow make up for the ones we
haven't been able to live. And probably the best way to foster
the dreams of our children is by dreaming a few of our own
and going about making them happen.

We often model hard work for our kids, imbuing it with
moral impetus for its own sake. We teach our kids that hard
work is a virtue, and that's bullshit. Work is energy. Thus, work
is inherently amoral. "Hard work" by itself is nothing but decon-
textualized labor. And hard work chosen not by but for a person,
whether by a cruel taskmaster or capitalistic notions of "success,"
is immoral; it is an offense to the human spirit. When we divorce
work from its source code—our dreams—it becomes a weapon
against our souls. Over the long haul, we can become so mired in
the drudge of the day-to-day that the world loses its enchantment. Or rather, we lose our enchantment with the world. What
a waste of human potential. What a scourge on the soul.

Parenting will always involve toil. But parenting devoid of
dreaming is akin to "drill and kill" teaching methods that have
been rightly criticized in K–12 schools. Today's "successful"
kids sure can put an equation in slope-intercept form, find the
main idea of that sentence, and support all their answers with
evidence from a text. However, they often do so with no connection to how these skills connect to *anything* in their lives that
actually matters to them. In classrooms, who traditionally gets

shamed? The kid who is sitting there, chin propped in hands, staring out the window. We chastise this kid for, all together now: *daydreaming.*

If I were teaching, I would plan a whole block of time for chin-propping. I would ask the kids, "What are you dreaming about?" I would say, "Oooooh, that's a good one! What should we do? Write a story? Plan a field trip? Learn how to cut and measure and sew and staple that dream into existence?" I would try to foster their capacity to dream as much as their ability to solve for *x*. Maybe I would even try to help them solve for *x* as a way to help them accomplish their dreams. I would hope that this daydreaming curriculum would translate into their adult lives, imbuing them with a sense of agency in their lives so that they will always know that when something isn't working, they have permission to dream a new dream and pull out the tools they need to fulfill it.

I call it acting out the cycle of dreaming and doing.

We dream, we do. We rinse and repeat, adjusting for each of our fuck ups—I mean, "opportunities for growth."

What is a dream, really? When we dream, we see in our minds that for which our heart longs. This upward motion, from heart to head, is key. There's a saying in Christian fundamentalism: "Many people miss salvation by about eighteen inches. That's the distance between your head and your heart." The meaning of this adage is that in order to get saved, you have to hear God calling to your heart. Override your logic because " . . . the wisdom of this world is foolishness to God" (1 Corinthians 3:19). What a lovely way to get people to bypass their intellects. Cue the emotional contagion music and drum up the altar call.

The saying does have a tad bit of wisdom in it, however. I think the salvation we actually need is to live our best, messy, dream-filled, fully human lives. And we often miss those best lives by about eighteen inches. Many of us spend years attempting to carry out the dreams that were handed to us. If we are lucky, we make it into our forties before we sputter out and end up wandering the self-help aisle, wearing the same look of crazed desperation we had when we were in Target searching for that pacifier. But when we turn inward and hear from our hearts, they provide the fuel to carry out even the most difficult of dreams.

Heart-conceived dreams are the inspiration from which our discipline springs. That discipline takes many different forms—anything from strapping on sneakers at 5:00 a.m. to poring over textbooks at all hours. Most of the time, it's also going to involve adulthood's dirty little secret: paperwork. Show me a dream, young human, and I will lead you to the form you need to fill out to make it a reality.

Dreams are so vital to our well-being that losing them can fuck a human critter up pretty badly. "Without vision, the people perish," right (Proverbs 29:18)? Lots of things can block our ability to dream: anxiety, depression, generational poverty, political upheaval at the hands of the power hungry. Over time, too many disasters and disappointments dogpile upon our dreams. When this happens, we subsist, down in the dirt. At best, our hearts beat out truncated visions, anemic dreams that lack the nutrition a human spirit needs to thrive. I wonder how much addiction is a substitute for unmet longing? How many opioids have been pedaled? How many drinks are downed because we are stuck unable to dream even the simplest of dreams—for a good day, a sweet date, a dinner laid out with love? Are our collective hearts so afraid to dream that we are being reduced to a society of malnourished spirits?

And what happens to a child when a parent becomes afraid to dream?

When I think about Jung's assertion that children suffer from the unlived lives of their parents, I am tempted to think that Jung meant the good, exciting, if-only-it-could-have-been parts. But I think that children suffer whenever a parent ignores *any* part of their life, grief included. Grief is part of life; sometimes it's the lion's share. While dreams can be stunted for many reasons, unwept grief is a powerful dream-killer. When a parent cuts off their grief, they are lopping off a huge facet of the human experience. And when a parent is busy trying to manage grief, their dreaming faculties get fried. I mean that pretty literally.

I found out recently that during pregnancy, the part of the brain responsible for daydreaming, mind-wandering, and thinking about others gets wayyyy supercharged.[26] This part of the brain, known as the default mode network, becomes more connected during pregnancy. When a part of the brain is more connected, via newly forged neural pathways to other brain parts, it becomes more active. So, it seems that, in an unsurprising turn of events, Mother Nature literally changed my brain to make me dream for my kids. In fact, that sneaky bitch had been working behind the synaptic scenes for *months* before I gave birth to Elijah.

Companion fun fact: Wanna know what causes *decreased* connections in the default mode network? That's right, *trauma*. According to Lanius et al. (2020), this network is less connected in individuals who have Post-traumatic Stress Disorder (PTSD).[27] In case it comes as a surprise that I probably have PTSD, let me offer that shocking reveal now. Okay: so now, consider the power that one small life entering and leaving this realm has on his mother's brain. Five times over, the part of my brain that connected me to each of my kids created more neural connections in my brain in general. And over the years, the trauma of losing Elijah may have created a pull against that push. So if I am a little slow to get going in the morning, maybe it's because there is a little neural tug of war taking place in my default mode network. Yes, I will have a second cappuccino, thank you.

I don't want to reduce Elijah's birth and death to a case study in neuroplasticity, but ... understanding that traumatic loss might have severed connections that, with the right machinery, are *literally* observable during daydreaming—and, importantly, during contemplation about who we are and what we value as individuals—does shed some functional, MRI light on the whole phenomenon. It also might explain why, when I lost Elijah, I was so tangled up in the trauma that dreaming began to feel unsafe. I felt like no matter what I did, another shoe would drop at any moment, sweeping away my best efforts to parent well.

In place of dreaming, an insidious companion took up residence in the dream nook of my brain: hypervigilance. It's not that hard to trace the origins of my overprotectiveness. I had failed to keep vigil over Elijah. The unthinkable had happened. Who was to say that it couldn't happen again? Lightning had struck, and contrary to the saying, it is actually more likely to strike the same place twice. *Clearly* the only logical response was to dress entirely in rubber and move into a fallout shelter about a billion miles away from the initial strike, then monitor the "weather" for all potential lightning strikes everywhere, all the time.

Hypervigilance demanded that I keep vigil . . . all the time.

Did I know that my hypervigilance was unhealthy? Look, I saw *Finding Nemo*, so I know the dangers of overprotectiveness. And I really didn't want to be like the stereotypical Jewish mother in the old joke, who wrote to her kids: "Start worrying. . . . Details to follow." But I couldn't stave off the feeling that another loss could happen at any time. Because guess what? It *could*. The problem with hypervigilance is that, rather than taking reasonable protective measures, the hypervigilant person moves into modes of control that make anything akin to living actually impossible. Sure, we are safe, but why bother? The payoff for safety is an existence so tepid that our souls might as well be in a coma. Perhaps they are.

Hypervigilance does not listen to reason because hypervigilance, like any obsessive behavior, has its own twisted logic. Elijah died in bed. This fact was particularly difficult for me. I think we can all agree that if there is one place that is supposed to be safe, it's bed. At least, that's what I thought. Hypervigilance reminded me constantly that beds weren't safe. Even the word "bed" was a trigger. For years, I made the rounds after I tucked my kids in—checking their beds for choking hazards or anything that could harm them. Is it normal to check your kid's bed for pennies or small bits of string? Sure, it is. Once. But multiple times a night? Every time you wake up to pee? Leaving a room only to return moments later to count the number of respirations per minute of your perfectly healthy three-year-old?

Addiction doesn't know the meaning of "enough," and hypervigilance doesn't know the meaning of "once." An alcoholic downs five bourbons in the span of two hours and craves more. For a hypervigilant mom, no amount of caution seems reasonable. My hypervigilance insisted upon the tic-like checks in order to protect my kids—and that was real, but it was equally real that I was trying to protect myself from ever again waking up to a child who had not made it through the night. So, I dutifully made the rounds, trying to regain some sense of agency. I couldn't control illness or random acts of violence, but this one, I could do something about. If God wasn't going to protect my babies, I sure as hell was.

My hypervigilance existed in tension with the part of me that knew my kids needed to take risks. Of *course* the kids need to climb trees, swim in the deep end of the pool, and learn to drive. Naturally, in order to thrive in the world, my kids needed to dream and flop and feel all the disappointment of wanting something really bad and it just not working out. As much as I hate it, I knew that my kids would only learn to navigate hardship through experience. Sure.

And, of course, right on cue, Brené Brown came round with her famous vulnerability TED Talk to remind me that "[my] kids are wired for struggle."[28] Really? Cause it seems like when they were little, they were wired to flail around on the floor and yell "Mommmmmyeeeee!" at the drop of a sippy cup. No shade to any kids here. It also seemed that at least one of my kids was wired to beat the shit out of their brother with Legos in order to protect their own little Lego camp. Was *this* the struggle to which Dr. Brown referred?

Turns out my kids agree with Brené. Yesterday, Marci and I were having coffee and talking about this passage of this book. I was like, "If I could make everything easy for you, I would."

Marci, the wise teen who is way smarter than me, took no time to say, "Yeah, Mom. Don't do that. That would not be good for me."

Anyhoo, the bottom line here is that hypervigilance and letting kids learn to flop do not mix.

Lest anyone want to chime in with some sort of memed-up word salad like, "Your struggle is your strength," allow me to revel in a bit of etymological back talk: "hyper," from Greek *hyper*.

Wow, thanks, so "hyper" is derived from, um, *hyper*.

And what does hyper mean, exactly? Well, I'll tell you. It means "over," "in excess," "in abundance." (Finally, some abundance in my life. I guess all those thirty-second affirmations paid off.) Here's my favorite definition of the word: "active." Ah, there it is. Hypervigilance is an *abundance* of active vigilance. This little prefix packs quite the punch, and I can't think of a situation in which the connotation is positive. Try adding the prefix hyper to the most amazing word and you will have an immediate *ew* response. Hyper-loving? Sounds controlling. Hyper-compassionate? Can't differentiate your own emotions. Whatever the Greeks intended, being hyper in any context just ain't good, y'all.

Hypervigilance is like having that one kid who just *cannot* stop turning the ball pit at McDonald's into a large-scale simulation of a confetti cannon living in the back of your brain. You know this kid. You may have this kid. You may be pissed that this kid turned your twelve minutes of afternoon escape from (I mean, quality time with) your own tornado of a toddler into a whole other level of chaos. Now, imagine *that* kid living in the back of your brain. You know you shouldn't triple-wrap your kid's baby tooth in Saran wrap only to worry that the Saran wrap will come unwrapped and get wrapped around your kid's pinkie toe (or worse). The adult, somewhat normal part of your brain knows this. But your trauma-informed toddler brain ain't having it. No reason, no impulse control, no chill. Gee, I wonder why my kids have anxiety?

The upshot of hypervigilance is that you don't have time to dream. When someone is anxious or hypervigilant, they say things like, "Anything could happen." Problem is, they don't really mean that. What they actually mean is anything *bad* can happen ... and likely will, unless they step in here and intervene. In response to catastrophizing, hypervigilance is *all* doing and no dreaming. I wasn't dreaming any good dreams when I was in this state. I wasn't peering into the future and seeing the computer scientist or artist or far-off Christmas Eve present-opening. I was just crisis-managing a scenario that had very little likelihood of occurring. Leave it to Mark Twain to sum up this type of thinking with a pithy little aphorism: "I've suffered a great many catastrophes in my life. Most of them never happened."

Brother, you have no idea.

I don't walk through the house like a demented hypervigilant heroine in a Jane Austen novel anymore. My hypervigilance has given way to a way more acceptable form of dysfunction: codependency. I don't really know how to do it another way, and there is no manual for knowing how much to let your kids struggle and fail vs. when it's time to step in and offer some parental micromanaging (ahem, support). This is a particularly hard line to walk when I start factoring in my intrusive thoughts—ahem, I mean *intuition*.

Sometimes I get these gut feelings about my kids, like my recurring dream that Ada was going to drive her car off the mountain in North Carolina. I didn't say anything to her because I didn't want to spook her. And then, not a month after she moved up there, she called me, breathless: "I am okay, but I just got in a wreck, and I almost flew off the mountain. I thought I was going to die."

Tell me, author of *Codependent No More*, what's a mother to
do with *that*?

When is a parent to speak up, and when are they to just let
those good ole "natural consequences" take over? And why, when
we speak of "natural consequences," do we use this term to mean
"Mother Nature will give your child a come-to-Jesus moment?"
Also, how many times are these consequences actually natural?
What people call natural consequences are actually often quite
preventable. In the name of letting a child experience "natural
consequences," I wonder if we are actually teaching them not to
ask for support, lest they be deemed some sort of natural consequence dodger. Yes, kids need to learn to solve problems, but
sometimes problems get solved by effing *asking for help*.

Take Marci again, for instance. My youngest is blessed with
my love of philosophical conversation. They live to make art.
They live in the world of words. And they struggle with this
little thing called keeping track of their things. About twice
a month, I receive a variation on this text: "Mom, I am really
sorry. I left my PE shoes at home. If you have time, would you
mind bringing them?"

Natural consequences parenting would encourage me to
respond, "Looks like you won't have your PE shoes today." The
thing is, not having those shoes is *not* an actual natural consequence. I mean, sure, shoes left at home are going to remain at
home. They won't magically transport themselves to my kid's
school. But neither does forgetting shoes at home need to be
some big moral brouhaha. What if, instead of allowing "natural consequence," I teach my kid that as their mother, I actually
enjoy supporting them? What if I say, "Let me check my schedule. If I can swing it, I definitely will. Love you." What if a natural consequence of living in community is that the community
does not expect perfection of people who are literally not adults
and whose bodies are mainlining puberty hormones?

Funny thing is, my kid hasn't become some entitled teen

monarch, sitting on their iron throne and demanding "Bring me my shoes!" They are grateful. In fact, they have recently started leaving their shoes in my Jeep so that they are unforgettable. They don't do this because I told them to.

Still, I don't think I've yet reached the closest approximation in my power to normal, caring, untraumatized, regular-vigilant parenting. I could be accused of having a martyr complex when it comes to my kids. I don't think so. I think that my kids just actually deserve a bit of reparenting. Here's why: The truth is that my PTSD did likely fuck up my kids. When they were younger, they missed out on some crucial aspects of parenting. First, they got Fundamomalist, then they got a mother who was simultaneously grieving, deconstructing from authoritarian fundamentalism, and dismantling their entire support system in order to maintain their sanity. I call that period The Great Unmooring: I had unmoored my ship from the shores of existential certitude, and I was paddling through an ocean of doubt and unprocessed grief. I was doing my best . . . and my kids deserved better. (Also, Lunchables were my friend.) Reparenting reparations are in order.

How much damage was done? In what ways? Fuck if I know. I'm not doing research here. I am living this phase of my parenting life *right now*, even as I try to document what doing the work of healing looks like. A storm swept through my home. A rupture occurred. I am not qualified to understand all the ways that my kids' psychological safety might have been compromised by my own ineptness. I am just rebuilding, trying to repair the psychological rupture that threatens not just my but my kids' ability to dream. How am I doing this? One road trip and heart-to-heart at a time. Do you see why I need Gigi to effing work, now?

I am not completely out of The Great Unmooring, but I am much more comfortable dog-paddling through the open sea. I no longer expect to one day land on a distant shore called Certitude. Instead, I put in at little ports where my own

Aunt Beasts reside. Remember Aunt Beast, the creature who cured Meg with her warmth in *A Wrinkle in Time*? I think we all need a few Aunt Beasts to soothe us.

I have a few—people who, rather than attempting to help me know how it all works, are content to simply know me. One Aunt Beast shares her extra Hello Fresh meals with me and lets me lay my head in their lap while I whine about how my life is just oh so hard. She just strokes my tangled curls and says, "I wish it wasn't so hard, too." Another Aunt Beast swaddles me in poetry of Louise Glück while we drink Topo Chico on his front porch. One of them buys me an "Elijah candle" to light when I need to slip into nostalgia. Mostly, my Aunt Beasts don't put a timeline on my healing. Years ago, an Aunt Beast biked me to yoga and made me watch all of *Battlestar Galactica* while I picked up the shards of my shattered beliefs. All of my Aunt Beasts mostly just let me be. They parent me so that I can try to repair the damage that fundamentalism and life's garden-variety hard knocks have wrought.

They also don't shame me for how I parent now, which is to say, as best and presently as I can. Last time I checked, the therapist who champions self-care isn't offering to come do the dishes.

It's easy to wave the self-care flag in a single parent's face when you are witnessing their struggle from the outskirts of the parenting arena. Bystanders cry "boundaries" like a ref hollering "Safe!" when a runner slides into homebase. My sometimes therapist, who is actually quite wonderful, used to end each of our sessions by telling me to take care of myself. I'd smile and think, "Shut up. I am literally being a mother-warrior right now." This mother's weapons consist of dinners on the ground in my too small apartment, late-night listening sessions, about 5,379 frozen pizzas, and an absolute unwavering commitment to create beauty out of the ashes of the fundamentalist hellscape of trauma that made me.

We are quick to say "family first," but what does that phrase actually mean when a kid is unpacking trauma, or learning what it really means to work with a neurodivergent brain, or just in need of a soft place to land? It means time, and lots of it. Time spent listening is time spent not doing something else. It's that simple. So when one of my kids needs to talk, I try to be available to listen. If I am codependent because my well-being is tied to the well-being of my living kids, so be it. If I come in swift and soft, it is only because I am trying to counterbalance the constrictive, authoritarian parenting methods in which I formerly trafficked. Doing so might be my real life's work. It's incredibly rewarding, and it is every bit as exhausting as middle-of-the-night feedings once were.

So, therapist, you can talk to me about self-care when you've got some skin in the game. When you are in my kitchen on your hands and knees, wondering from whence that weird stank emanates, or sweeping up kitty litter at midnight after you co-regulated with my trans kid who is freaking out because their ability to medically transition is being threatened by a regime that calls the assault on queer people's bodies "family values," you can share your self-care wisdom with me. Are you planning to be around when something preventable befalls one of my kids that I foresaw and didn't mention? Are you going to sit with me and help me clean up the pieces when a kid tells me that their mental health is in the toilet?

Sans action, cries for self-care amount to little more than thoughts and prayers. Bring over a battle lasagna and some kinda of booze. Then we'll talk.

Currently, my parenting is both intense and gentle, guided by these ideas:

1. Your emotions are welcome in this house.
   All of them.

2. It is okay not to be okay.

3. It's okay to not be okay *with me.*

4. Conflict doesn't shut down communication, or affection, or your rights or thoughts or anything. Navigated with care, conflict can actually lead to good things. We will find our way through.

5. You have inner wisdom, and you are *learning* to use it.

6. Parents are human. When we mess up, we need to repair the rift.

7. Sometimes I am not okay, and that is not your fault. You don't need to fix it.

8. You don't have to be on the fast track to "success." Be on *your* track.

9. Let's not think about what you "should" do in this situation. Instead ask, "What would nurture my soul? What feels like healing?"

10. Newsflash: You can ask for help *before* you are in crisis.

11. Independence is not the goal. Nor is it even possible. Inter*dependence* is where it's at.

12. You can quit things that don't work for you. You don't have to gut it out. This won't turn you into a narcissist. It will equip you to care for yourself (and others).

13. Nothing about you is evil—not your music, not your desires, not your thoughts, and certainly not your identity.

14. You haven't been angry in a bit. You all right?

Number fourteen is super important for a family of kids who were once taught that anger is a four-letter word. When I was Fundamomalist, repression and submission were the tools of the trade to deal with this "negative emotion." Learning that anger is not negative but in fact instructive when it comes to figuring out our desires, needs, and dreams is an ongoing process.

I do still have a bit of "ten-hut" in me, but I try to only use that energy when danger or discipline is called for. When the family returned to New Orleans after Hurricane Ida, the apartment had clearly succumbed to the humidity of a Louisiana August sans air conditioner. The result? Surface mold on the carpets and chairs. We were lucky, all things considered. But after driving home in Labor Day traffic and arriving around 10:00 p.m., nobody felt like dealing with the situation, but there was nowhere else to sleep that night. When I insisted that we get to work making two rooms habitable, I met with a bit of exhausted resistance.

I tried to be gentle, but then the Southern Woman in me took over. I felt the blood of both my grandmothers coursing through my wrists as I commanded: "It's time to work. We are cleaning these rooms tonight. You think I like it either? My room is the worst, and I will be sleeping on the floor of your bedroom. We are *doing* this." I even brought in every mother's favorite twist-your-kid's-arm tool: a good old-fashioned guilt trip. "You think this is bad? People lost *everything* in Katrina . . . . like some did in *this* storm. Let's not conflate discomfort with *disaster*. You can sit on the bayou and cry about it later, but right now, it's time to clean."

So, *that* might not have been my finest parenting moment, y'all. Or maybe it was. Do we really even know what our finest parenting moments are? We just love to measure and rank things in the West. And parenting doesn't get a pass from this hyperfixation. (See? *Hyper.* Not good, y'all.) Some people would say I was just leaning into my masculine energy and helping my kids do what needed to be done in a crisis. Others would say I could have slowed down a little bit and made room for them to process their emotions before moving out the moldy ottoman. I say I was tired AF and doing my best to make a call in the moment. I drew upon my Alabama roots of folks who work hard to overcome and don't make a big deal about it.

And I trusted that we would be able to talk about it later. Which we did. We do. With laughter. The point is not whether or not I got the gig exactly right at that moment. The point is that I trusted our relationship and knew that I had a bank of relational capital with my kids that I could draw from. We are learning. Me from my kids and my kids from me.

The above vignette represents times when I have played the parent card, but it's a card I hold in reserve. It does rest upon some felt sense of "I am the adult here, and I am taking charge. Fall in line." But in most cases, this authoritative approach to parenting feels downright icky to me. Collaboration and cooperation feel more true to my proclivities as a human and to my kids' development. What no one tells you about parenting that loses the top-down approach is that it takes, once again, a fuck-ton of time. Training up kids to be soldiers involves a time-sink up front, but once the kids are trained (gross), you speak and they obey. Pretty simple. But parenting in creative collaboration with a child's spirit, parenting them toward dreaming, is anything but.

Parenting toward dreaming involves listening. It involves getting out of efficiency mode. It involves entering into the child's world. When you are still navigating your own trauma and suspect your kids are doing the same, prepare for some middle-of-the-day drives where you shut the fuck up and listen. . . . Bring Kleenex. Stop and grab a coffee for you and your near-grown kid. Drive nowhere in particular. Hand them the Spotify reins and let them play their comfort songs.

This is not your teachable moment, parent. This is not your time to offer your unbidden "wisdom." When they start sharing the inner recesses of their heart, don't say anything but "That's beautiful, darling. More of that please." Whether those inner recesses are full of rage at everything they missed out on, or anxiety about their crush, or fear that their identity is being legislatively assaulted—whatever their sorrow, just listen. Open up a spacious place in your soul that is able to hold your child's words. And just know that this act of healing listening is not going to happen on your timetable. You may have to cancel a meeting or lose a little bit of professional *whatever*.

At least, that's how it has worked for me. We joke about scheduling our breakdowns, but like Gigi, our hearts seem to run on their own schedule. I am about this critical work of restoring and maintaining a sense of psychological safety.

I call upon the words of Christ here: "What does it profit a man if he gains the whole world and loses his soul?" (Mark 8:36). My soul will not be right if my kids are not more or less okay. I am not talking about the regular ups and downs of adolescence. (Of course, nowadays, those seem to include worrying about the literal end of the world due to climate change.) I am talking about when a heart missile scuttles my child's ability to dream. I am talking about healing family trauma *in the family itself*. Sure, a child can go on and find their way to healing without ever addressing issues that hurt them with a family member. Oftentimes solo healing is necessary, but isn't it better, especially when dreams are on the line, for the line of repair to be direct? Trauma happens in relationships. Trauma is healed in relationships. If that healing comes with a literal price tag of less money or fewer promotions, so be it.

I am willing to pay this price. I figure that later on—like when I am eighty three—I can focus more on my career. Perhaps this view is controversial, but if a job doesn't work with the needs of my family, I quit. If I sense that I am about to lose my sanity because I am doing too much and I can't find a way to pull back from a job, I leave. Period. And sometimes I do it without notice. I think of this trade-off as a resource switch. I'm from the poor, rural South, and my mama taught me how to stretch a dollar. I will always make sure that our basic needs are met, but I will also choose to be rich in time if I see that the eyes of my child are growing dim. Protect the dreaming. Protect the healing. Give the time. Sorry, any future employers, it really is family first around here.

I sensed a change was going to be needed in late 2019. It seemed to me that Navis, who was living up North at the time, was having a rough go of it. Truth be told, I wasn't too happy living one thousand miles away from them, either. Mothers know things. Like old-timers who sniff the wind and know that some weather is about to roll in, mothers sense when a storm is brewing in their child's heart.

In fall of 2019, my gut told me that a storm was coming. My child needed me in some way that was beyond my means to deliver if I stayed tethered to a local job. I needed it too. I was exactly one semester into this job, which was a local gig at my alma mater. The decision to leave wasn't entirely con-scious, and I didn't so much make it as it made me. In the words of my own song, "Sometimes your heart walks right in and makes up your mind." So, I quit my university job between semesters, most likely burning a professional bridge.

Relief that I could morph into "Mobile-Mom," armed with a laptop and a fully remote job, flooded my middle-aged bones. I was ready to fold up the highway and head north as often as possible to tend to my kid's, well . . . whatever came up. Then a lovely event known as "The World is Going to Shit, March 2020" occurred. So, instead of flying across the country, I found myself completely cut off from physical contact. What the actual fuck, universe? Down in Ft. Richter, I paced in my lair, knowing that Navis was in pain and feeling pretty damn helpless.

Everyone knows what early Covid was. We know it writ large even as we all lived our own sequestered stories. For my part, I had long been disabused of all "it happens to other people, but not to me" exceptionalist notions. I stared down my own mid-life mortality in ways that perhaps others who hadn't faced a truly against-all-odds, perfect storm type of death didn't. Not once but twice my kids experienced this type of perfect storm; once it ended in a death and the other time in an emergency delivery of a son who simply did not breathe when he was born.

He made it and is fine, but I have never forgotten what it was like to have doctors tell you that something is growing inside of your newborn, making its home between your child's spine and aorta. "No, it's not operable. No, we don't know if it's an aggressive tumor or a benign little bit of blood vessels. I guess we'll just have to watch it for like, oh, you know, two years or so and keep you posted."

I remember figuring when Covid hit that I could easily be taken from my kids. And when children started getting very sick with Covid-mediated hyperinflammation, it took all of my rational powers to stave off the message gut's trauma response: "Don't quote me the odds." It certainly wasn't all lemon drops and family nights with *Bob's Burgers* within the confines of Ft. Richter.

Of course, we all seem to have moved on from the over seven million deaths, each representing someone's child, great aunt, sister.[29] I understand that we need movement in order to heal, but these people did not beat the odds. Where is the national day of mourning for their loss? What potential did the world lose? Moreover, it's not like the world was all coming up roses prior to the pandemic.

My kids are coming of age in the Age of Anxiety, and their fears are founded. Young climate activist Greta Thunberg urged us all pre-pandemic: "I want you to feel the fear I feel every day. And then I want you to act. I want you to act as you would in a crisis."[30] Of course, Thunberg was referencing the mother of all dream-killers, climate change. Her anxiety is warranted, and so is that of my own offspring. Their world is inhabited by bogeymen and about a million reasons to feel anxious. This coming-of-age milieu seems to be branded with that word or its less turbulent cousin, "languishing." My heart is broken in a thousand ways when I observe Zoomers being shamed as lazy or noncommittal. This is simply not true. These kids are simply acting like we're in the midst of a worldwide crisis—because we are.

In response, Thunberg has taken up the activist's call. This work always involves a dialectic: activists are both afraid and dreaming. Their dreams may not be for an ideal outcome but to move the needle of the cause by a millimeter, to wake people up. Thunberg is discomfiting because she won't shut up about the problem. She won't let adults ignore what should not be ignored. She will not be quieted. Good on her for finding agency and perhaps hope in the dark. In her book *Hope In the Dark*, Rebecca Solnit quotes these words by Virginia Woolf: "The future is dark, which is, on the whole, the best thing a future can be, I think."[31] Activists engage in defiant dreaming. They grab that dark future by the balls and begin marching light toward the world which they stubbornly envision. They do this without knowing the outcome. That's bravery. That's dreaming. That's being alive.

The reason I'm attempting to not let my PTSD fuck up my kids (too badly) is because I believe in healing. I may not ever be entirely healed from losing Elijah. I don't suspect I will. Or maybe I haven't had access to the right resources. Or maybe part of me wants to cuddle up with my loss because I falsely believe it connects me to my son. Who knows? But maybe I can be a wounded healer. Maybe I can facilitate healing not from some far-off temple, wishing everyone love and light. Maybe I can teach from the middle of the mess. Maybe my wounded healing can engender a bit of courage, and maybe that courage can infuse the anemic dreams of a few with some enthusiasm.

What if, instead of waiting for some sense of closure about all that has transpired, I can dream dreams from the middle of my own mess?

What I dream for my kids now is what I want for myself: healing. I want continued healing so that my kids can dream. I want them to flex their dreaming-and-doing muscles. I want them to find their own places in the world with people who love them. I want them to flourish and feel safe. But most of all, I want them to jump out of the plane and hang-glide on the wind of their own dreams.

Please kids, please. Please dream. Dream big and deep or small and intimate or supple and sensual. Dream of video games or grandeur, of getting rich (but don't be a dick about it) or living in a wilderness yurt. Eat ambrosia. Or Tofurky. Or, worse, Vienna sausages. Okay, don't eat those because they are not food. Just dream a good dream for your life and go about making that dream come true. May some of your dreams exist, as theologian Frederick Buechner advocated, at the intersection of your great joy and the world's great need—but may some of them be just for you alone, held in the intimacy of your heart. Water your dreams with kindness, and don't demand that they provide you with what the world calls success. Dream dreams that let you live in your skin with a sense of abundance. Dream dreams that water your spirit. Dream dreams that connect you to your truest self and to your neighbor.

And when life surprises you, as it will, when the wrecking ball of loss demolishes a dream, have the courage to dream a new dream. Perhaps it will be a small dream at first: a garden, an oil painting, an exquisite meal of beans and rice on the bayou. May your hearts house dreams even if your houses are never tidy, or your bank accounts large. May your dreams give you courage to face some demons you didn't even know you housed. May you find some wonderful dream-weaving companions with whom you will jostle and joyride. Most of all, may you find a dream that lets you know that you belong in this world just as you are. May you continually unwind from your mind any vestiges of the lies you were told as children, for your hearts are good, good, good, my children.

I am here to help you dream. I know that my job is not to keep you close but to help you know that if your dreaming wings have been clipped, you can regrow them. Sure, they may look a little different than if they had emerged from hearts that had not been wounded, by me, by fundamentalism, by the times into which you were born—but those wings can still have lift. My dream is that I have done enough and done it with enough care that you will dream lives that you can't wait to wake up to.

None of your dreams will go as planned. I won't offer you bullshit couched as wisdom and say, "But it's better that way." Because sometimes broken dreams threaten to break our spirits. This is why we need dreamkeepers who will put a splint to our wings and sing to us the songs of the brokenhearted. So, in your dreaming, I only ask that you surround yourself with people who will commune with you in your dreams and invite you to commune in theirs. May they be your home even as I have tried to show you what home can be like, even if home is messy and cramped and we only have one bathroom and never enough privacy. May you dream of home, may you make it.

And can I come visit sometime when I am old and need to dream a few more dreams while I sit on a rocking chair on your porch? And can I hold your babies and look on in awe at the life you dreamed? This is what my heart needs, not a fat retirement plan, not a huge "impact," not accolades. I don't want to be special. I don't want to live "large." I want to have the simple privilege of beholding the dreams each of you weave.

That is my dream.

Hadestown was Heaven

The house is so full right now, fuller than it has been in decades. Navis, Ada, Marci, and all our felines are living it up in an apartment situated under James' lovely large, mid-1920s home in Bayou St. John. We are tucked away, ensconced in a basement apartment that I mistakenly thought would be a home of one—a little writer's refuge from which I would exist, more or less, in solitude.

I began preparations for the move into my little nook of a place in September of 2020, but I had first met my home-to-be earlier that year, during lockdown. Needing a place to work remotely while my brood occupied Ft. Richter, I reached out to James. He lent me a key; I was grateful. Laden with laptop, electric kettle, and tea, I trekked across the neighborhood to perform my patchwork quilt of remote jobs.

The place wasn't much to look at. It had been partially renovated by James and, I think, his first wife of forty years ago. Renters had come and gone through the years, leaving various accouterments scattered throughout the rooms. It had, back in the day, been the home to some ragers. At least, that's what I pictured. Each day, I plopped down on the red velvet couch and did what we all did during the early days of 2020: act like work was normal while scores of people were dying. I hated it. I hated having to trudge through pages of dissertations and spreadsheets while the world was in such pain.

When that phase of lockdown ended, I figured my days with the red couch were done. I returned to working from my two-bedroom shotgun. By all measures, the shotgun apartment is nicer. Finished. Spacious. Steps away from Jazz Fest. Importantly, this more modern home possessed two necessities I swore I would never live without again: a dishwasher and en-suite laundry.

The problem with dreamers is that we see the potential in everything. Back in my actual, sensible apartment near Esplanade, I dreamt of James' little basement abode. I realized then how I'd failed to notice that I was noticing its potential. Bit by bit, I'd begun to admire the way the light filtered through the French doors in the red couch room. I'd appreciated the patina of the old clawfoot tub that I had taken to bathing in. I'd eyed the fingers of exposed beams and felt the comfort of the cool concrete floors contrasting with the hot humidity.

Mostly though, I'd noticed the serene quiet. The house had the feel of a place that could tell stories, but was keeping its trap shut. I imagined musicians rendezvousing in this space, certain that some LSD had been dropped there in the seventies, maybe some jazz written under its influence. I hadn't consciously known it, but something about this home's imagined, slightly wild history implanted itself in me. When I would visit, the silence was palpable—except for when the sounds of James' playing would waft down through the wood floors. James has the focus of a musician who knows that it is his job to wake up and compose as surely as it was my job to wade through scores of dissertation manuscripts. His ministrations tempered the studies I was helping to shape.

When one guides research, one quickly learns the language of problem framing. Social research is almost always nested in real world problems: the achievement gap, underrepresentation of women in STEM, teacher attrition. As I waded through literature reviews about just about every societal ill one could fathom, I would be jarred from my reading by a riff that took flight into the experimental. My researchers were planning the harmonics of their research, and each word would be tested by an audience of doctoral committee members, many of whom knew less about research and writing than me. I would dutifully help them conform to the expectations of their committee so that they could emerge newly minted doctors in education, psychology, and healthcare.

Meanwhile, James transgressed the boundaries of trad jazz again and again, tromping through harmonies that my ears could not quite place. I was jealous of his freedom to stand above me, the dissertation consultant, and write whatever the eff flew from his fingers. Jealous, in awe, and grateful.

Though I was fond of this little haunt, I had no plans to inhabit it, which is the surest sign that I would one day inhabit it. In fall of 2020, I found myself living alone. The older kids had moved out over the summer, relocating to a small college town in North Carolina where jobs awaited. Suddenly the two bedrooms loomed large. The rent seemed impractical. And, I dreamed of traveling to where my four kids now lived. Instead of evenings with my children all nestled around my kitchen table, I pictured myself jet-setting across the country to their respective tables—weekends split between New Orleans, North Carolina, and up North, where Navis and Marci were living.

I called James. Without hesitation, he offered it to me, and I know he did it out of love for me and my family. That's what James does. He acts with love and no strings. His offering was no small gift to me: the rent was cheap. Move in would be immediate. I rented out my old place and called in the help of friends to pack it up and help me make the new home habitable.

I started with the trash, of which there was plenty. The home had no built-in kitchen, and the room that would become one contained many things that were not ideal, like the seat of a minivan. Whose? No idea. Old paint cans and plastic tarps hearkened back to home improvement projects long since abandoned. A metal shelf held an assortment of screws, paint cans, and CDs. What was this place? Treasure lay amongst the trash: ornate chopsticks, an original Fats Waller poster. The real find was the dark-stained drop-leaf table, which I just knew would become my writer's desk. I envisioned many quiet evenings at that desk, the solitude of my new dwelling forcing me to create. It was a solitude I didn't particularly want, but I was sure going to make verbal lemonade out of it.

I carried loads and loads of trash out of that room and others. Friends pitched in to help paint. On Marci's recommendation, I purchased a steam mop, then bought the largest shag carpets I could find to cover the mahogany-painted floors. What goes with mahogany-painted concrete? Turns out, nothing. But no worries. I cleaned each of the exposed beams by hand, removing grime and impregnating the wood with the best mold-remediation products I could find. Dank, musty odors were replaced with new smells: Murphy's Oil Soap, freshly steeped tea. It was a work in progress, but the place was coming alive.

Two days before I was set to move in, I received this plot twister of a text message: "Have you heard from Navis today?"

I had—in the form of an earlier text asking whether or not I would be willing to cosign on an apartment for them. Navis was seventeen, an early graduate of the Covid senior year high school class. You know, the one that got royally effed over and didn't get to have a normal prom, or graduation, or much of anything? Of course you do. These losses are not lost life— and, if you are seventeen, and it's your last year not only of high school but life as you've thus far known it, they are going to matter. More than one thing can be sad at a time.

I knew the year had been hard on Navis, and I knew that I wanted closer contact. Still, I tried not to think too much about these texts. After all, I was about to become jet-setting, middle-aged, writing Mom of the Bohemian Bungalow, right? I needed to get moved, settled, and start planning spacious, totally non-urgent trips, yes?

Yeah-no. What I needed to do was drop all my belongings

in my new digs and get on a plane. Immediately.

For reasons that shall remain private, it turned out that Navis had departed from home unannounced. There is a word for those who do this type of leaving: runaways. I had a hard time wrapping my head around the fact that I was a parent of a kid who had run away from home. The whole situation was scary but also legally complicated. Given that Navis was seventeen, they existed in a sort of legal limbo: Running away from home was illegal, but seemingly unenforceable.

Navis was in contact with me and okayed a visit, so I booked a ticket and locked the door to my apartment. The place was far from turnkey. It was disheveled, half-finished, packed to the gills with too many belongings.

Two days after receiving the plot-twisting text, I landed up North and drove my rental car to Navis's small city, which I figured I would hate. But it's hard to hate the Midwest in the fall. The northern air is crisp. Apple cider is literally everywhere. In the Midwest, fall is actually fall. So I wasn't padding around barefoot on my newly ordered shag carpets; I was suddenly thrust into sweater weather, albeit under less than ideal circumstances.

After I landed, the buzzer in my belly turned into a homing beacon. I just needed to see Navis. I didn't arrive in the land of apple pie in order to grill them. I didn't fly north on the cusp of the anniversary of Elijah's passing to judge whether or not Navis had justifiable cause to run away. My job was twofold: a.) hear out my kid's heart and b.) get my kid out of runaway status. The order didn't really matter. Part c.)—get them to return to New Orleans with me—was a little more aspirational.

Our reunion took place at a Hungry Howie's.

Navis, who was on shift, greeted me cheerfully enough, but they had the lean look of a haunted thing. A waif. There was something very *Oliver Twist* about their visage. Or maybe it was more *Into the Wild*. There was a jumpiness to them, like a small animal that had just escaped one of those snapping traps and had been scampering through the forest for days foraging for food. I felt that if I touched my child, they might bolt . . . or bite. So I allowed a calm veneer to spread across my face and greeted them.

"Hey, kid."

"Hello, Mother. Would you like to share a chicken Caesar salad with me? I have a special way that I make it."

"Sure."

So we did. We sat and ate a Hungry Howie's chicken Caesar salad in late September in a strange Northern town. We talked. We jested. A casual observer would not have noticed anything unusual. Just two people who certainly seemed related sharing a meal together. Strange, how the outsides and insides of situations can be so mismatched.

During the meal, I met the store manager, the man who had been (illegally) housing my child for the past few days. And by meet, I mean, he barely looked up and waved at me. That did not sit well with me, and I told Navis so later (that was my first mistake). It's not that I totally disliked him, for I have somehow managed to maintain my optimism about people and start them all out at one hundred percent and subtract from there. But damn, dude. Something felt off about this situation, and She-Beast was starting to sharpen her nails—and there was the rub. My cub was nearly of age—nearly of age, and had already shown a stubbornness that they surely inherited from both their German ancestors and my Southern clan. I come from a motley lot of ancestors and kin who, if not always wise, are damn sure not going to be trod upon.

Take my sister, who spent the better part of two decades working out her own salvation (from fundamentalism). She needed an ocean's width between her old life and new in order to heal. Even as I felt the pain of this separation, I always knew that she was working out some wounds and that she needed the time and space apart. Then there is this gal right here, the one munching a store-bought salad in her sweater.

She spent almost four decades entrenched in fundamentalism before choosing to dismantle her whole life—and still can't exactly pinpoint every reason for doing so.

However healthy or unhealthy our methods, I do know that Billy women don't seem to grow up gently. We have a history of pushing back *hard* as we cross into our own adulthoods. So hearing that Navis had chosen this way of individuating, while scary as hell for a mom to watch, was not completely surprising to me.

It was to the other kids. I remember Isaiah in particular exclaiming, "They did WHAT? Of all the kids, I wouldn't have thought it would be Navis." Yeah, son, there's a reason they say to look out for the quiet ones. While some family members engage in honest, old-school rebellion, some of us turn the tasks of individuation inward. Instead of risking the ire of our parents, we sit in the roiling stew of doubt and self-loathing.

I admire family members who got their individuation out of the way early. I felt no such ability. But it was not only from fear of leaving my faith. It was fear of the pain I knew my leaving would cause. I had seen my mother's sorrow over losing her other daughter to a worldview that she believed was harmful. Eventually, I could see no middle path for myself. When one is raised to think in binaries, breaking hard in one direction first is natural. The pendulum swings wide.

I wonder if Navis felt the same. If, by the time Navis's situation had reached its boiling point, they believed that only drastic measures would work. Like I said, my kin don't seem to grow up easy. The good news is that we do, eventually, grow into ourselves, and the strength that we discover by giving a big *fuck you* to, oh, just about everything that isn't our own desire for a while does serve us well. It is a strength hard won, and sometimes, we do some pretty stupid, destructive things along the way. But, hey, doesn't Kali do a bit of destroying along the way to creating drastic change?

Perhaps we are in the company of an ancient goddess who

won't be tamed. Or perhaps we should have a special diagnosis in the DSM-V: "Grows up hard no matter what." I don't know. I do know that not all kids survive their own adolescent attempts to grow up. I know that it is out of my control. And yet, I am here. I am here, hoping that some middle ground can be found.

Navis informed me that they got off at 11:00 that night, and I told them I would pick them up after work, which I did. Settling back into my rental, which I also surprisingly did not hate, I began to take stock of my surroundings. I was still recovering from the whiplash of what I thought I would be doing on this day—settling into my new digs—and what I was actually doing: sitting on a leather couch 1,100 miles away from home. It was a big ole bro-couch, the kind made for men in their mid-forties to knock back a few brewskies while watching their alma mater take on their arch-rival—yet again.

I sat alone, cupping a mug of tea and trying to catch up with myself. I noticed a crispness to the air, such a welcome respite after yet another grueling New Orleans summer. My father had been right: fall in the Midwest did indeed call the Garden of Eden to mind. I grabbed a flannel blanket to insulate myself against the leather couch and surprised myself with this thought: "I think I . . . *like* it here."

But still, edenic or not, it wasn't home. Would the apartment my seventeen-year-old wanted me to cosign for be anywhere near as comfortable as this cozy house away from home?

My musings were short-lived as I backed out of the drive and returned to the little strip mall where Navis and their too quiet boss/host were closing up shop. Navis seemed a little more settled than earlier. It wasn't until I saw them carrying out their belongings, a backpack and cardboard box filled with the sum total of what they had deemed worthy of bringing on the road with them, that my heart lurched. My child had chosen this, at age seventeen, over living in a home that I was quite sure included more fine amenities than I could ever afford. What the hell was going on here?

This is damage control, Desi. Just get your kid "home."

If there's one thing I know the look of, it's trauma, and this kid had been through some. That twitchy look of the hyper-vigilant was easy to recognize after battling my own PTSD after losing Elijah. We are all, at some point, in some measure, haunted. Each heart knows its own joy and sorrow. Has even been thus; will ever be the case. Even though we can comfort each other in those sorrows, we cannot entirely bear them.

So, here I stood with my child, a kid who I just loved as intensely as all of my children but with a special spark of joy that ignited when all nine pounds of them first arrived on the scene. Navis had always been an easy child. Ineffably quirky. Placid. We used to joke when they were a baby that their fussing (if it could be called that) had an air of "Hey, I know you are taking care of those two kids who are constantly getting into mischief, but if you could, if you don't mind, could I pretty please, you know ... *eat?*"

And eat they did. At another 11:00 p.m., seventeen years prior, Navis arrived home to our 835-square-foot Toronto loft, and they arrived hungry. I had only so much to give before my milk came in, and though I nursed them repeatedly, I spent most of their first night alternating between having the end of my middle finger suckled and giving them all the colostrum I could. Navis was my fourth child, but our table went from two kids to three when they came on the scene. Elijah had been gone for just over three years when they were born. With their arrival, the nest felt more full. And I felt lighter.

I mean that, in part, literally. With Navis, I had been very large with child, so large that a kid on the elevator unabashedly stared at my belly all twenty-three floors of our ascent.

I stared him down from over the nose of my rotund abdomen. "It's really large, isn't it?"

The kid didn't answer but gave a slight nod. I think he was scared of the giant pregnant lady.

After Navis was born, the need to roam kicked in, winter

be damned. We set off with their stroller into the Canadian tundra. Not patches of ice, snowdrifts, nor chilling cold could keep us inside. Navis slept through all these escapades, seemingly made for the wildness of winter.

And now, we were on the edge of another winter, and this kid wanted, if nothing else, to be free, free from something that I had only an inkling of understanding about.

When we arrived at the Airbnb, I helped Navis settle in.

Navis to me: "You want to hear some music?"

God, yes.

In this strange land into which both Navis and I were thrust, music was a way to kindle familiarity. Music had always been our point of reference—our go-to way to connect. This was true with all of my kids. We didn't leave home without CDs. At first, I shared my musical tastes. (Sorry about that Jason Mraz phase, kids.) But as the kids grew into their own, it was they who brought the new music to me. Isaiah got me into Logic. Ada brought in Panic! At The Disco. Marci has now infiltrated my Spotify with all manner of tunes. I might even like a few songs by vocaloids, but I won't say which ones. (Kids, if you are reading this, I will *never* like the "Two Trucks Fucking" song. Never. Eww. On so many levels. Eww).

Navis had shared their own tastes, but I wasn't as familiar with them. And in this moment, music seemed like such a welcome respite for us both.

"It's called *Hadestown*," they said.

Navis had just gotten into this musical—a masterful synthesis of musical traditions and the melding of two tragic tales: Orpheus and Eurydice and Hades and Persphone. Since leaving fundamentalism, I have accumulated quite a bit of knowledge about topics that are not Jesus or, rather, fundamentalist Jesus, but I still have holes in that knowledge base. This was one of those times where my kids helped me complete my education.

Navis filled me in on the whole Hades/Persephone spring

thing. In Anaïs Mitchell's retelling, Orpheus is a poor boy who loves Eurydice, and Eurydice ends up in the underworld not because of a serpent bite but because Hades tempts her to flee the cold. It is a winter that Hades himself has brought on by insisting that Persephone return home too soon, and Hadestown proves to be the undoing of all who enter it.

I listened, not fully entering into the musical's magic but appreciative that we were together. For the time being, my kid was safe. For then, that was enough. In hindsight, I can easily see how a kid who was going through hell on earth would be drawn to this story.

What strikes me now is that music was acting for my child in a way that it had for me many times in my life. Over the years, I have written many words about grief, but I am aware that words can only do so much. In grief, the most primal parts of ourselves emerge. Only these visceral parts of ourselves are capable of processing the rending of our soul's fabric in ways that can do that rending justice. No tome, no logic, no math can make sense of our insides being torn asunder. Music transcends the words and carries us right to the depths of our longing.

I didn't fully understand then how important music was to Navis, but I think now that it might have saved them. Faced with the prospect of leaving behind both their childhood and their home, this kid was doing their own music therapy. They found comfort in the ancient, and not just in any ancient: in tragedy.

Wow.

The most gut-wrenching sequence in Hadestown is when Orpheus and Eurydice begin the ascent out of hell. They are given permission to leave—on one condition: They can have no physical contact with each other. No comforting hands. No words of care. They are permitted to walk the road out of Hadestown together, alone. All of this is taking place against the backdrop of a reprise—Euridice intoning Orpheus to wait for her. Though Euridice pleads, Orpheus cannot hear her. He only hears the Fates questioning his ability to lead. The walk was rigged by Hades as sure as the snake's gambit with Adam and Eve was.

It ends, as we know it will, with Orpheus turning back to see if Eurydice is still with him only to hear the door of a boxcar slam. Eurydice is already being ferried back to Hadestown. The audience is slain by the loss. But we relate to the words, a call for connection as simple and plaintive as God's asking Adam and Eve "Where are you?" in the Garden: *Wait for me, I'm coming!*

"Wait for me, I'm coming!" I call to my kids as I try to catch up to parenting without dogma. "Show me the way!"

But what of Navis, and Hungry Howie's, and the wintry North? After a few more plot twists, my kid did land at home in New Orleans. And when *Hadestown* landed at the Saenger for the holidays, I got tickets.

The gift almost didn't happen. Tickets were pricey, and trying to schedule with the out-of-town friend who was planning to accompany us proved a little tricky. But several trips down the Stubhub aisle later, I emerged with three little balcony right seats. At the last minute, the friend couldn't come, so Navis and I donned our theater best and headed out for the spectacle.

It seemed the whole city needed a night out. Ah, yes, here was my New Orleans, with the ladies done up and the men donning red velvet jackets and vests.

I had told Navis before we went that the night would be life-changing. Little did I know that the magic would find us both. The tale was retold as can only happen in real time on the stage. We were far away by Saenger standards, but the Saenger is not large, and from our vantage point the stage framed the unfolding drama so well. Such a story of heartbreak needed some sort of container or it would be too much to bear. The play opens with something that we could all be second-lining to: the 'bone blows, the musicians are part of the story, set up on risers at the back of the stage. One of the Fates plays an accordion. It was Acadiana meets Jazz Fest meets Ibycus. And I think Ibycus would have been pleased.

I don't know how to encapsulate what it felt like to be enraptured. But seeing this retelling felt like more than a mother and child taking in a show for a Christmas present. It was catharsis in the truest sense of the word. So much of the premise of the play is that the earth's troubles are a direct result of the gods forgetting. In this case, it was Hades' forgetting of the song that split his heart open with love for Persephone. But Orpheus has found that song and offers it to Hades, rending it up in floaty high notes that *Les Misérables'* original Valjean, Colm Wilkinson, would be jealous of. Orpheus was sung by a seventeen-year-old kid. I am not kidding. And this kid sang the stars off the ceiling of the Saenger.

More salient, though, is that he sang Navis's slender shoulders into silent little sobs. He laid open their pain. It was not Hades' song that was remembered in that moment; it was Navis's, it was humanity's. And it was mine. All of the pain, the sense that the world has just been too damn much for the past two years and then some, finally found a place to be unpent. Up in that upper balcony, row W, seats two and four, I clasped Navis's hand. Those slender fingers entwined with mine, and we wept. We wept for it all, for Orpheus, for Hades' amnesiac heart, for our own forgetting, for our own heartbreaks. It was a deep well of sorrow that Orpheus's song tapped. And as we watched him sing from the depths of Hades, we were reminded again that there is always a way out; that those who climb out of hell do not do so unscathed; that even though Orpheus was ultimately unable to overcome his own demons, thereby dooming Eurydice all over again, still, he sang.

The play ends by winding up the tale all over again, as if the gods somehow knew that more important than the ending is the living. This is what *Hadestown* taught me. What happened that night cannot be summed up in a neat little essay about the power of art. *Hadestown* didn't really fix anything. But it provided a space for the unspeakable to live. It did remind me that this is what art can do. It reminded me of why music is as vital as plasma and as rich. It told me that I am part of the family of humans who have loved, who keep sinning and singing, who do not dare to stop doing so. It made me so happy to cry. It made me so hopeful that I can have a good life. In spite of it all. Because of it all. It made me want to dream of some sort of healing for this world even though I will never see that work completed in my life. It was the medicine that I needed. I couldn't have known that going in, but perhaps the gods did.

I dream of being a healer, to myself and others. Music is my medicine, and judging by Navis's response, it is theirs too, or perhaps theater's.

When we left, they said, "I want to do something like that." Now, this is something I have felt about Navis for a while. About all of my kids, actually. They have the hearts of artists. And you know what? So do I. Even as we drove around town and talked about a melancholy song of heartbreak, Navis shared their musings. I said, "You do realize that not everyone does this, right?"

Hadestown was heaven. And in that heaven, I heard the fullness of my kid's heart.

That was almost two years ago, and we continue to walk the healing road. Navis is stage managing a set of Tennessee Williams plays at school. Another plot twist: Another of my grown children has decided to come home and walk their own road of healing. The basement-garrett that I thought would hold one now holds four. On this path, we all hear each other quite well through the thin walls. At night I text: "Going to bed and requesting quiet." We all take to the bayou to find respite. Or we take to the third spaces of the city.

My drop-leaf table became not a writer's desk but a coffee station that greets visitors. James still practices not dutifully but with the frenzy of a fiend who knows they've got the shit and are gonna share it. So, no, the Bohemian Bungalow isn't exactly host to my vision of the artist in self-chosen solitude. But it *is* the home of a different, more collaborative kind of art, the art of living and healing that can only happen in concert with loved ones: making home together. Choosing home together. We fuss about laundry and who's doing the cat litter. We just decided to start a family movie night.

What has surprised me most about this healing tapestry is that I once had the audacity to think I was going to be some purveyor of healing. I was going to lead the way out of *Hadestown*. As it turns out, nothing could be further from the truth. My kids being near for this time has healed me. And I don't mean that in a direct or concerted way. I am healed osmotically by their presence—and when it is time for them unfurl from our little nest, I will move the writer's desk back to the big room, probably long for the nights when the house was too loud, and make a cat cuddle with me.

I think those days are still a bit in the future, so for now, I will welcome the afternoon and remember another truth about the road to healing from *Hadestown*, sung by none other than Hermes himself. The most important road we walk is the one between our ears. The road of our mind can be one of our own making or undoing. Hadestown and Heaven are within our grasp on a given moment every single day. We create them for ourselves and extend them to the ones we love.

The road I am walking has at times felt very lonesome, but my little family, living it up down low in the basement, reminds me that I am not walking it alone. In some ways, my kids are farther along the healing path than me. That road can be mapped in conversations where they are leading me to new ways of thinking and being.

Wait for me, I'm comin, kids. And I'm gonna keep coming, and comin', and coming down the road that lies between my ears and behind my eyes. That is my promise. I'll keep chipping away at the beliefs that got built between my ears before I knew better, and I'll keep forging new neural connections that tell a better story about this life than the one we were handed. In this new story, we are not broken, just dinged up a bit, and so, so worthy of holding each others' hands on the road out of hell.

Sad Hour:
This Round's on Me

I know that whoever Elijah would have become remains mostly unknowable to me. I know this because I have been constantly surprised over who my living children are becoming. I can backtrack and see the seeds of their temperaments at play, but really, the whole human forming thing is pretty much a mystery to me even though I have watched four of them get pretty grown in front of my eyes.

One thing I feel pretty certain of, though, is that Elijah would have loved music. How do I know this? Because Elijah *loved* music. His little toddler heart moved to the beat of all the music we shared with him.

One of my favorite memories of Elijah is him stomping down the oaken hallway of The Vintage Home by the Park, which is what we called our home in Florida. It was really more like a toddler-sized gallup stomp. Elijah rocked his way down the hallway, planting the heels of his feet as loudly as he could on the oak planks. There was an intention to his movement that seemed to extend beyond being as loud as a little boy could be.

Perplexed, I asked: "What are you doing, Elijah?"

"I play Oh-No," he replied, literally without missing a beat. "Ohhhhhhh."

"Oh, No!" was a song from the very popular Evangelical cartoon series *VeggieTales*. In this particular scene, evil anthropomorphized leeks walk to this beat as they plot the demise of a young man named Daniel. At least, I think they are leeks. Marci thinks they are celery. We shall not let this important disagreement come between us. At any rate, these rap*scallions* sing a banger of a Christian ditty as they scheme against Daniel—*the* Daniel. You remember the guy? The one who ends up in the lions' den for refusing to pray to a king? Yeah. That one. Anyhoo.

Apropos to this memory is the fact that the song opened with a heck of syncopated drum solo. It was this solo that Elijah was attempting to recreate via the pounding of his feet. Elijah did this because he was a musical kid. He loved this song, just like he loved all the songs on our CD player. That small player sat atop my childhood piano. Whenever we arrived home from an outing, the first words out of Elijah's mouth were, without fail: "D? Oh please." It took a minute for me to realize that he meant "Play a CD? Oh please." Understand that the word "hyperfixation" does not do the frequency of this request justice.

Elijah had no nuanced vocabulary to describe the songs he heard. So, he parsed them into two categories: slow and fast. When he asked for songs, he would ask for a slow one and then another slow one. How about a fast one to mix up the pace? In this way, our little DJ filled the house with music.

Toddlers love repetition. Like G. K. Chesterson's toddler version of God raising the sun each day just for fun, Elijah curated the same set list over and over. What we found monotonous, he found infinitely fascinating. Good on him.

In the immediate wake of his loss, it is no surprise that I listened to all of his songs on repeat, sucking the marrow out of that music even as the memories of Elijah's interface with those songs began to fade. Still, nothing connects me to Elijah like hearing his songs. After a while, I kept them tucked away, revisiting them only on his anniversaries.

I was a little surprised when new songs started coming. I

had written a song or two in my life, but around a decade after Eijah passed, the muse found me. At first, I hoped for commercial success, but these songs just didn't feel like the stuff hits would be made of. I tried making an EP of my music and found the process exhilarating. To create in this way felt like life returning to some part of my psyche. But the songs never went anywhere much, and that's okay.

Then, yet another crop emerged. These songs felt like a direct working out of an issue. They are a song cycle.

Song cycles predate concept albums by roughly a century. The first recognized song cycle is credited to Beethoven (of course it is) and was composed in 1816. *An die ferne Geliebte* contained the traits for what would eventually become codified into the form—that is, "three or more clearly individual songs with related tonicities and a central poetic theme."[32] I haven't listened to it yet, but given that the title translates to "To the Distant Beloved," I am going to guess that the central theme is not super upbeat. Each of the six songs render the speaker's longing for the beloved via an interplay with the pastoral:

> *These breezes will playfully caress*
> *Your cheek and breast,*
> *Toying with your silken locks.*
> *If I could but share this pleasure!*[33]

Nailed it.

I didn't set out to write a song cycle about grief, just like I didn't set out to write a book about living with loss, but it appears that is exactly what I did. The songs are less of a window into the private yearnings of bereaved parents than these essays; strangely, they took on an instructional tone. I am reminded of bereaved parent Colin Campbell's instructions in his brilliant essay in *The Atlantic*: "Never say, 'There are no words' to the Grieving."[34] He's right. While this sentiment is born of the desire to lend weight to the grief of the parents, it misses the mark. It turns out that there are plenty of words that both the bereaved and those in conversation with them can and should use.

Still, I would argue that in some cases, especially those of the newly bereaved, words should be saved. My song "Lend Me Your Heart" speaks to this need:

Don't ask me questions
I can't explain
Words are like echoes
The pain still remains

I've no wish to reason
I haven't the will
Words get all caught in my mouth
I've had my fill

What the newly bereaved may desire is simple:

Come with compassion
Come with your tears
Come with your mind full of peace
And wrestle these fears
Come close beside me
Here in the Dark
Wait in the silence
And lend me your heart

Where "Lend Me Your Heart" is a call to friends and the larger community, "Don't Leave Me Alone" calls to the intimates in the life of the bereaved. There is a progression from simply sitting in the dark night of the soul to offering some tangible comfort, acceptance of the bereaved's imperfect attempts at meaning-making with the loss.

Love, don't leave me alone tonight
Cause I can't fight the good fight with no home
And you're my home
And if my soul slips out in a song tonight
Please don't treat my words at trite
Just give me grace's alibi
Oh Love

Love, read me a story tonight
Cause I can't face the real thing hurts too bad
Summon up, summon up all your best strength tonight
Hold me in the darkness
Don't let me go
Don't let me go

This song was ten years in the making, and all because of that sticky wicket of songwriters far and wide: the bridge. The bridge is supposed to bring it all together, right? It's supposed to drive the theme *home*. I both love and hate that this bridge took so long to write because these songs are as much about me working out my grief on the page as they are my grief working its way through me to the point that I could name it. So, the writing of the bridge speaks to the slow slog that any recovery requires as much as it names the dysfunction that we, the bereaved, can engage in as we try our damndest to heal.

Cause baby, I'm still grieving
A long lost love that I believed in
And I'm so tired of these hard feelings
Of all the missing those who've gone
And though I've done my share of leaving, too
Tonight, I'm barely breathing

There is humility in this bridge even as the last verse shows that this bereaved speaker is kind of full of it.

So, Love, don't leave me on my own tonight
It's more than one heart's meant to bear alone
Stay with me a little longer tonight
Just another hour and I'll be all right
I'll be all right, oh, love

Really? Just another hour and you'll be all right? Methinks I spy an unreliable narrator on the page, y'all. Yes?

If "Don't Leave Me Alone" reminds us that the grief-stricken community exists, "Sing the Sad Songs" is a reminder to the bereaved to stop it. Stop all the trying to square it. Stop repressing. Stop the agitated movements. These songs both call for the bereaved to be still.

You can sit with your sorrows
Let them stay for a while
Let the tears roll down your cheeks
You've walked such a lonely mile
And I hope that tomorrow will be better by far,
But tonight's for singing sad songs
On your old worn out guitar

You've been runnin' for so long
Tryin' hard to forget
But her memory just won't leave
It's the worst at 3:00 a.m.
And the darkness shines a light
on the days that are long gone
On the ring she never wore
On the bet you made and lost

The speaker really gets down to it in the third verse:

You've been blaming, naming names
Yeah we all know how she lied

And you were true and she was not
No matter how you tried
You've been fired up. Gettin' drunk
Like a cowboy in a fight
You've been every kind of angry
Son, sit down, be sad tonight

The cycle meanders its way towards hope with a little chorus that wrangles with the ways a broken heart starts to come alive again. Though the outcome is uncertain, the broken heart can't help but see the potential.

I didn't choose, but I guess that's all right
Sometimes your heart walks right in and makes up your mind
I guess if I lose, I won't be fine
I'll take those odds
Steppin' onto the wire

But the journey of a bereaved heart is not linear. And though we yearn for the renewed connection, a new love, a purpose with which to fill our days, we can get thrown off our Blue Bikes in the blink of an eye. New losses open up the need to revisit what we thought we had fully grieved. We think we have navigated the worst, and then a new worst comes along and we're back to square one. Grief work is exhausting. "One Too Many Tears" speaks to the compounding interest of loss and how, sometimes, we just need to let it lay us low again for a while.

One too many tears on the floor
One too many loves walked out the door
One too many days spent in heartache
So I sit in the darkness alone

For one too many times I have tried
One too many dreams hung out to dry

Too many prayers sent up to the sky
Unanswered, so I'll leave to roam

As a psyche remolds itself, the bereaved often turn inward, picking up the shards of their old life and trying to fashion them into a different type of vessel. If Leonard Cohen's catchphrase about how the cracks let the light shine through applies, my janky vessel could allow the light of a thousand blazing suns to shine right through. Cohen's astute aphorism captures the importance of acceptance—but the metaphor overlooks the fact that whatever liquid that vessel originally could have held is long gone. When we remake the vessel of our lives after loss, we are setting the stage for a new type of psychic brew.

"Take a Look" shines a light on what the beginning of that introspective process might look like: honesty. Calling out the bullshit of our old ways that no longer work and calling *in* contemplation.

You know the place you live between your waking and dreaming?
The one where you come clean cause you just can't lie to yourself?
There's a garden there reminds you a little bit of Eden?
There's a love you've lost cause you're living under a spell

Take a good long look at your life. Take a good, long hard look at
your life. Are you a phantom of who you could be.

The light penetrates closer in verse two:

You know the face you paint in the mirror to please all these people?
The one that wears you down cause you just don't feel like yourself?
You know the games you play where everyone comes out a loser?
And the stories you leave just to try to prove you are well?
Take a good long look at your life.

Unlike the bridge for "Don't Leave Me Alone", this bridge showed up all preachy-like with no delays. It's so highly prescriptive that I could cringe, but I won't. If the bridge fits, walk it.

Take a walk to the hills. Lift your eyes to their heights.
Feel the rush of the wings in their flight.
Take a train, take a trail, I don't care just go anywhere.
Anywhere that you can feel alive.
Say a prayer, say your peace
Close your eyes, get some sleep
And listen to the deep, the deep, deep beat
Tells the truth

Yeah, I dig the call to authenticity in that bridge. That song led me to take off my mask and get into the deep waters of my own heart, asking myself the hardest questions a human might need to ponder: "What is true for me in this life?" Grief has a side effect of de-bullshitting our lives . . . if we'll let it. At least, mine has. My life has much less sheen to it now than it did when I was trying to turn Elijah's death into something. Instead of some structured, ill-aimed attempt to "bring glory to God" through Elijah's death, these songs represent what grief wrought in me. They, too, are catharsis.

But who would listen to them? These songs aren't bangers. They aren't slick or riffy. If I had to place them in a lineage, I would call them descendants of old country music. They are simple. They are raw, underproduced reckonings born of the hardest times I've ever known. I'm not worried about their success, but I do think that country star Rodney Crowell was onto something. In Ken Burns' *Country Music* documentary, Crowell dropped this little truth hammer: "When an artist gets it right for themselves, it's right for everyone."

For a few years now, I have had the strangest desire to start "sad hour." Sad hour is exactly what it sounds like. Instead of clinking our half-price matinees together and pretending that all is well, at sad hour, we get to let it all hang out. Picture this: On a random Friday, accountants at the height of their careers and grandmas who have buried babies boohoo their way through songs like the ones that I and others have written. What if, instead of collectively avoiding our universal experience of life, at times, royally sucking, we circle up around it, knock back a gimlet or two (or not), and give our grief some space? Doesn't that sound like ... fun? Perhaps if we gave our sadness an hour or so together on Friday night, it might not have to sneak up on us Saturday afternoon. Let us enter the holy honky-tonk and take our grief to church.

This is not therapy. This is not "fixing you." This is just regular people in need of some company and a place to be honest about how effing hard the world is right now. Welcome to sad hour, folks. This round's on me.

In the Cool of the Eve

"In the beginning God created the heavens and the earth. The earth was without form and void, and darkness was upon the face of the deep; and the Spirit of God was moving over the face of the waters. And God said, 'Let there be light,' and there was light."

These gorgeous words are the opening to the Genesis creation narrative. They are, in fact, the very first words of that book, which anchors both the Torah and the Bible. It's a passage about beginnings, and that in itself holds merit for this girl who has felt the murkiness of her own heart to be as formless and void as that soon-to-be-born baby Earth. In this moment, we encounter God, hovering, encountering the vast dark. Musing. Perhaps wondering exactly which direction He would take with this dark, wet, mass of void. The curtain has not yet risen on the great narrative known as Project Universe. What a pristine moment.

These verses don't find God infamously urging Satan to "Consider my servant Job." No. It's far too early in the story for that. It's too soon for wrathful OG God—the God we see in most of the Old Testament—to admonish the Israelites to commit genocide on some fallen foes with these words: "Go and smite Amalek and utterly destroy all that they have, and spare them not; but slay both man and woman, infant and suckling, ox and sheep, camel and ass" (1 Samuel 15:3).

Seriously, why do all the cattle get such a bad rap when OG

God shows up on the scene? Like, even the ox and the ass need to turn tail and run when Yawheh gets his panties in a wad. When this version of the Almighty rolls in, the good times are quickly forgotten.

I like chapter one Genesis God much better. Unlike the God who told Job to piss off because ... "I'm God. I said it. That settles it," this God is just hanging out in the dark, contemplating little things like, you know, the creation of the cosmos.

I picture EG (Early Genesis) God as a gray-headed man in a red flannel puttering around in his woodshop, wondering which project to take on next. His whiskers are unkempt. His black coffee slops over the edge of God's favorite mug—the one he got from Ray's Radiator Shop back in the day when his Harley needed a tune-up. Yes, I like this God very much because a.) this God owns a Harley and b.) even God has vehicle troubles.

Anyhoo, God floats around, slopping black gas station coffee all over the cosmos, scratches his head and decides:

"Ah, yes ... Let's get some light on this subject."

This God is starting to resemble my grandpa more and more. My Papa might have tugged a piece of yarn jury-rigged to a broken off bit of chain attached to a bare bulb and lit up some crevice of his well-worn home—probably the laundry room where I tried and hated cigarettes when I was eight.

Grandpa God's method was much simpler: "Let there be light."

And just like that ...

Brilliance envelops the cosmos

The face of the water shimmers.

God smiles.

"Yeah. Some Effing Light. That was a good call."

It's groovy, right?

I think God was at his best in this moment, calling to the creative potential of the universe. When the story continues that humans are made in God's image, I believe the sense of likeness refers to this creative potential. Humans, like the God in whose image we were made, or the god we made in our image,

are at our best when we are making shit. I love this image of creating because it is so different from the other C-word: conquering. Unlike conquering, which invariably involves winners and
losers, victors and captives, creativity is about cooperation. It's
an alchemy of the elements. It is about calling forth possibilities.
Creativity is not about control but about releasing potential into
the universe. Some of our best work begins in the dark.

As much as I love the opening to the creation story, my
favorite passage in the entire Book of Genesis is this verse: "In
the cool of the evening, the man and his wife heard the LORD
God walking around in the garden" (Genesis 3:8).

Isn't this such a lovely thought?

The same God who had hovered above the dark, who had
spoken the whole shebang into existence, drew nigh to His
handiwork. He stopped hovering and began to walk, visiting
the young world in the cool of the day.

There's something comforting to me about this idea. I get
the idea that God was in the habit of taking this little evening
stroll, checking in on all the critters He had crafted. I like to
think that God walked around high-fiving himself whenever
he encountered a millipede or a mustang. *Good job, Yahweh! You
really nailed it with that spider monkey. You might want to reconsider
the mole rat—nah. We all need a good chuckle now and then.*

Maybe I had it wrong earlier when I fashioned a grand-
fatherly God. Christian apologist G. K. Chesterson certainly
seemed to think so. Rather than a wizened elder, Chesterton's
God is more like a toddler (that would certainly explain a few
things). Chesterton here:

> "It is possible that God says every morning, 'Do it
> again' to the sun; and every evening, 'Do it again' to the
> moon. It may not be automatic necessity that makes
> all daisies alike; it may be that God makes every daisy
> separately, but has never got tired of making them. It
> may be that He has the eternal appetite of infancy; *for*

we have sinned and grown old, and our Father is younger than we" (emphasis mine).[35]

What if we, rather than God, are the old curmudgeons? What if, in our oldness, we drudge through our days, taking each sunrise in stride? We barely glance up at the orb that makes our existence possible. Of course there are all sorts of reasons we may fail to do so. Most of us are just trying to pay the bills with enough left over to take the kids to Disney. But what if the greed that comes with our oldness and our conquer-at-all-costs mentality has given rise to the even bigger sin of forgetting the ways that daisies dance in a field?

Maybe Christ was hearkening back to this young God when he said, "Consider the lilies, how they grow: they toil not, neither do they spin; yet I say unto you, Even Solomon in all his glory was not arrayed like one of these" (Matthew 6:28-31). I think he probably could have just stopped at the first part: Consider the lilies. Just do that. Who cares about Solomon? The dude had like three hundred wives and concubines and once recommended cutting a baby in half to solve a maternity dispute. Yeah. Let's just consider the daisies.

Why?

Consideration and its close kin, contemplation, often begin in murky stillness. We hover over the void of our unformed potential. We strike a little thought match, hoping to shed light on the subject. Sometimes we get a crack of light that splits our cosmos. More often than not, we feel our way through relationship conundrums, career, whatever the situation that needs some illumination. In this way, we navigate our lives.

But when grief comes in and leaves us gaping, it's hard to consider much of anything but the presence of our loved ones' absences. Old wounds may open. Contemplation gets yoked to one incredibly painful subject. The generative darkness births only more pain. There is no change, no spark, no movement.

Most days now, I get by. I would even say that I thrive. But

I feel very aware that a spin-out could be around the corner, especially where my kids are concerned.

Cue life mirroring art: A few days ago, I was hovering over the darkness of this essay, doling out yet another oh-so-wise revelation about living life with your guts wrenched out. I barely noticed the text: "I'm on my way. Be there in ten minutes."

The text was from Navis—Navis, who was riding a bike over to grab coffee before class.

I looked back at my laptop. Tapped a few more words. And then it happened. *Buzz* went the little timer in my belly, the one that goes off when I need to check on a kid. Okay, it's not an actual buzz because that would be weird, and clearly I am a very normal parent. It's more of a tightening in my gut that says, *Something is wrong.*

It's the same buzzer that went off one day when Isaiah was about eight weeks old. From his little carseat, I heard a cough. It sounded funky. That's all I could really say. Maybe a little squeaky, but then again, new human kids make all kinds of weird noises. Nevermind. I was spooked. I called the pediatrician. Thank God I had one who didn't downplay my instinct. The diagnosis? Pleural effusion and collapsed lung. Score one for mother's intuition.

When Navis didn't arrive on the scene after ten minutes, I texted, "You all right?"

"Yeah, don't worry; just Baby's First Blue Bike wipeout. I'm okay except for a couple of scrapes on my arm and probably bruises on my knees. You are now allowed to yell at me if I leave the house without a helmet."

Important Fact 1: Blue Bikes are pedal assist, meaning that they can go about twenty miles per hour.

Important Fact 2: When it comes to bodily injury, Navis is a minimizer.

Me: Oh honey. Where are you? I am so sorry. Do you want me to come get you?

Navis: Walking. I'm genuinely all right!

Me (inwardly): *The fuck you are* (grabs keys).

Me to Navis: I'm picking you up. Is that okay?

Long story short, I found my kid amped up on adrenaline, walking down the street with a very banged up knee and gouged out hand.

About thirty minutes later, the adrenaline left their system and they shed a few tears, realizing that while it *hadn't* been bad, it certainly *could* have been. Navis had skated around a threshold but a lesson was still surfacing. As they sat next to me, calming down, they spoke the truth: "It's just that sometimes you realize we are all basically held together with a bit of duct tape and glue."

Amen, kid.

The truth of our duct-taped reality is too much to reckon with, so some of us barrel through grief, pretending that life is much the same as it was, even as we subsist within the blast range of our loss. Others can stay frozen in grief. That would be yours truly. My tendency is to sit, shell-shocked and alone. I don't want anyone to see me in deep sorrow. And I don't want to have to function. At all.

But when we are wounded, we need to stop. We need to be held. We need to be seen. We need someone to help us bind up our soul wounds and not insist that we act like Grief Zero didn't just happen. We need the old longhouse fire to tend, a glow to remind us that the elements are still with us and us with them. That tending is the first blush of movement after the freeze of early grief. We light the long dark one strike of the flint at a time. But we do need to exist in the dark until we are ready to show our changed faces in the full light of day. We need the dark as much as we fear it.

And, if healing is to come, eventually we need movement. Like a limb after the cast comes off, our souls need movement. Literal movement.

Limbs pumping blood.

Legs in locomotion.

Bare feet feeling their way through grass.

So, back to the Garden of Eden for a moment . . . the site of a very famous wipeout. Remember that Fall? Of course you do. The story has been recast so many times, codified into a myth that conveniently lays the burden for humanity's mess at the feet of a crafty serpent, an ingénue-like Eve, and one missing-in-action Son of Red Earth. Once again, we find God padding around in the twilight. Only this time, He is walking after the first humans' epic oopsie has taken place. On this walk, EG God isn't high-fiving. He is looking for His kids.

And there you have it. Four chapters into the book of beginnings, and we find that grief has entered the scene. The garden had become a blast zone. God is cut off from his children by the choices they've made. This was the real pain, the real death in the garden. This was God's Grief Zero. God walked in the cool of eve, perhaps not wanting to know what He already felt to be true.

Omniscience is a bitch like that.

EG God grew older that day, each step moving him closer to the flood-wielding, plague-sending deity who would command Joshua to slay the all Amalekites. But God wasn't the only one who felt the loss. To his children, the Creator's steps became a menace. The hum of their own contemplation and connection was replaced by the protective freeze of fresh grief. In this protective stance, I imagine that they huddled, probably bickering over the whole knowledge-of-good-and-evil debacle.

Eve: I *told* you! The serpent was crafty.

Adam: Well, I didn't know what crafty was yet, dear, as I didn't know what good and evil were.

Eve: Whatever. Go find me another fig leave because I guess for some reason my nipples need covered and yours don't.

* * *

What does all of this hearkening back to the Genesis tale have to do with the loss of a small child, or the working out of a life with grief braided through it? It has to do with healing. Whatever else Genesis is about, it is definitely about grief. God's grief in the garden. The grief of young families and tribes. Grief: there is no Genesis—or genesis—without it.

The book leaves out as much as it reveals. We learn that Eve is a bereaved mother, her son murdered by his brother. This tragic fact is somehow glossed over, and the focus remains on the march of humanity through these early days, when the thorns and thistles of their own missteps create mishap after mishap. The stories of Genesis are stories of disruption and reconnection. In Genesis, we find humanity walking across deserts and into furnaces. We find a brother being sold into slavery because he was the favored son. The Kardashians have nothing on Joseph's brothers. We find humans walking through centuries of enslavement, prophets being called forth. It's all very messy and disruptive . . . and real. I feel a kinship to the humans in Genesis.

Take Rachel, for example, the wife of Jacob (his, uh, *favorite wife*, by the way, but that's a whole other story). Jacob was on the outs with Rachel's father and decided to cut ties. On their way out, Rachel decided to steal Daddy's household gods and hide them in her camel seat. This is some straight up Alabama shit happening in the land of Paddan Aram. When Daddy came looking for his gods, Rachel ostensibly lied and said she was on her period, so, "Sorry, Dad, I can't stand up." That story feels so palpable and honest. I'm pretty sure that whoever told it first was some ancient ancestor of Mark Twain.

At any rate, I can relate to the mess of these Genesis kinfolk much more than I can Job's acquiescence and tidy end. If Job is about tying off the story of grief, Genesis is definitely about letting the loose ends hang out. It is a bloody book, a recounting of heroes who are as fucked up as they are formidable. Yeah. Genesis people are my people, a motley lot of breathing, passion-fueled, ragtag citizens of antiquity. Their foibles and grief are hidden between the folds of tedious geneaologies of "so and so begat so and so." Shem begat Arphaxad. Arphaxad begat Shelah. Shelah begat Eber. Who knows what any of these folks did. They were small and noteworthy, and in the pages of Genesis, humans continued to boldly and bravely create.

Some would argue that the creativity was corrupted by Adam and Eve, and it does seem that EG God leaves the scene pretty early on to be replaced by paranoid OG God, who is threatened by humans banding together to build a tower. Plot twist here: God becomes the destroyer and scrambles the languages. But I wonder if the joke was on God here, as humans just spread out over the land like a virus with new languages to beget. They walked, sometimes in the cool of the eve, sometimes under the the cloud of fire, carving out gods from earrings and stories that endure.

In Genesis, God's grief and the grief of humanity form a double helix that spirals through the ages, embeds itself in the very nature of existence. Somehow the loss of one small boy fits into this lineage of humanity's great grief. Like my kin in Genesis, I have had to learn to walk again. After every loss, I have had to freeze. Freezing gives way to the thaw of contemplative thought, of a renewed sense of curiosity. Movement is threatened. What once was normal—walking in the cool of the eve—becomes a walk through the valley of the shadow of death.

Remember that breakup I mentioned a few chapters back? The one that left me reeling for well over a year? A side effect of that was that I shuttered myself, fearing to be alone in the dark. But one night, I decided to move.

Bayou St. John is no large body of water. It's really a sliver of a thing that a child could throw a stone across. But its history reaches back to pre-Columbian times. The Houma called it Bayouk Choupic. Once an important trade waterway, the bayou is now primarily used for recreation, though every St. John's

Eve, a voodoo ceremony ensues. The drums beat into the night. Under cover of dark, all are welcome to the head-washing ceremony that offers renewal of the soul at the summer solstice.

No public events took place the night I decided to slink out, feeling so brave to do what once had seemed like second nature.

April 4th, 2018

Last night I did something that I haven't done in over twenty years. I left my house well after dark, and I left alone. I left simply because I wanted to and for no other reason than to walk like God used to, in the cool of the eve. My neighborhood is a veritable bower right now. The jasmine is in full bloom. So are the roses. Everywhere I turn, the smells beckon and never more so than in the evening. I know the hot is coming. I have felt it creeping in these past few days as I've walked to my coffeeshop, my grocery store, the little cafe in the Tremé that I like to frequent. I've felt that stickiness between my legs and my boobs, and I've thought, "Here we go again."

I haven't walked alone at night in years. When I was a young woman in my early twenties, I worked at a Girl Scout camp in Michigan. It was a job that rarely stopped. New buses of Brownies arrived weekly each Sunday, and I would welcome them to our campsite, teach them the basics of camp cooking, console them through their inevitable bouts of homesickness and bug bites. The room and board part of the package sweetened the pot of a low salary. So did, of course, the girls. We all basically lived in the woods, in these camping cabins that kept out the mosquitos but not much else. And we were out at all hours leading night hikes, returning from horseback rides, walking alone. Yes. Alone.

Each counselor got one day off a week and two hours off

each day, which we usually spent in the counselors' quarters. Those quarters consisted of a few air-conditioned rooms, a kitchen, showers, and some sort of communal living room where we could watch TV. I'm pretty sure this was pre-Internet, and definitely pre-Internet addiction era, so mostly we watched videos or TV, read, or played cards when we were off.

But what I remember most is the walk to and from that cabin. I grew accustomed to walking at night and doing it without a flashlight. I loved the sense of feeling my way across the terrain. In Michigan, there was actually terrain to traverse. My feet nimbly navigated the slopes, whether they were soaked with summer rain or dusty from the lack thereof. I felt free, like a creature connected to her heart and body and the earth.

I was naive then. Sheltered both physically and psychologically from the harm that can befall a woman walking alone. Of course men can be harmed, are harmed when outside at night, but I don't think that they carry the same fears that women do about leaving their houses unattended at night. I don't know a single man who texts a friend with "Look for my body if I'm not back in an hour." None of my male friends carry mace or pepper spray or sign up for self-defense classes. They all seem relaxed about going out at any time, day or night.

The fears that women carry, or rather the fears that I carry as a woman, have been laid down slowly year by year, generation by generation. They are the sediment of stories that I've heard through the years, stories of joggers in Central Park whose bodies are found in shallow graves—or no grave at all. When the stories hit closer to home, as they inevitably will, they weigh upon me even more. When I was in college, I heard my sister tell of her friend who was dragged from her car at a stop light and murdered. This woman was simply driving and made the "mistake" of not having her door locked at a stop light. She paid for that miscalculation with her life. My sister was called in to ID the body.

Then there are my own #MeToo moments, which hardly seem worth mentioning in light of these tragedies, but I mention them because if the more grisly tales of murders, rapes, and domestic violence are the large rocks that keep me inside, these smaller transgressions are the gravel that fill in the spaces around the rocks. Catcalls aplenty, unwelcome sexual advances of the aggressive variety, a man masturbating on the bayou in broad daylight a few feet away from my friend and me—the upshot of all these stories is a constant sense of unease around walking after dark. It's just too easy for women to disappear.

And so, I didn't walk alone at night anymore. Not until last night.

When I was partnered, my boyfriend and I would walk the bayou each night. Sometimes we strolled hand in hand. Other times he would jog ahead and we'd meet up at our lamppost. A byproduct of this union is that I felt completely safe in my skin as we walked. I rediscovered that feeling of playfulness that I felt as a child, riding my bike to the 7-Eleven to grab some Twinkies. Mickey and all her playfulness re-emerged, or at least someone akin to her. I would slip my sandals off and let the grass massage my middle-aged heels, slowly sipping in the humidity and centering myself. I no longer felt my skin bristle as shadows approached. I didn't scan them for their gender, put my hand on keys, or plan an escape route. I felt completely unencumbered to enter that state of reverie that I had so enjoyed as a young child. Maybe it sucked that it took being with a well-muscled male to free me from the weight of all those stories, but at least I was free.

When we broke up, I felt the fear return. Maybe because I had swaddled myself in the comfort of that man's presence, maybe because I hadn't really been walking much prior to that relationship, whatever the reason, when we split, I felt a strange pissed off-ed-ness toward him. It was different from the usual break up blues. I, the dumpee, was heartbroken. I wasn't dealing with all the usual breakup thoughts: "What did I do wrong? Why wasn't I good enough?" Blah, blah, blah. We all know that tape.

This was different. This time, the pain of the breakup seemed to cascade along with every other loss. Loss piled upon loss, and I felt like I was re-grieving the loss of my child, my marriage, my faith, and most of all, I grieved the woman I had hoped to be by now. That woman is settled, centered, and, most of all—free.

I could have called other friends to walk with me, but I didn't want to. I could have walked a little earlier. But pain like this is best tended to at night. During the day, we do the great work of simply showing up to our jobs, performing tasks in a perfunctory manner. If we have kids, we try to shield them from our sorrow (we never do, not fully). But at night, something wild awakens, and grief is nothing if not a wild force akin to every natural disaster out there. Grief is a tsunami, a blizzard, a forest fire. First it razes our mental highrises to the ground, then it sweeps them all out to sea, and finally, it freezes us in some sort of soul trance, barely blinking our lids as we lie in the space where all we had hoped for used to be. It is in that great empty space that we can start to rebuild.

But we must inhabit it. And though friends can help, ultimately the work of grief is solitary. And for this work, I needed the shroud of darkness to look at the barren landscape and begin to imagine planting—first, one small dream seed, then another. Grief is the great dream stealer; perhaps this is one of the hardest things about it. We grieve because we actually did try. We put our powers of dreaming and vision-making to work. We effen *invested*. Hell, we have often gone *all* in.

I used to tell my ex-boyfriend that when loss sweeps in— whether a loss of a partner, a parent, or, in my case, a child—we need time to let that particular dream die. We should probably be giving these dreams funerals, eulogizing them as much as we do the people who have left, but we would probably feel guilty about doing so because we are taught to feel bad about honoring our losses. Similar to when a child enters a world and all attention turns to the baby even though the mom has been oftentimes literally torn asunder and is experiencing great emotional upheaval, when death comes, we turn most of our immediate ritual to the one who has died. I don't know if it's exactly a bad thing. Wakes, sitting shiva, planning elaborate final send-offs are all part of the process, but we seem to collectively suck at tending to the bereaved.

In the throes of this new grief, I needed my bayou, my Cabrini Bridge. All I wanted to do was sit and watch the spiders spin their resilience. I had started the spider-staring during the year that my kids and I lived in separate states. I was grieving then too as I tried to make my arms stretch across the one thousand plus miles and imagine bedtimes, school plays, all the milestones I was missing. During those years, I began to notice the spiders diligently spinning their silk houses. These threads would capture the last rays of sunset, turning each truss into a sort of silken stained glass. I'm pretty sure if I had been a fly, I would have died on one of those beguiling threads. As it was, I stared at them, knowing that even if they got rained on or blown away, a little spider weaver would be back to rebuild her home.

It was at this point that I began to make friends with spiders. I admired their resilient faithfulness to their task. I would not have attended to their art had I not learned that grief requires both stillness and movement.

Some people look to the butterfly as the ultimate teacher of resilience. And I get it. I especially get it now that I know caterpillars basically turn into goo before they transform into their future glory. It's a nice metaphor, though I don't know how butterflies feel about being nature's poster child of resilience. I think I prefer the spider who, whilst making something beautiful, remains perfectly able to deliver a bite that says, "Back off. I'm hemming off this little patch of air to be my lair; I suggest you give me some space." It was the spider I needed to observe at sunset in order to start the slow, slow process of disentangling my heart from my now former partner. I didn't want to do it at 3:00 p.m. I wanted to take the mask off and just be wrecked. And I couldn't. I didn't. Until last night.

Buoyed by the liquid courage of a white wine aptly named Liberated, I decided for once to *not* do the smart thing. I would never tell my daughters to do what I did, but I needed to do it. At 10:30 p.m. or so, I strapped on my Chacos and set out, sans mace, sans text to a girlfriend, and definitely sans man. I was alone. It might be one of the most vulnerable things I've ever done. As I walked, I channeled Cheryl Strayed, who with each step of her journey on the Pacific Coast trail told herself that she was not afraid. I echoed her sentiment, and even though I wasn't braving the wilderness, I felt courage propel me down my steps, out onto the pavement, and into my neighborhood. I was immediately greeted by the cool night air, invited into the smells and the rhythm of my own feet. My feet remembered what freedom felt like. So did my heart.

Not one block from my house, my left big toe caught the corner of the sidewalk. It was a sharp pain that quickly gave way to a blunt throb that is still with me. *This is the definition of irony,* I thought. *Girl goes out to reclaim the night, chants against her fear, and immediately stubs toe.* God, that is so Desi. It was a rude awakening. It reminded me that even if no one molested me, I still had the potential to trip, take ill, or worse at any moment. Fucking fragility of life. Just about the time you think you've settled into safety, some little irritant or malady writ large arrives to remind you that you are in the big picture, a weak little organism that can be extinguished at the whim of the cosmos. So be it. What else is there to do but keep walking?

In the quiet, I took my familiar path past the coffee shop, past the grocery where I buy my avocadoes, around the little green space where my youngest and I used to eat takeout and play river fairies. Inevitably, I passed my ex's apartment, the one where we listened to Indigo Girls and John Denver, the kitchen where he took me into his arms and we swayed in front of the microwave, the room where we first made love. I felt some breakup angst and anger, and couldn't decide whether to flip that apartment the bird or revel in the memories of the early days of our romance. I decided to do neither and simply let that house, and all the memories in it, stay asleep. Tonight wasn't about us. It was about me.

When I got to the bayou, I noticed that few people were out. I was nearly alone, and it felt fantastic. I also noticed that those who were out were in groups of two. A stray male or two jogged in the moonlight. There were bikini-clad twenty-somethings on paddle boards or rafts full of beer-drinking Bayou Boogaloo goers. All of these people I love, but I didn't want to meet them tonight. Tonight, there was only one person I wanted to meet: myself.

I couldn't help but stay aware of the others. I felt my ingrained defense mechanisms kick in. I remembered that I used to have a pretty good roundhouse and can throw a decent jab. I felt anything but ferocious, but I hoped that I could put up a fight. In between those contemplations, I slipped into a type of mental ease. I felt like the twenty-something version of myself, the one who was unencumbered with the news of joggers and Amber alerts and the awareness that what I was doing might turn out to be incredibly unsafe. Sometimes in order to reach liberation, we need to do something a little bit reckless. Or at least I do.

As I strolled, birds whose names I don't know took their respite along the shore. The breeze tousled my hair. Dogs off-leash came up and nuzzled me briefly then scampered off with their owners. I saw couples, and rather than envying their ability to walk unhindered, I simply nodded and kept walking. While I felt that twenty-year-old girl with me, I also felt my middle-aged, dented self along for the ride, too.

I didn't cry about the breakup. I did something else. I talked to myself. I dialogued with the bruises. I thought about my kids. It felt meditative, not in a mantra-driven way, but more in the "just let thoughts come and go like the clouds" kind of way. I didn't have an agenda for my thoughts. And it felt good to let them ramble, much like my feet, in any direction they wanted to go. They flit across the landscape of my brain. Snippets of things I've read recently: "Option A is not available. Let's kick the shit out of option B" (Sheryl Sandberg).[36] I thought of my kids, all of my kids, and I let my heart swing open, sending that love downstream to where they were sleeping at their dad and stepmom's house. After about forty-five minutes, I was ready to return home, so I stepped it up, a little more healed, a little more me. I had been brave.

What is the point of including an old missive about a woman who literally took a walk in one of the safest neighborhoods in her city? Glad you asked. I write about taking a damn walk because I think it is important to remember that bravery is not a one-size-fits-all proposition. When we are wounded, we often judge ourselves by what the former version of ourselves could accomplish. We want to get *back* to that version of ourselves. But there is no going back. Just ask Adam and Eve. Ask Arphaxad, or Eber, or whoever else. Ask God. What better way to epitomize this than by laying down the bricks of our healing—one step at a time in the dark?

We need to remember on our healing journeys that bravery can mean taking an evening walk, or picking up the phone to call a loved one, or not picking up the phone to call a loved one, or painting a hummingbird in watercolor, or making a peanut butter and jelly sandwich because we deserve a bit of joy in our days. Bravery can be listening to country music while sipping limoncello and letting a man gain access to your inner world, even if that world is pocked with the memories of your losses. These small acts of bravery are scaffolds toward a different version of ourselves, ones that can hold all the losses we are called to encompass.

When loss swoops in and all the thresholds we have ever crossed create a wormhole from which it is difficult to function, we can want healing to come in equally as grandiose a fashion. Elijah's loss was so public. But healing from Elijah's loss, and each subsequent loss, has been a small, private affair. As much as I have needed to be held and broadcast some of the pain, I have needed small steps, slipping silently through the grass—sometimes I feel more like the serpent slithering through the garden than like a goddess bringing light. I remember that before the blaze of light, there was God, hovering. Like God, I hover over the shadows of my unhealed wounds. I exist, hovering between the formless parts of my heart and the inscrutability of a future I have yet to dream.

I remember that some things are best mended—or created—in the dark.

In the cool of the eve, tears can slip out unbidden. The great heat of grief that I still sometimes want to spill onto Mister Linen's chest needs to be stilled by the cool of the eve. Grief must expand and contract. Every so often, it seems to erupt, but it also needs to be tempered. Sometimes the soul needs to skinny dip and be seen by nothing other than a lone gosling or a shrouded moon.

I don't know if my creator is out there walking with me, but in the evening, I feel no shame. I just feel creature-like, padding around the bayou like a lone wolf who might need to sit on her haunches and howl at the moon, only to return to a glass of pinot noir and a hug from one of her offspring. In the cool of the eve, I don't find closure, but I find that the darkness acts as a salve. Some wounds don't need debriding. They just need a good soak in the epsom salts of my own memories. Closure is not the goal. Making peace, one stubbed toe at a time, is.

September 24th

Hey Buddy,

How are you?

I'm sitting here in this little corner of my coffee shop, thinking of you. It's been twenty-three years since we've had this type of relationship, the one where I find a quiet place to crawl off and try to hold the magnitude of this day. I think when a little soul exits the world, that day is worth taking note of. Son, I love you. I hold you in my heart today. I wish there weren't a world and a whole life's worth of loss between us. Today, just for a little bit, I let myself slow down and remember. Of course, I woke up thinking of the day. I cried a bit—am crying now. I started on the floor and lay there for a bit in my cutoffs and sweater. Navis came in and saw me and asked if I was okay and why I was down there. They wondered if I had hurt myself. Well, of course the answer is yes, but not in the way they meant. I quipped, "Don't worry, if I were physically injured, I would let you know, and then, because I am hyper-independent, I would begin walking a mile to the doctor all by myself." Cause I'm healthy like that, son.

But today, baby boy, or grown boy, or ethereal spirit, or memory that resides in my bones, I don't want to hide my hurt with a quip. I don't want to deal with it, either. I don't want to make something of it. I just want you. I want you with a longing that is etching its way from some primal part of me into where you are supposed to be, or where I want you to be. Son, I want you here. And I don't want you here in my heart. I want you here grown, as you would be at this age, with Ada's eyes and Isaiah's build and Navis's wit and Marci's brightness and, of course, your own. I only reference the other kids because I have no real point of reference for what you would be like.

But today, I will allow myself to imagine it. I imagine you just went away on a long journey, and sure, the years have changed you some, but you are still you and our souls recognize each other. I wish you would come back and scold me, tell me that you narrowly escaped death but that you went off to live with a bunch of healers or scientists on a secluded island. I want you to come back and tell me it's okay. You're okay, and I am okay, and you are proud of me for the mother I have tried to become even though I am such an imperfect one.

I would like you to tell me that you visited your dad and he's doing okay too because he deserves to be, son. He really does.

Today, that won't happen, but today, I am trying to make contact with you in my mind, through my fingertips and my longing and my just letting it all be. I wanted to write you a letter like we used to do back in the nineties, when you were little. We would head off to an office supply store and buy some godawful mass-produced stationery with a hokey little Christmas scene emblazoned across the top heralding the birth of Christ and the death of a few more trees, only we didn't think about the trees because, you know, Jesus, and because the nineties. I would write a letter to extended family, all the people that I wasn't close enough to for whatever reason, and catch them up on the comings and goings of the family.

That letter would be written to mimic script, because for some reason we thought this gave it a personal touch, and it would have innocuous subsections like this one:

We Moved!

Wow! Last year our family had quite the adventure! We packed up our young brood and started a new chapter in Missouri. Everyone is settling in nicely. Here's a pixelated image I scanned of a kid sucking their mitten.

We would all carefully curate the contents of those letters, letting people into a linguistic Polaroid of our lives and always ending with best wishes for a happy new year. I kind of miss those little family letters, Elijah. Nowadays, we have the Internet, which was just coming into fashion for the masses when you were little. Back then, we called it the World Wide Web. We connected to it by plugging in our computers to the phone line and dialing up our provider. I think if any of us had to go back to the Internet the way it used to be, we would have even more intense road rage than we do now. Trust me, son, we don't need that.

Two days ago, on the bayou where I live with three of your younger siblings, I saw a prissy little white hybrid car honking its way along behind a car going about twenty-five miles an hour (incidentally, that's the speed limit). The whole world these days just seems to be in a damn hurry. I get it. I am pretty prone to the efficiency illness myself, truth be told, but it saddens me to see its creep in my little corner of the world.

Anyway, the Internet. I guess we don't need home-printed Christmas letters like the ones I used to make anymore. Now, we all carry around phones and upload pictures of our soup to Instagram and are like, "I just took a bite of this crawfish bisque, and I feel mentally ill about it." And weirdly, son, saying things like that means that we are complimenting the soup. It's a strange world, son, where we all act like we are infinitely connected, yet we are all lonely as fuck, your mom included.

That's not strictly true, buddy. I am not lonely in the largest sense of the word, just like I am not anxious about everything all the time. I am lonely for you, Elijah. And I think I am just sad. Last night, I had another round of intrusive thoughts, and I wanted to check the beds. Okay, I did check the beds. Okay, I checked one bed—Marci's. I don't really do that anymore, but yesterday Ada and Marci rearranged Marci's room, and something in my body signaled to me that this day, today, was coming, and it was a Saturday just like the day that we built your bed, and I was tired, and for no reason and every reason, I tiptoed into Marci's room and found some bullshit excuse for going in there. I moved a few piles of things around and got them some water and basically succeeded in disturbing Marci's sleep. Yeah. Your mom ain't quite right all the time, son. So be it.

So, Elijah, here's what's been going on around here this year—the high points.

Your little sister is big. Like, bigger and taller than me. Remember when you were little and she was newly home from the hospital? You seemed fascinated with her and you showed it in your little toddler boy way. Ada had great baby blue eyes, just like you, and you were just learning to count, so you put two and two together, walked up with your index and middle finger, poked her little baby eyes, proudly proclaimed, "Two eyes!" I'm pretty sure I said something like, "Yes. Let's be gentle with her eyes." You complied with as much tenderness as your chubby fingers could provide.

My favorite memory of you and Ada begins with Ada propped up in her bouncy chair, just being a baby, taking in all that her little eyes could behold. She could not likely behold too much because she was so little that her eyes could probably see about as far as my boobs—hey, let's face it, that's about all she needed at that point. Anyway, you came over, carrying your Winnie-the-Pooh blanket, the one we had gotten you when you were born. It was well broken in, much in the way a good pair of jeans just get better with time. That blanket had been part of your bedtime repertoire since your own infancy, and you liked to carry it around the house. You *loved* that blanket, had been comforted by that blanket, had dragged that blanket through field and mud and many a car trip.

But this day, you saw that Ada might need it. I think she had been fussing, or maybe she was already asleep. I can't remember, but you "gently" laid that blanket over her tiny frame—all the way up to her eyes, if I remember. Of course, I rearranged it, but I saw that act for what it was: the most generosity a young chap could offer his baby sis. You gave Ada your best.

God, I miss you, baby.

How incredibly sweet of you, son. And what evidence that we little humans contain all the fodder of what we can become. Little toddler you contained the raw material that can become explosive anger in adulthood along with the best parts of our humanity. That day, you showed the best, and I felt your little heart of compassion. What a gift.

As for Ada, her eyes are still sparkly. She sees so much farther than she used to. She sees the whole damn world and loves it. She has the eyes of an artist, never hurrying past any small, mundane miracle. She just moved back home to do some recovering from a few hard knocks of her own. I gotta be honest, Elijah. I love having her here. It's not always simple, and yesterday we had a little tiff. She's twenty-three, you know, a woman, and I know it can't be easy for her to be living in our little Bohemian Bungalow on the Bayou (that's what I started calling our place back in 2020, when I thought that I would be living there alone).

Did I say alone? I am far from it. We never had a pet when you were little, Elijah, but right now that little bungalow is bursting at the seams with six cats, two snakes, and four humans. Okay, it's a basement apartment, son, not a bungalow. And it's not the first house we have dressed up with a name to remind us that what started out as a basement partially refinished by the landlord's first wife has the potential to be . . . a home.

I don't know if you know this, but when we were house shopping in Florida during residency, we looked at a slew of houses. Money was tight even though we thought the low $30k-range salary your father was about to draw was pretty amazing. We decided on a home that cost $65,000. It had been inhabited by an older couple, and word had it that the husband had passed from dementia. Apparently, he had the habit of sitting on the porch and taking in the neighborhood's view dressed only in his tighty-whities. I mean no disrespect to him, son. I mean, in a way, good on him for losing some inhibition. "Naked I came from my mother's womb, and naked I return to the dust," right (Job 1:21)?

Anyhow, the house had become too much for the elderly couple and had fallen into disrepair. We had fallen into the habit of calling the house The Big Ugly, because it was cheap. It was also big. It was also ugly. Someone had decided that it would be a good idea to glue industrial-grade mauve carpet directly onto the oak floors. By the time we happened upon the Big Ugly, it had been donated to the Baptists, who didn't seem too interested in the mauve carpet or the faded turquoise walls. Your dad and I, however, were undaunted, and we overlooked those aesthetic sins because the house was effing huge. We'd cycle through the list of potentials but always return to The Big Ugly. Finally I was like, "I just don't think I can buy a house called The Big Ugly," so we christened it with a new moniker: The Vintage Home by the Park.

Technically, this name was equally true as The Big Ugly, in the way that an impeccably restored 1950s Harley Panhead and a Tweety Bird PEZ dispenser caked in mud and carrying remnants of your Aunt Bessie's can of snuff can both be from the same era. Let's just say that this house more closely resembled the latter.

We bought it and began the process of renovation, painting and peeling back that dark pink carpet. We moved in after the paint and floors were complete, and we played with you amongst the rubble of renovation. I was already pregnant with Ada when we moved into that house, having conceived her in some Berlin hostel not too far from the train station. Wow, this letter is going way back, son, and here I was trying to give you a touchpoint from life today. I guess my mind returns there because, well, because that house is the last place I lived with you.

I may take out the scrapbook today and revisit one of my favorite pictures of us in that house. In it, I am pretty pregnant with Ada, but my lap still had a bit of real estate, and upon its outskirts you are perched. We were reading *The Christmas Mouse*—a rousing tale of how an incredibly cute, anthropomorphized rodent did something or other at Christmas that must have been book-worthy. Yeah. It was clearly a riveting read. The point is that in this photo you looked content, engaged in the world of words in the way only preliterate children can be, listening to my voice, pointing at the pictures. I am pretty sure that brilliant baby you was jubilantly exclaiming things like, "Mouse!" I loved reading to you, Elijah, entering the world of story and little books about how the world works. Reading to you is one of the million things I miss about you.

But back to the present. Here's a little tidbit about the family. We are . . . a beautiful mess, son. Look, I don't want to make every issue that has ever happened about your passing. But the scars of that loss have worked their way through the wood of our family. If our family really was a tree, someone could look at a cross section and see exactly when you left, much like how an arboriculturalist can examine growth rings and tell exactly when an avalanche hit— mechanical damage, they call it. So, our tree has been growing, but the mechanical damage was pretty massive. We have grown twenty-three rings, and some of them show signs of malnourishment, blight, or the blunt trauma of your loss. However, this past year's ring is pretty robust. So here's the update.

Navis is in college studying theater. And son, I can't think of a better thing for them to do. Their days are very full, moving between barista-ing at the coffee shop where I am writing this letter, attending class, and stage managing an upcoming show. Navis is a force. I think you two might have sparred, but I feel like some of your gentleness would have always found its way into any fights.

Isaiah is living in North Carolina. What to say about him? Well, your little brother is also big. Like, way big. I just saw him a couple of weeks ago when I went up North to help Ada move. He is dating the coolest girl. He is working back of house at a restaurant, saving money, and also making art. I don't know how to describe to you the precision with which Isaiah paints his little Warhammer figurines. He started painting them as a coping mechanism for when his girlfriend was spending the summer in Alaska, and he never stopped. Let's just say that if the number of figurines is directly proportional to the sadness Isaiah felt when his girl was gone, that girl ain't got nothing to worry about. I see the way he walks out his love for that girl in the smallest ways: setting an alarm to remind her to take her meds, making time for her, planning dates. It's a young love, son, but it's really love.

And your littlest sibling, Marci. Also not little. Marci is about to make sixteen, son. That's how we say it in New Orleans, and I love that little saying so much. In New Orleans, we don't *turn* an age, we *make* it. Isn't that cool? We get to *make* that year something, using our inclinations and our dreams. I would say this year is the year that Marci is in movement with dreams. Marci draws, has a crush, has so much wisdom and rational thought.

As for me, I'm nearly fifty-one, and I am not really sure of what I am making of it. The days are so full now, son, fuller than they were when you were little. Or perhaps I am just tireder. I feel young when I am playful, and I feel old when I feel into my dents. When I was teaching piano a few years back, a student's father, a widow, talked to me about loss in this way: "We all have our dents." I like that idea.

Sometimes, I trace the dents in my heart. There's a huge one where your physical life used to be. Sometimes, I feel like I have tried everything, Elijah, to pull out the dents. I've been to lots of spiritual dent-pullers in the forms of books, retreats, walks, therapists, and preachers. I've tried to get the axle unbent so that I can just drive straight and hold down the same job for years, grow a career like it seems other grown-ups do. I tried to be normal again. I think this cockeyed car is just what I have. Sometimes it pulls me over and I just sit by the side of life's highway and let my tears spill onto the engine. It's not so bad, really.

In many ways, Elijah, I am so lucky, but luck doesn't cancel out hurt. Some of that hurt and whatever healing I have found, I bundled up and put into sentences. Those sentences turned into essays, and those essays became a book. So, your mom is going to publish, and I really hope I have honored the import of your humanity as it touched my own. I'm sure I have both fallen short and overshot; such is the nature of love. Some days we pirouette into the perfect expression, like when we find the Christmas present and just *know* it's going to light up the heart of our loved one. Other days, we are stingy with our love or fail to aim our arrow true, like the day I tried to love you and failed to see. Intent does not equal execution, and learning to maneuver in love in ways that feel like love for my beloveds has become a lifelong quest.

And what of today? Of this tiny moment? It's just me, clad in cutoffs and consuming coffee on a leather couch in my little patch of the city I have come to love. I sneaked away early, before anyone could find me, because I wanted it to be just me and you. Remember when it was just me and you and I would nurse you at night? Or me and you on the swings at the park by The Big Ugly, I mean, The Vintage Home by the Park? Remember the time we sat on my bed and I fed you too many Goldfish as I fed myself with fiction? God, I was young when you came on the scene, son. Twenty-five. That's two years older than Ada is now. I felt grown, but I don't think I really was. Anyhoo . . .

So, today, dear, I am just here, hurting that same hurt, knowing that tomorrow I will get up and this day will be filed away as one of the many anniversaries I have made it through. I don't feel stuck in trauma today. I just feel tender, like a portal into the wonder that we live at all has opened in my heart. I feel warmth, like I will be cared for today. And that feels good, because most days, I feel like there is too much to do and not enough me to do it.

But I wonder about you. I still wish you could show me some sort of sign that you are okay. I wish you and I could just sit in this coffee shop the way Ada, Navis, Marci, and I will. I wish you could talk to me about my love life. I've been seeing this guy, Mister Linen, and I broke things off with him a couple of weeks back because he can't commit to me. And Elijah, when I say he can't commit, I really mean it. He has all the signs of someone who wants to love me, who does love me, but for reasons that he tries to explain over and over but that my heart can't quite grasp, just isn't able to. I would be up there with him in Baton Rouge today, Elijah; he would hold me and listen to me talk about you and life in the Bungalow and the six cats and two snakes. I know that he would make me the most beautiful cocktail with a garnish of dill or sage. He would put on my favorite record by Mickey Newbury. He would know that my favorite song contains lines about wishing to be three men, wishing for a .44 pistol with two bullets, wishing to put one in the heart and one in the brain, leaving the third man free of his humanity and the pain of the loss.

He wouldn't think I am morbid for loving those lines, but he would understand them as a cry of longing for the one I have lost. He would soften this day for me and take me home and remind me that sexy and sorrow can be very good bedfellows indeed. But he won't, because I told him not to come calling out until he's ready to commit, and I don't expect he ever will be.

Even so, the first text I saw this morning came from him. Now, I'm sure your younger siblings would call out how he didn't "respect my boundary," but I am so grateful that he didn't, Elijah, because on this day, more than I need silence, I just needed to hear from him. I need to remember you today especially, but it's just so wonderful when other people remember you, too, or they remember me on this day and understand the nature of this anniversary.

Here's what I woke up to, Elijah:

"My best friend will wake up to a complex day, and I want to be there to support her in every way. I know a lot about this day courtesy of her amazingly explicit writing that has the power to reach untold hearts— and will, when her wonderful book is available. My role, given all, may be to stay silent and offer my love in an indirect way, or it may be to speak to her directly and be solace by means of loving ears."

Can we just talk about what a beautiful turn of phrase that is, Elijah? "Solace by means of loving ears."

In all the long years of missing you, son, the solace of loving ears has perhaps been the most solacey solace I have received. Over the years, many different people have taken up the mantle of listening to your sad mama recount her sorrow. Bless 'em. Bless 'em for not growing tired of hearing how my heart shakes. Bless 'em for not trying to save me from my sorrow but just sitting with me as it leaks from the radiator hoses of my little grief-heated heart car.

Mister Linen has been so good in this regard for me, Elijah. Perhaps I have put him on a pedestal for this. Perhaps I have overlooked red flags. (By the way, son, red flags are what we now call basically anything about another person's personality that makes us feel a tad bit uncomfortable . "That person is sooooo into ASMR." "Red flag!" [Okay, maybe, actually.]). If I have overlooked behaviors in Mister Linen that others knew meant he couldn't commit, I did so because he seemed to know what to do with my heart. Whenever I entered into the world he curated via his bar, his bed and cowboy boots, a little valve in my heart that normally feels constricted would open up. If I held on too long to Mister Linen, it's because he made his way into my heart by loving you, or letting me love you with all the rawness, fierceness, and braveness that I hold.

I have feared that men would fear me because I am not all the way healed in the wake of your loss. It's too much for me to handle your loss, son. It's like trying to grab the tail of a hurricane, unravel it, and send it spinning in the opposite direction. But my storm didn't seem to phase Mister Linen, even as it doesn't seem he can fully embrace all that a life with me would mean. Whatever life I am still building in your corporeal absence is so full-bodied. The twin forces of your entrance and exit from my life still blow through me, making and unmaking me all the time. I am better and worse for you coming and going, and today, I just want to let the wind rip through me again. I want to let the grief churn up the waters and let the riptide take what it may. I really do.

Isn't it strange, son, that I can be sitting here, one foot propped up, skin around my jowls sagging, clicking away at my keys? There's a whole Milky Way of galaxy churning in my chest right now, and no one knows it—not the baristas, not the neighborhood philosopher reading the paper with his lady friend, not my coworking couch companion with whom I banter.

But Mister Linen would know it. Or, rather, he would lay back if we were in bed, slow me down, smile that slow grin of his, and say, "Now, darling. Tell me about this complicated day." And I would.

It's so strange, son, because I know he wants to. Or, if he *is* a player, I am standing up in my soul screaming "Bravo!" for the stringing-along of the century. I choose to believe he's telling me the truth. After all, a man who wears only bell bottoms and owns about two thousand ties just can't be *that* good a liar, right? Even though he can't deliver right now, or maybe ever, Mister Linen knows that he could handle me as a partner. The second part of his text tells me so:

> "I love you, Desi, and I see how I could be the man you
> lean on and into. I haven't felt I could really be that

for anyone else, as time shows. You are beautiful, and I'd have to explain that to you in bite-size pieces each day, over charcuterie and rosé."

Mister Linen knows that what I need more than someone to name all of my cognitive distortions or point out how well I am doing "all things considered" is someone who sees me not as too much, not as "the lady who lost her son and never quite recovered," but as something else—beautiful.

Son, I think I am beautiful, even if my beauty is charred by the day that led to lowering your ashes into a plot of ground that my mother patted and kissed. Mister Linen sees my mess and calls me beautiful, and he takes me to bed, or at least he did until I chose my dream of having a partner again over the solace of his sweet lips.

Wow, I guess you being not around in the physical means I am prone to quite a bit of oversharing, son.

I guess I will close now because Ada texted that she wants to have coffee. The house is a nightmare wreck of absorbing another human into an already too small home. One of the cats has probably peed on something. Marci has a cosplay to make. Ada wants to have coffee. Gigi is coming back from the shop again. I guess she just had a loose hose this time . . . or she is biding her time to go on her next overheating adventure. Something resembling dinner needs to be slapped together. I don't mean to gripe, and I am not really. I just know that we have shit to do and that my little time where I hold you extra close in my heart today is coming to a close.

I am reminded of the day I defended my dissertation. In front of about sixty people, I sang my way through the stories of the teachers who had opened up their lives to me. It was such a high point. Papa was there and he cried with pride. What a big heart your Papa has. I wish we could have found our way to healing; perhaps we still will, but I know I have to heal more first. After that highpoint, I went out, celebrated all night with a few friends. The next day, I woke up and bought toilet paper.

That's how life goes. We move in and out of the viscera of big emotions and tiny tasks. We are the top number of a fraction that, when converted to a decimal, is 1.25e-10. I know you didn't really get to this place in math, Elijah, or you have now transcended and are up there saying things like, "It's all part of the great math of the universe, Mom, chill out." However, 1.25e-10 is this number written out: .00000000000125. That's a decimal so small, I can't wrap my mind around it. It means we are such a small part of the whole thing that I don't even know why we bother being so preoccupied with our 1.25e-10-sized lives.

But we do, son. We remain trapped in skin that houses a brain that churns out solar systems of emotions, thoughts, and stories. All I know is that you remain a huge part of my solar system, and that your loss still holds the gravitational pull of a black hole. If I let it, it could still pull this whole life I have tried to make in your absence into it. Don't blame me; blame my neural networks, which your quickening quite literally rewired. Baby, your birth bore me this way.

So did your siblings', and so, I am signing off now, Elijah, just loving you, holding you, wanting you, but glad I could revisit the crater of your loss and find that some flowers have grown there. Perhaps I will pick one and put it in my hair much in the same way people in New Orleans pin money to their clothes. Or perhaps there is no need because your life is emblazoned in these lines around my eyes, in the hollow of my cheeks, and in the strength of these hands that hold the vastness of all that it has meant and still means to be your mother.

Oh god, here come the tears. Love you, baby. Let 'em. Let's just end it here today:

"And Desi looked upon all that she had made—the messy house, the burnt bagels that she forgot about, the jalopy of a Jeep that never works quite right, the arguments she smoothed over with her kids because she was too opinionated about their 'life choices' and can't bear to let them fail, the three jobs she quit because she was too exhausted to give another damn damn and her dig-down-deep button was broken, the lovers she hoped could be her solace but who she finally had to let go, the six thousand breve cappuccinos that will probably give her a coronary before she's sixty, the relationships she failed to salvage, the albatross of unpaid student loans around her neck, all the sunrises she forsook in her sor-row—and she called it 'good.'

"She made her peace not with the life she thought she would have when she was eight years old and still thought she had a chance to be a gymnast. That was before she realized that she could barely make it across a room without stubbing her toe on a lava lamp, let alone rival Romanian prodigy Nadia Comăneci. She tiptoed up to that log cabin of a gentle life that she has been build-ing, sometimes by flailing around a dull ax, other times by meticulously laying the best of plans. She welcomed it into her heart with the fierceness of a woman who accepts what is . . . and then got to work building some-thing beautiful, messy, and wild. But not before her sec-ond cappuccino. God knows, never before that."

God, I love you, Elijah. I just fucking LOVE YOU. Bye for now, baby. Have a wonderful day, or millennia, or nanosecond, or however it works in whatever form your stardust is in. If I find a particle of that dust, I shall hang it around my neck and let it charm me just the way your little chipmunk grin used to do.

Love,
Mom

Afterward: On Journals, Healing, and the Sins of the Parents

To write is to name. It is to explore, to romp, to placate, and to upset. To write is to mark our making, our meanings, and our current understandings. Much of what I have written the past few years has circled around overlapping concepts: grief, parenting, romantic love, and work. I have written letters that never need to be sent, processed the pain of losses. Mostly, this practice of writing has been for me. On this private plane, I have poured it all out. Sometimes I have felt better for my musings. Sometimes worse. Sometimes, I haven't felt much at all. Much like a clarinetist who heads to the practice room to run their scales, I have simply ordered a cappuccino, flipped open my laptop, and diligently written out whatever is in my soul.

By writing most mornings, I have created a password-protected inner sanctum. That sanctum has likely been my salvation. A journal never tires of you telling it your woes. So what if twenty years after the fact, I was still chewing on some facet of how Elijah died, or how my life has never quite felt like the life I was supposed to have lived up to? In my journal, I can be as honest as I want about just how hard some days can still feel. No one will judge my resilience or lack thereof. I can just be. And that is fantastic.

And then along came the opportunity to publish these musings, to create a public artifact of motherhood in grief. I questioned the value of going public with a grief that many have felt but few seem to talk about. After all, isn't privacy part of the bereaved's dignity? I faltered in revision, wondering if sharing these essays had a larger purpose. I have since come to believe that sharing the private pain that has informed most of my adult life could bring some good into the collective grief sphere.

Here's why: Grieving mothers walk two roads. We traverse the unseen labyrinth of the usual societal expectations about mothering, even as we tread the tracks of our own deep sorrow. We are rarely seen because our loss is seen as just too hard to bear. And in some religious circles, the idea that "God won't give you more than you can handle" still gets a good amount of play. Incidentally, I have seen way too many people who were given more than they could handle. The result of them "handling" whatever was supposedly not too much was the ruination of their spirits and the destruction of their bodies through addiction or other forms of self harm.

Losing a child is too much to bear. And so are lots of other losses in this world. When grieving mothers seem to be doing mostly okay, we are held up as bastions of bravery. *I couldn't do what you do.* Truth is, we never know what future us will do. *There are no words.* Actually, there are. The bereaved have many, many words to share if we are willing to listen to them.

I decided to go public with, as I've often said, "whatever the fuck living with long-term, deep loss looks like," in part because I want to do my part to help normalize grief. Grief is a universal fact of life that somehow feels like life's dirty little secret. Grief remains shrouded from polite conversation as if mentioning it means we have just brought the verbal equivalent of a torpedo into the cocktail party.

Like many with deep loss, bereaved mothers keep on keeping on. We buy fruit snacks for our remaining kids or rock other people's babies in the shadows of memories that feel too painful to share—and, by not sharing, by complying with our society's unspoken yet potent norms, we cut ourselves off from some of our own healing. Sure, support groups exist, but even these groups make me feel like my loss is allowed, say, on Tuesdays at 6:00 p.m., but let's not talk about Elijah on Wednesdays at nine in the morning, because that would interrupt the office banter. Let's compartmentalize and cubbyhole our grief so that we keep the wheels of work moving. God forbid someone have a breakdown at work over their own humanity peeking around the edge of their cubicle.

Why does the fact that one of my children didn't live past the age of two mean that I can no longer mention his name in casual conversation? Is it me that has the problem, or are we so grief-phobic that the mere mention of Elijah's name twenty-three years after he passed away inevitably casts a pall? I don't think we need to get over our grief, but I do think we need to get over our grief-phobia. If reading about a woman who is not afraid to trot out some pretty hard truths in one sentence and talk about her disdain for the tooth fairy in the next can help normalize what living with grief is actually like, then some good has come of this book. (But also, when did the tooth fairies unionize and start demanding five bucks a tooth? I am pro-union, but this is a wee bit much.)

Writing this book has allowed me to reframe not just what living with grief is but what healing means. There is no one great healing from the wound of waking up to Elijah's loss. With any deep-soul wound, we don't get the privilege of having one big come-to-Jesus moment and then waltzing our way to healing. "Well, *that's* done. Anyone want a s'more?" Maybe that truth seems obvious to others—but I have been to so many revival meetings, have walked down the aisle so many times hoping that *this* time when I lay it on the altar, my issues will fucking stay dead, that I have had to learn to envision healing differently.

Healing is not a one-and-done proposition but more like spinning a web one strand of silk at a time. Healing is a series of moments, some of them like the one in *Sense and Sensibility*, where

Marianne sits out in the English countryside in her wheelchair after her fever has broken. Alan Rickman's Colonel Brandon reads to her from Edmund Spenser's epic poem *The Faerie Queene:* "Nothing's lost but may be found, if sought." Sometimes it's peaceful like that, and I really wish that Alan Rickman's ghost would visit me and read me poetry. Just putting that out there, Universe. Cause I am a bereaved mom. And I need to find a few things that I lost.

More often, though, healing feels like a wound debridement, or a choice in my saner moments not to self-flagellate. Healing is as much about unlearning old ways as it is learning new ones.

Healing is allowing myself to be humbled by the relatively small impact I have on the world at large but my ability to cause immeasurable harm in the lives of my children. Elijah's accident hammered this truth home to me. Healing is allowing that truth to humble me.

Healing is also the kindness I show myself when my mean side shows up, like in a sharp word to one of my kids. A couple of days ago, I asked Marci how their day was. The kid tried to explain that they felt aimless and that the day had been just "okay." Some weird switch tripped in me, and instead of being gentle, I berated: "What do you mean? It seems that unless someone is planning something for you and doing something with you all day, you just aren't happy."

WTF, Des? Where did this come from? The kid had spent much of the previous day profusely thanking me for the birthday party I had planned for them. Marci does not suffer from ingratitude. I tried to stop, but I just kept picking at them. "You have to learn to plan your own day, and it can't always involve other people. You have hobbies. Do them." At least I had the good sense to walk myself out of the room and regroup.

Time for repair. On my bed about twenty minutes later, I repented:

"Marci, you did absolutely nothing wrong, and even if I did

think that you were focusing more on the negatives than the positives, my way of talking to you was absolutely uncalled for. I attacked you. This is me telling you I fucked up. I am open to hearing your perspective on this, and I will try to do better in the future."

Writing this book reminded me that I can actually mess up loving—because loving is a skill, just like washing the dishes. Okay, maybe not *exactly* like washing the dishes, but you get the point: You can realize you missed a spot and rewash; you can realize you were less loving than you wish you'd been and seek healing. Yes, I just compared relationship repair to rewashing dishes. Fun. But really, relationship repair is a privilege that I no longer take lightly, and I don't know if I would have learned that lesson so well without having to accept that my time with Elijah is over, as far as I know, permanently. Realizing the fallibility inherent in loving—alongside the renewable resilience of relationships that are built on love—is itself a form of healing.

Finally, healing is the commitment to keep pulling the shards of fundamentalism out of my psyche, neither ruminating on nor ignoring them. I pick out the glass splinter, and then I try to get on with my day.

Memoir writing is, on the whole, a brave affair. It's audacious. As memoirists choose to excavate a little corner of their souls, they believe that when readers sift through the soil of their story, they will find at least a mineral or two that shows up in their own. My story is particular to me. But the soil in my soul is really not so different from anyone else's. I believe that if we let them, grief and loss can become great connectors. Nothing humbles us like loss. Nothing lets us know just how small we are like yearning. When we feel the pain of separation from loved ones and get the opportunity to draw nigh to their hearts, whether through the page or other kinds of communion, we are lucky.

If I have learned anything from this book and reexamining the ancient texts about sorrow, it is that the via dolorosa runs long through the years when I have written of my September 24ths—the day Elijah left. Each year as I return to that day, I am reminded that every day is someone's September 24th. If today is yours, my heart is with you.

A few September 24ths ago, I wrote, in list form, things that feel true to me about grief. This is the closest I have come to any sort of on-the-nose advice-giving about the big G. Here it is:

DESI'S ALMOST-ADVICE ABOUT WHATEVER THE EFF LIVING WITH LONG-TERM GRIEF IS

1. Grief does not go away. It just gets a little easier to live with.

2. Grief cannot be managed, bargained with, or tied off neatly with a bow.

3. Grief is not a feeling; it is a force, an energy that wants to move through you. Let the tsunami in.

4. Grief changes throughout the years.

5. Grief has no endpoint.

6. Grief doesn't automatically make you a better or worse person.

7. Grief remembers the moment you lost your loved one. Grief will make you forget yourself.

8. Grief is simultaneously isolating and connecting.

9. Grief settles into every single one of your cells. It beckons you from your bones.

10. Grief does not exist in isolation. It will be with you when you shop, have sex, and sing your favorite songs.

11. Sometimes you don't want the grief to get better. Good on you. That's just fine.

12. Grief requires us to accept our lives as they are, not as we had planned them to be.

13. Others will remind you of your loved one. This will both hurt and heal you.

14. Guilt and grief go hand and hand.

15. Grief is the thing you both can and can't live with.

16. Grief needs to be observed.

17. Honoring your loved one is not something you add to your to-do list. It's a way of life.

18. Healing and forgetting seem to go hand in hand. Sometimes this is painful to realize.

19. Sometimes you will want to feel bad about your loss.

20. Other people will rarely know what to do with your grief. And you will rarely know what to do with theirs.

21. No one can heal your grief for you, but they can make it a little more bearable. Choose your grief-bearers carefully.

22. If you don't like your grief finding you at 2:00 a.m., make an appointment with it at a better time.

23. Repressed grief will make you sick. Period. Like, very, very sick.

24. Grief has very bad manners.

25. Grief is not a zero-sum game.

26. Grief is a small child.

27. The only way through is to turn toward your grief. You will want to numb it; avoid substituting sex, work, nicotine, or some other substance

so that you don't have to deal with your grief
because it's so exhausting to heave it around with
you. It won't work.

28. Grief needs forgiveness. So do you. Even if you
    don't feel you did anything wrong and you lost
    someone due to entirely "natural" causes, you
    may still feel guilt about being here when your
    loved one is not. You cannot "enjoy life for two"
    or pretend this guilt is not present. Like the grief
    itself, you need to forgive your guilt. This too
    requires acceptance and a recognition that much
    of what comes with grief doesn't seem to make
    sense. It simply *is*. Create a file called "Mysteries
    of Grief and Loss" and place this feeling in it—not
    to bury it, but to have some sort of label for it.

And there you have it: twenty-eight findings about grief,
pared down into aphorisms. I couldn't have written them
twenty-three years ago, and I will likely add to them over the
next twenty-three.

Even as I hope that this book will offer some measure of
insight into how a life that is framed by sorrow can be a good
life still, I think much of its value has come from clarifying
just how deeply I was shaped by fundamentalism and how
that grid colored everything, especially my parenting. I can't
thank my editor Chelsey Shannon enough for asking me the
questions that moved this narrative from being only about a
single loss to naming how that loss was informed by beliefs
that are presently being co-opted by Christo-fascists, who, in
my opinion, are neither Christian nor democratic. But that is
a book for another day, and others can write it better than I
could. However, I will say that this movement scares the beje-
sus out of me because I understand the roots of its thinking
from the inside out. It is nothing short of an authoritarian
regime that masquerades under the banner of Christianity.

But, back to this book.

Writing this book has been a reckoning. If journaling allowed me to beat a path toward a life that makes some kind of sense, fleshing out these musings has allowed me to feel my way through my failings in a way that is kind. Old Testament Scriptures speak of OG God "visiting the iniquity of fathers on the children." Writing this book has caused me to reckon not with how God visited anything upon me but rather how institutional abuse and indoctrination led me to parent in ways that I can only name as harmful now. Elijah's death jump-started musings that led me out of fundamentalism.

Fuck if I have figured that all out, but I have recently been embracing an idea that has been touted in the child psychology literature for years: "happy mom, happy baby." And, as John O'Donohue aptly pointed out, we are all a bunch of ex-babies romping around with the power to buy stocks and fuck.[37] So, while I can't undo past choices made, nor rightly take credit for all the sources of inspiration for the isms that have rooted themselves in my kids' psyches, I do acknowledge that continually allowing myself my own joy and being in that joy in front of my kids is a very powerful force. My brand of *laissez les bons temps rouler* may be of the quieter, contemplative variety, but I am now committed to joy as much as I was once committed to the idea that I was evil.

Writing this book has reminded me to be defiantly relentless in my pursuit of joy. Joy is needed not in spite of the sad state of our world but because in joy, we may find the seeds of this world's healing.

Let us live toward joy, losses and all.

1. Cecelia Hock, "Was an 1812 hurricane the worst storm to ever hit New Orleans?," The Historic New Orleans Collection, June 11, 2021, https://www.hnoc.org/publications/first-draft/was-1812-hurricane-worst-storm-ever-hit-new-orleans#:~:text=In%20September%20.1812%2C%20French%20consul,knocked%20down%20buildings%3B%20and%20otook.

2. Louisiana Office of Public Health, Infectious Disease Epidemiology Section – Annual Report, accessed July 1, 2024, 2, https://ldh.la.gov/assets/oph/Center-PHCH/Center-CH/infectious-epi/Annuals/LaIDAnnual_YellowFever.pdf.

3. Brené Brown, *Rising Strong: How the Ability to Reset Transforms the Way We Live, Love, Parent, and Lead* (New York: Random House, 2017), 183.

4. Kate Dwyer, "Lidia Yuknavitch Writes to Break With the 'Tyranny' of the Past," *The New York Times*, June 23, 2022, https://www.nytimes.com/2022/06/23/books/lidia-yuknavitch-thrust.html.

5. Sophocles, *Antigone*, 4.66–70.

6. Kahlil Gibran, "On Children" in *The Prophet* (New York: Knopf, 1923), 21.

7. Michael and Debi Pearl, *To Train Up a Child* (Pleasantville, Tennessee: No Greater Joy Ministries, 1994), 46.

8. C. S. Lewis, *A Grief Observed* (New York: HarperOne, 2009), 4–5.

9. Lewis, *Grief Observed*, 10–11.

10. Lewis, *Grief Observed*, 57.

11. Martin Shaw, "On Job: A Strange and Rewarding Adventure," The House of Beasts & Vines, July 2, 2023, https://martinshaw.substack.com/p/on-job-a-wind-from-the-des-

ert.

12. John O'Donohue, *To Bless the Space Between Us: A Book of Blessings* (New York: Doubleday, 2008): 47–50.

13. Francis Weller, *The Wild Edge of Sorrow: Rituals of Renewal and the Sacred Work of Grief* (Berkeley, CA: North Atlantic Books, 2015).

14. Anderson Cooper, interview with Francis Weller, *All There Is with Anderson Cooper*, podcast audio, November 29, 2023, https://www.cnn.com/audio/podcasts/all-there-is-with-anderson-cooper/episodes/30f07496-476a-11ee-a898-7b5f17aa3b47.

15. Weller, *The Wild Edge of Sorrow*, 73.

16. Francis Weller, "Drinking the Tears of the World: Grief as Deep Activism," Daily Good, October 22, 2023, https://www.dailygood.org/story/2214/drinking-the-tears-of-the-world-grief-as-deep-activism-francis-weller/.

17. Weller, *The Wild Edge of Sorrow*, 74.

18. Weller, *The Wild Edge of Sorrow*, 16.

19. Dwyer, "Lidia Yuknavitch."

20. Cheryl Strayed, "The Love Of My Life," *The Sun*, September 2022, https://www.nytimes.com/2022/06/23/books/lidia-yuknavitch-thrust.html.https://www.thesunmagazine.org/articles/25205-the-love-of-my-life.

21. "Heaven's Gate Event Poster, 1975," We Are the Mutants, February 9, 2017, https://wearethemutants.com/2017/02/09/heavens-gate-event-poster-1975/.

22. Claire Weinraub, Christina Ng, Acacia Nunes, and Haley Yamada, "Heaven's Gate survivor reflects on the cult's mass suicide 25 years ago," ABC News, March 11, 2022, https://abcnews.go.com/US/heavens-gate-survivor-reflects-cults-mass-suicide-25/story?id=83213680.

23. *The Vow*, season 1, episode 8, "The Wound," directed by Jehane Noujaim and Karim Amer, aired October 11, 2020, on HBO, https://play.max.com/video/watch/3ea6b645-014a-4544-a2ba-d97174fea33a/6acad0fc-8ca1-43cd-9421-5b616a-942/ba.

24. Steve Hassan, "Dr. Steve Hassan's BITE Model of Authoritarian Control," Freedom of Mind Resource Center, last modified 2023, accessed July 1, 2024, https://freedomof-mind.com/wp-content/uploads/2023/08/BITE-model.pdf.

25. C. G. Jung, *Development of Personality*, vol. 17, ed. and trans. R. F. C. Hull (Princeton: Princeton University Press, 1954), 78.

26. Elseline Hoekzema et al., "Mapping the effects of pregnancy on resting state brain activity, white matter microstructure, neural metabolite concentrations and grey matter architecture," *Nature Communications* 13 (2022), https://www.nature.com/articles/s41467-022-33884-8.

27. Ruth A. Lanius, Braeden A. Terpou, and Margaret C. McKinnon, "The sense of self in the aftermath of trauma: lessons from the default mode network in posttraumatic stress disorder," *European Journal of Psychotraumatology* 11, vol. 1 (October 23, 2020), https://pubmed.ncbi.nlm.nih.gov/33178406/.

28. TEDx Talks, "The power of vulnerability | Brené Brown | TEDxHouston," YouTube, October 6, 2010, video, 20:44, https://www.youtube.com/watch?v=X- 4Qm9cGRubo.

29. "Coronavirus Death Toll," Worldometer, last modified April 13, 2024, accessed August 14, 2024, https://www.worldometers.info/coronavirus/coronavirus-death-toll/.

30. Greta Thunberg, "'Our house is on fire': Greta Thunberg, 16, urges leaders to act on climate," The Guardian, January 25, 2019,https://www.theguardian.com/environment/2019/jan/25/our-house-is-on-fire-greta-thunberg16-urges-leaders-to-act-on-climate.

31. Rebecca Solnit, *Hope in the Dark: Untold Histories, Wild Possibilities*, 3rd ed. (Chicago: Haymarket Books, 2016), 1.

32. Katrina Gingerich, "The Journey of the Song Cycle from 'The Iliad' to 'American Idiot,'" Musical Offerings: an undergraduate journal of musicology, last modified October 2011, accessed July 2, 2024, https://cedarvillemusic. wordpress.com/the-journey-of-the-song-cycle-from-%e2%80%9cthe-iliad%e2%80%9d-to-%e2%80%9camerican-idiot%e2%80%9d-by-katrina-gingerich/.

33. Ludwig van Beethoven, *An die ferne Geliebte*, Vienna: S. A. Steiner & Co., 1816.

34. Colin Campbell, "What Losing My Two Children Taught Me About Grief," The Atlantic, March 1, 2023, https://www.theatlantic.com/ideas/archive/2023/03/how-to-talk-about-grief-support/673232/.

35. G. K. Chesterton, *Orthodoxy* (London: Bradford and Dickens, 1908), 93.

36. Adi Ignatius, "'Above All, Acknowledge the Pain,'" *Harvard Business Review*, May–June 2017, 142–147, https://hbr.org/2017/05/above-all-acknowledge-the-pain.

37. Krista Tippett, interview with John O'Donohue, "'John O'Donohue: The Inner Landscape of Beauty," On Being, podcast audio, last modified February 10, 2022, accessed August 14, 2024,https://onbeing.org/programs/john-odonohue-the-inner-landscape-of-beauty/.